Preface

Human beings love to beauty and admire it. For that purpose they try to beautify them and their surroundings. For this purpose they share the feelings and ideas of other persons without keeping in mind caste, creed and colour. When civilization progressed and people had more means and time at their disposal to make things beautiful and artistic, they produced many works of art, such as imposing buildings with ornamental gardens, paintings and sculptures. Tourism provides a ground to improve the culture of a nation and relations with others.

Tourism is a major growing contributor to jobs, wealth, investment and cultural understanding—with unique potential across developing states. Transportation, accommodation and hospitality are integral parts of tourism. The lacking of one of these detains whole process of tourism industry. Transportation itself is an industry and consists of railways, roadways, airways and waterways. International tourism depends on air travel while domestic tourism depends on roadways and railways. Hospitality also plays an important role in promotion of tourism.

Tourism and Hospitality is potent instrument for eliminating poverty, for ending unemployment and promoting dialogue among civilization. This is the industry, which helps the nations to improve relations along with their economy. For a nation it gets tax revenues based on lodging, food and recreational activities and also improve the capital investments in real property, amenities and infrastructure development. Tourism industry worldwide has emerged as an important sector of an economy. Owners of hotels, restaurants, cruise industry, airlines, recreational centres, amusement parks, theme parks are competing with each other for the hospitality dollar all over the world. Modern management and marketing principles most facilitate breakthrough in the tourist system in-take the appropriate desired and realistic market share with the flexible market plan, keeping in view the capacity to do business, image of the business, future scope, risk factors, human resource availability, technological development, means of communication as well as competitiveness in tourism marketing.

Tourism sector's potential for employment generation is immense both in terms of numbers and cost effectiveness as well as employment opportunity in rural and backward areas without causing migration to distant places, foreign exchange earning industry, a tool for sustainable human development including poverty alleviation, environmental conservation and regeneration, job creation and advancement of women and other disadvantaged groups.

Present effort is being done with the co-operation of the educators; researchers and persons related with Tourism and Hospitality to discuss the management, marketing, research and other related aspects in present scenario. I am thankful to all contributors for their support. We wish to our my heart-felt gratitude to Prof. Ramesh Chandra, Hon'ble Vice-Chancellor, Bundelkhand University, Jhansi, who is always a source of inspiration for us.

Mukesh Ranga
Ashish Chandra

Contents

1

Protecting the Environment Through Accreditation of Ecotourism Operators: A Planning Tool

*Malcolm Cooper**
*Patricia Erfurt***

Abstract

Ecotourism is nature-based tourism that involves education and interpretation of the natural environment and is managed to be ecologically sustainable (Ceballos-Lascurain, 1987; Buckley, 1994; Beeton, 1998). As such it has the potential to a be very important environmental conservation tool for tourism and land-use planners throughout the Asia-Pacific region. Key elements include dependence on the natural environment, ecologically sustainable de.elopments, contribution to conservation, involvement of education and

* Professor Malcolm Cooper PhD LLM FPIA is Dean, Wide Bay Campus, University of Southern Queensland, PO Box 910, Hervey Bay, Queensland, Australia.

** Patricia Erfurt BA (Geography and Planning) is an Honours Student at the University of New England, Armidale, New South Wales, Australia.

interpretation, sustaining local communities, and adventure, leisure and fun. Worldwide there has been massive growth in the ecotourism market, despite some adverse comment on the true nature of this 'greening' of the tourism industry (Wheeller, 1993: Hall, 1994), and this has important ramifications for tourism planners.

A number of behavioural standards and regulatory regimes have been developed in an effort to assist tourism operators in developing practical environmental impact monitoring measures, or to regulate their activities. This Chapter discusses a range of these techniques, but concentrates on the Nature and Ecotourism Accreditation Program (NEAP) developed in Australia. This program has been developed by industry for industry, addressing the need to identify genuine ecotourism and nature tourism product in Australia, and is a joint initiative of the Ecotourism Association of Australia (EAA) and the Australian Tourism Operators Network (ATON). It is functionally similar to Green Globe, and the two are seeking ways to extend the accreditation process world-wide. Using such tools would allow tourism and planning managers in all countries to more easily control and regulate that part of their tourism industry that is based on the natural environment.

Key Words: *Ecotourism Natural Environments Tourism Planning and Management Environmental Accreditation NEAP Green Globe*

Introduction

Ceballos-Lascurain (1987) first identified sustainable or ecotourism as a form of travel that primarily focussed on the natural environment; involving travel to (unspoilt) natural environments, and experiences relating to those natural environments. Since that seminal article, debate about the nature of and the impacts associated with ecotourism has raged across academia and into the public consciousness in most countries. The term has become a catchphrase that encompasses numerous tourism forms, including 'nature tourism', 'wilderness tourism', 'low impact tourism', 'green tourism' and 'sustainable tourism' (Wearing and Neil, 1999). In turn the debate has ranged from what constitutes an ecotourism product or experience, to the concept of ecotourism as a way of living (organising interactions between humanity and the environment in which humanity lives). It is the latter concept that operator accreditation in the tourism industry attempts to address.

Underlying this debate is a belated realisation that the natural environment is not static but is itself constantly undergoing change as a response to changed conditions, including the impact of tourists. However, in order to take this into account operationally there is a need to develop flexible management regimes and therefore tourism enterprises that are responsive to those changes. As the market for environmentally sensitive tourism facilities continues to expand on a worldwide basis it is vital that local businesses meet global expectations and standards associated with sound environmental practice. Adherence to these has the following advantages:

- Saving money by cutting running costs such as those for energy and water and waste disposal;
- Giving business an environmentally responsible image and appeal to a new and growing market;
- Confirming the position of tourism as a valued industry in the local community and economy; and
- Ensuring future viability by maintaining the resource base on which tourism depends.

Manidis (1994) developed an enterprise quality assurance continuum that indicated levels of conformance with sound environmental practice through increasing regulation. Regulation provides business, protected area managers and tourists with an assurance that a specific tourism product is backed by a commitment to best practice environmental management and the provision of quality experiences. As part of this, the development and acceptance of standards provides the following recognised benefits:

- Criteria to assist operators to plan and develop tourism product based on principles of ecologically sustainable development;
- An opportunity for operators to continually improve performance to a standard recognised as best practice;
- A recognised means of identifying genuine ecotourism operators and to encourage improved practices that lead to less environmental impact; and
- A tool to help local communities determine a mix of tourism activities that maximises benefits and minimises negative impacts.

Tourism Management Through Accreditation

Since the 1980's Australia and other countries have realised the importance of quality assurance as a means of gaining a competitive advantage in the market place. This realisation has prompted the growth of a range of quality assurance programs, notably the internationally recognised ISO series. Many industry sectors and individual businesses have invested considerable emphasis and resources in demonstrating best practices and continuous improvement, including the tourism industry, through an increasing focus on using quality assurance standards and accreditation by an independent body to distinguish products that have met those standards. Table—1.1 gives an outline of the range of regulatory mechanisms that could be applied to tourism developments in order to achieve such conformance, but we stress that it is important to design *local* systems to fit both the demands of the environment as well as the requirements of central and local government and industry. On achieving this, an ecologically sustainable future for tourism may be possible.

Beyond the level of codes of behaviour, accreditation or certification schemes allow businesses and individuals to be formally recognised for implementing, and to market their attainment of, industry quality standards. Numerous professional organisations have processes for individuals to achieve certification. With respect to individuals in the Australian tourism industry, bodies providing recognition of the quality standards of individuals, through membership, certification or accreditation, include the Australian Institute of Travel and Tourism, the Australian Federation of Travel Agents, the Inbound Tourism Organisation of Australia, the Restaurant and Catering Association of New South Wales, and the Meetings Industry Association of Australia.

With respect to businesses, the accreditation options can include generic programs that are open to all businesses within an industry, and programs that can apply to specific types of businesses or operations (such as travel agents), specific industry sectors (such as ecotourism), and geographic regions (such as a particular state). Generally speaking, accreditation processes give businesses the opportunity to:

- Clarify and document their policies, management systems and procedures;
- Improve control over operations and increase consistency in performance of functions;
- Enable a better understanding of expectations, roles and responsibilities within the business;
- Receive recognition for their quality status, and be able to maximise the competitive advantage from that recognition; and
- Develop a framework for continuous improvement (Taylor et al, 2000).

One feature of accreditation programs is their *voluntary* nature, with industry members able to choose whether or not to participate. Licensing, which requires the support of government legislation, is the next step on the quality assurance continuum, and some licensing arrangements already exist, for example with retail travel agents. However, in the current climate of deregulation in Australia,

Table—1.1 Ecotourism Industry Quality Continuum

Criterion	Codes of Practice				
	General Behaviour Guide	Behavioural Code	Accreditation System	Quality System	Certification System
Status	Informal	Formal	Formal	Formal	Formal
Requirement to participate	None	Voluntary	Voluntary (National)	Voluntary (International)	Compulsory (Government)
Origin	None	Complying with codes	Administered by industry or other body	Externally driven	Externally approved standard
Benefit	Little	Can possibly require the signing of an agreement	Involves local standards of skill, experience or activity	Conformity with external standard or best practice	Regulatory
Enforcement	None	May involve enforcement	Involves audit of individual or organization	Involves audit and benchmarking	By regulation
Penalties	None	Rare	Withdrawal of membership	Withdrawal of status	Court imposed
Examples	Ecotourism Association Publications	Tourism Council Code of Conduct	National Ecotourism Accreditation Program	ISO 9000/ 14000 (Quality in Service)	Travel Agents

***Source*: (adapted from Manidis, 1994)**

governments continue to encourage the tourism industry to manage quality assurance itself.

Tourism Accreditation Schemes in Australia

There are a number of 'generic' tourism business accreditation schemes within Australia's tourism industry. The Tourism Council of Australia's *National Tourism Accreditation Program* (NTAP) was developed following a decision of major stakeholders in early 1997 to pursue a national framework for tourism accreditation. The result of this meeting was the establishment of an Australian Tourism Accreditation Authority (ATAA), and an accreditation program aligned to Australian and International Standards for Quality Management Systems—ISO 9002/14002.

Some 1000 businesses have been accredited in the TCA Western Australia/Tasmania/South Australia program that began in December 1996, with an attrition rate in WA of about 5 per cent. The *Better Business Tourism Accreditation Program* in Victoria also commenced in December 1996, and is built on a framework established in 1993 by the Victorian Tour Operator's Association, but essentially similar to the TCA one of ISO quality assurance standards. Its initial membership of 250 businesses rose to over 500, but has had an attrition rate of around 10 per cent in recent years. TCA State branches in the Northern Territory, Australian Capital Territory and New South Wales are currently investigating the establishment of tourism accreditation programs in their respective jurisdictions.

The Nature and Ecotourism Accreditation Program

There is an array of other large and small-scale accreditation or quality assurance related schemes that are relevant to specific industry sectors or types of operations. Of these the *National Ecotourism Accreditation Program* (NEAP) was developed in 1996 to address the need to be able to identify 'genuine' ecotourism operators in Australia. In 1999 the program was launched under a slightly modified name as

NEAP II—Nature and Ecotourism Accreditation Program, featuring revised criteria and a distinction being made between nature tourism product and ecotourism product. It is designed to provide a range of benefits for nature tourism operators, ecotourism operators, consumers, protected area managers and local communities. NEAP has been developed to apply to two industry sectors: nature tourism and ecotourism, and to cover the accreditation of establishments offering accommodation, tours and attractions. As at 2000 there were approximately 230 NEAP accredited products spread across 90-odd businesses.

The quoted benefits to nature tourism and ecotourism operators from accreditation under NEAP include:

- Competitive advantage in marketing nature tourism and ecotourism products (e.g., discounted advertising and logo inclusion in the Ecotourism Association of Australia's *Australian Ecotourism Guide* and opportunities for cooperative advertising and logo inclusion in the Australian Tourist Commission's *Australian Tourism Source*);
- Financial savings resulting from extended tenure in protected areas;
- Baseline criteria for operators to determine the degree to which their product meets the standards of nature tourism and/or ecotourism;
- An opportunity to promote products as genuine nature tourism or ecotourism;
- A framework within which performance can be continually improved to a standard recognised as best practice; and
- Information on ways to improve the quality of products.

The benefit to tourists themselves essentially reduces to a recognised means of identifying genuine nature tourism and ecotourism products, while the benefits to protected area managers include:

- Improved tour practices that lead to fewer negative environmental impacts and more efficient use of natural resources; and
- Criteria to assist in identifying genuine nature tourism and ecotourism products.

Importantly, the benefits to local communities include:

- Criteria to assist in identifying genuine nature tourism and ecotourism products;
- A tool to help communities determine a mixture of tourism activity that helps maximise benefits and minimizes negative impacts.

Different Levels of Accreditation

Eligibility for nature tourism accreditation under NEAP is based upon the following four principles. The *nature* tourism product seeking accreditation:

1. Focuses on personally and directly experiencing nature;
2. Represents best practice for environmentally sustainable tourism;
3. Consistently meets customer expectations; and
4. Is marketed accurately and leads to realistic expectations.

Eligibility for ecotourism accreditation under NEAP is based on the following eight principles. The ecotourism product seeking accreditation:

1. Focuses on personally and directly experiencing nature;
2. Provides opportunities to experience nature in ways that lead to greater understanding, appreciation and enjoyment;
3. Represents best practice for environmentally sustainable tourism;

4. Positively contributes to the conservation of natural areas;
5. Provides constructive ongoing contributions to local communities;
6. Is sensitive to, interprets and involves different cultures, particularly indigenous culture;
7. Consistently meets customer expectations; and
8. Is marketed accurately and leads to realistic expectations.

Each of the above principles is reflected in specific assessment criteria that establish three categories of accreditation: Nature Tourism, Ecotourism and Advanced Ecotourism (See Table—1.2). Each category of accreditation incorporates a more stringent set of assessment criteria. For Nature Tourism Accreditation, the four principles of eligibility outlined above are reflected in core assessment criteria, of which a product must achieve 100 per cent to be awarded accreditation. The provision of interpretation is not mandatory to achieve Nature Tourism accreditation; however, where it is provided it must satisfy core criteria. Exemptions to core criteria are permitted only where the criteria are deemed inappropriate (convincing evidence from the operator is required). Operators undertaking Nature Tourism accreditation are encouraged to implement a continuous improvement program and, if desired, seek ecotourism accreditation.

Table—1.2 Two Sample Components of NEAP Accreditation

1. A Natural Area Focus

Core Criteria

Nature tourism and ecotourism focus on directly and personally experiencing nature.

(a) The majority of each customer's time is spent in nature;

(b) The product is based around activities that help customers to personally experience nature, e.g., by the provision of opportunities for customers to use at least three senses (such as observing natural features, listening to bird calls, smelling the oil of leaves, tasting bush foods, or touching the bark of trees);

(c) Each transport-based tour has no more than fifty customers per guide;

(d) Each non-vehicle based tour (eg., guided walking, horse riding or snorkelling) has no more than 25 customers per guide;

(e) Accommodation is within or adjacent to a natural area. The applicant must justify how the product has a natural area focus in the comments column;

(f) The majority of marketing images for the product incorporate nature as a feature or background.

2. Interpretation

Core Criteria

Customers of ecotourism products are given access to interpretive opportunities through a number of techniques.

(a) ***Nature Tourism:*** The provision of interpretation is *optional* (tick box if interpretation is provided);

(b) ***Ecotourism:*** Customers have the *opportunity* to learn about the natural and cultural heritage of the environment they are visiting;

Note: *The operator must provide at least three interpretive opportunities from a list provided. It may be necessary to demonstrate that reasonable access to interpretive materials/activities is available for those customers who wish to participate—but it is not necessary to demonstrate that all customers are exposed to interpretive material or activities.*

(c) ***Advanced Ecotourism:*** Interpretive activities and materials that allow customers to learn more about the natural and cultural heritage of the area are a *core component* of the product.

Note: *For tours and attractions, the operator must provide at least four interpretive opportunities, one of which must be a personal technique. For accommodation, the operator must provide at least four interpretive opportunities, a personal technique is optional. To satisfy this criterion it is necessary to demonstrate that* all *customers participate in activities that allow them to learn more about the natural and cultural heritage of the area they are visiting. Exposure to interpretation is guaranteed through integration of interpretive materials and activities throughout the ecotourism experience,* all *customers are given interpretive commentary / self-guiding leaflet, or join an activity such as a bushwalk or slide show.*

The eight principles of eligibility outlined above for Ecotourism product accreditation must be met 100 per cent. Exemptions to core criteria are permitted only where the criteria are deemed inappropriate (convincing evidence from the operator is required). Operators undertaking Ecotourism accreditation are encouraged to undertake a continuous improvement program that will allow them to seek Advanced Ecotourism accreditation.

Fore Advanced Ecotourism accreditation, the eight principles of eligibility outlined are also reflected in *bonus* assessment criteria, of which a product must gain a set percentage to be awarded advanced accreditation. Extra points may be awarded to products that provide examples of innovative best practice. To be eligible for Advanced Ecotourism accreditation, the operator must include interpretation as a fundamental component of the product.

Continuous Improvement and Self-Assessment

NEAP is based on the principle of continuous improvement, and is designed to assist the tourism industry to continually improve standards. The criteria are reviewed on an ongoing basis to reflect industry standards and performance, and more stringent standards are likely to be put in place following each review. The next major review of criteria is due in 2003. Accreditation is valid for a three-year period. Operators with accredited products are required to lodge an annual return to advise the Administrator of any operational changes that affect their products' ability to meet relevant criteria, along with an annual renewal fee.

At the end of the third year of accreditation, a new application with appropriate fees must be lodged. A complete review and assessment of the products against the current set of NEAP criteria is then undertaken. An operator with existing accredited products, an applicant for accreditation, or an operator re-applying for accreditation, has a right of appeal if their accreditation is removed or application refused. However, a caveat exists in that there is no right of appeal for applicants disputing a panel decision on whether or not they meet core criteria.

NEAP is also based on *self-assessment* in the first instance. Nevertheless, the use of referees, monitoring and auditing play crucial roles in the program. Four forms of monitoring are used: reviews by referees, feedback from customers, paper audits and on-site audits. The NEAP panel will investigate customer or other feedback that indicates that a breach in accreditation standards may have occurred.

Across-the-board paper audits of selected criteria are conducted on all operations every year. These will involve formal justification and verification that the product is meeting selected criteria (such as guide qualifications, licences, verification of stated contribution to conservation, etc.) Each year, operators are informed of the criteria selected for auditing. Operators have ninety days in which to respond to the audit.

Application fees for accreditation range from AUD175 to AUD540, depending on business turnover. In addition there is an annual licence fee of between AUD275 and AUD2,060, again depending on business turnover. Fees are charged quarterly. If an operator wishes to upgrade a product from Nature Tourism accreditation to Ecotourism accreditation, or from Ecotourism accreditation to Advanced Ecotourism accreditation, they must submit a new application with the appropriate application fee and annual fee.

Complementary Programs

Better Business Tourism Accreditation Program

Operators are welcome to apply for NEAP as a stand-alone program, however the Ecotourism Association of Australia (EAA) and the Australian Tourism Operators Network (ATON) encourage tourism businesses to link the principles of this program with those relating to the financial viability of their business. The *Better Business Tourism Accreditation Program* is a business-focused accreditation program that is complementary to NEAP. As a joint initiative between the two programs, operators that have their business or product accredited under one program will receive a 20 per cent discount on the fees associated with the second accreditation program undertaken.

Nature and Ecotour Guide Certification Program

NEAP encourages operators to build on the principles of this program by providing suitably trained and qualified interpretive guides and staff. From November 2000, one way this can be achieved is by ensuring that guides employed are certified under the Nature and Ecotour Guide Certification Program (NEGCP), or that relevant in-house training conforms to the benchmarks set by this program. It is anticipated that NEAP Edition III (due January 2003) will require lead or head guides to comply with certification program criteria and/or qualifications for all operations conducted in protected areas.

International Equivalents

The *Green Globe* scheme is an independently verified international certification program for travel and tourism that was re-launched in Australia in 2000, in partnership with the Cooperative Research Centre for Sustainable Tourism based at the Gold Coast. The scheme seeks to brand good environmental performance and increase consumer awareness and participation in sustainable tourism development, and it may include some linkages to the NEAP scheme in the future. It originally derived from Agenda 21 principles for sustainable development endorsed by 182 Heads of State at the 1992 United Nations Earth Summit in Rio De Janeiro. Green globe has been designed to achieve environmental, social and cultural improvements in tourism at global, national and local scales. It encourages and facilitates compliance that recognises national and provincial legislation and accommodates local regulations as required by agencies or authorities. It is a private organization, which includes an international Advisory Council, and seeks peer review of its standards and technical supporting information.

Green Globe is managed by the joint venture partners Green Globe Ltd (London), Green Globe Asia Pacific (Canberra), the Caribbean Alliance for Sustainable Tourism in Puerto Rico, and most recently, the Entrepreneurship Academy in Africa, each of whom has different roles and functions within the organisation. Green Globe (London) is responsible for global policy and marketing, while Green Globe Asia Pacific oversees development of the green globe product and Green Globe Americas, taken on by CAST, handles the Caribbean and South America. There are also strategic alliances that include Société Generales de Surveillance (SGS); Anglo Japanese Registrars (AJA); BM Trada, WTTC, the Tourism Industry Association of New Zealand, and the Ecotourism Association of Australia. These partners and alliances make it possible for Green Globe to operate on a global scale.

Discussion

The variety of schemes and programs highlighted above provides an indication of the importance placed on quality assurance by the tourism industry. However, this arguably represents potential for some confusion among consumers of ecotourism-related products. This issue was one of a number pertaining specifically to accreditation that were identified by participants involved in a national scoping study of regional tourism issues and priorities conducted recently by the Centre for Regional Tourism Research (Prosser, 2000). Other accreditation related issues noted were: a need to design effective schemes, encouraging participation in these schemes, and false advertising by regional operators of the value of such schemes.

In particular there is a widespread concern in the industry about the need to monitor, report and evaluate the implementation of accreditation schemes and standards. Despite acknowledgment of the importance of monitoring and evaluation to ensure adherence to accreditation standards and to ensure that accreditation systems are operating effectively however, there is limited evidence of widespread take up of the current accreditation schemes.

The perceived weaknesses of these programs are the cost implications for some (smaller) operations, the lack of follow-up monitoring after the initial documentation phase, poor recognition and credibility of the program within the industry, and a lack of public knowledge about the importance of the 'tick' or accreditation level reached. The fact that the NEAP program and its Green Globe international equivalent are not mandatory, and the lack of public recognition of their symbols, does little to promote commercial interest in this form of quality assurance. ISO quality frameworks are more attractive.

Participant businesses have not necessarily achieved significant direct benefits from accreditation and have a range of concerns about the programs as a result. Specific positive effects to business operations have included improved health, safety and risk management, increased business esteem and staff morale, and streamlining of procedural systems, but these appear to be outweighed by negative perceptions. The latter were the lack of customer and industry awareness of accreditation, poor program or government support, inadequate entry standards and program monitoring, and the lack of increased customer numbers and profitability resulting from accreditation. Potential avenues for addressing these issues include overcoming awareness and image deficiencies, enhancing accreditation delivery and management mechanisms, and improving business-level performance measurement.

Despite these negative issues and the relative infancy of NEAP style programs, the increasing involvement of businesses and Governments in such programs, and the commitment to accreditation indicated by those who have taken them up, suggests that there is potential for them to expand further at a National and International level.

Conclusions

There should be only one accreditation and/or certification system on a national basis. In this regard it is important to note the on-going discussions between NEAP and Green Globe Asia Pacific. For the NEAP model (in its Green Globe guise?) to be of use to other countries however, the accreditation process should be simplified (without compromising standards) and *replace* ISO accreditation—for example streamlining the process for *small* businesses for whom some of the requirements may not be relevant or appropriate, and minimising perceived deterrents to entry into tourism accreditation, such as concerns about fees, is necessary.

A range of financial and non-financial incentives should be developed to encourage businesses to become and stay accredited (particularly for those programs where no incentives are currently offered)—for example discounted or preferential access to marketing, insurance, membership and or awards initiatives on a National or International basis. In addition, the appropriateness and stringency of entry standards should be reviewed locally to determine whether these are high enough to produce consistent quality outcomes and provide for differentiation from non-accredited products and services.

Support for accreditation programs like NEAP is required at grass roots and at National level, to enhance communication, commitment and ownership of programs at the point of individual businesses—for example setting up local or regional networks of accredited businesses. Each country therefore needs to develop a comprehensive national framework, based on the NEAP/Green Globe criteria, before the benefits of such programs can be fully realised.

REFERENCES

Beeton, S. (1998) *Ecotourism: a guide for local communities.* Land Links, Collingwood.

Buckley, R. (1994) A framework for Ecotourism, *Annals of Tourism Research*, Vol. 21, No. 3, 661-669.

Ceballos-Lascurain, H. (1987) The Future of Ecotourismo, *The Mexico Journal*, 27 January.

Hall, C. M. (1994) Ecotourism in Australia, New Zealand and the South Pacific: Appropriate tourism or a new form of ecological imperialism? In: Cater, E. and Lowman, G. eds. Ecotourism: A sustainable option? 137-157. Chichester: John Wiley.

Manidis Roberts Consultants. (1994) *An Investigation into a National Ecotourism Accreditation Scheme*, Department of Tourism, Canberra.

Office of National Tourism. (1997) *Ecotourism Snapshot: a focus on recent market research*, Department of Industry, Science and Tourism, Canberra.

Prosser, G. (2000) *Regional Tourism Research Scoping Study.* Centre for Regional Tourism Research, Southern Cross University, Lismore.

David Taylor, D., Rosemann, I., and Prosser, G. (2000) The Effect of Accreditation on Tourism Business Performance: An Evaluation, Occasional Paper Number 3, Centre for Regional Tourism Research, Southern Cross University, Lismore.

Tourism Council of Australia. (1998). *Code of sustainable practice*. TCA, Sydney.

Wearing, S. and Neil, J. (1999) Ecotourism: Impacts, Potentials and Possibilities, Melbourne: Butterworth Heinemann.

Wheeller, B. (1993) Sustaining the Ego, Journal of Sustainable Tourism. Vol. 1, No. 2, 121-129.

2

Ecotourism and Community Development: Diaoluoshan National Forest Park, Hainan, China

*Mike Stone and Geoff Wall**

Introduction

Ecotourism, Protected Areas and Community Development

Ecotourism has received much attention in recent years, especially within the developing world. It has been linked to sustainable development initiatives, protected area conservation efforts, and regional and community development strategies in many places (Wells, 1997; Ceballos-Lascurain, 1993; Nenon and Durst, 1993).

While no widely accepted definition of ecotourism exists (Campbell, 1999; Weaver, 1998), at a minimum, it is thought to involve travel to natural environments (Eagles, 1998). Others define ecotourism more strictly, suggesting that it must be environmentally and socially responsible travel, that it should generate funds and support conservation efforts, and

* Faculty of Environmental Studies, University of Waterloo, Waterloo, Ontario N2L 5X4, Canada

that it should provide benefits to local host communities (Ceballos-Lascurain, 1993; Western, 1993). Parks and protected areas have been among the most common ecotourism destinations (Boo, 1990).

Behind a strict definition of ecotourism lie high expectations for the generation of a wide variety of benefits. While there is evidence that ecotourism's espoused benefits can be realized (Eagles, McCool and Haynes, 2002; Mitchell and Reid, 2001; Slinger, 2000; Hatton, 1999; Norris, 1992), there are equally as many (if not more) cases where ecotourism has fallen short of its proposed objectives (Lee, 2000; Nepal, 2000; Walpole and Goodwin, 2000; Ross and Wall, 1999b; Place, 1991). Indeed, ecotourism's impact has been highly variable.

While some countries and destinations have benefited from ecotourism, the fact that others have not has led some to conclude that significant gaps exist between ecotourism's potential and actual contributions in many areas (Nepal, 2000b; Ross et al., 1999b; Brandon, 1996; Wells, 1997; Lindberg, 1991; Ziffer, 1989). Nevertheless, countries in the developing world continue to turn to forms of nature-based tourism as a means of contributing to national, regional, and local development. Given this, one must ask if such tourism is really contributing to sustainable development. What have the socio-economic, cultural and environmental impacts been? Are the espoused benefits of ecotourism being realized? While these questions have been addressed to some extent in the literature, Ross and Wall (1999a) have criticized the lack of practical assessments of ecotourism's status in specific areas. Indeed, relatively few assessments of ecotourism's impacts at the local level have been performed (Lee, 2000). To address this research need, the impact of ecotourism at specific destinations in developing areas should be examined. This study is an exploration of the delicate relationships that exist between tourism, nature (protected areas), people and development.

Study Objectives

The central purpose of this study is to assess, through an evaluation of the existing tourism-park-community relationships and impacts, the current status of ecotourism at two protected area destinations where it is being promoted as a regional development strategy. More specifically, the following research questions are addressed at each study site:

- What is the destination's administrative body's definition and expectations of ecotourism?
- What infrastructure, facilities, programs and attractions exist at the ecotourism destination?
- What is the current state of management at the destination (active/passive, policies, etc.)?
- What are the host communities' perceptions of tourism at the destination?
- What is the relationship between host communities and natural resources at the destination?
- What is the distribution of socio-economic impacts at the destination, and what are the sources of economic leakage?
- What strategies could be used to strengthen the tourism-park-community relationships at the destination?

This research focuses on ecotourism, or at least what is being promoted and developed as ecotourism, at Jianfengling National Park and Diaoluoshan National Forest Park in Hainan Province, China, Hainan, although endowed with a wealth of natural resources and possessing an established tourism industry, is one of China's most economically backward provinces. Ecotourism has been identified as an important provincial strategy for balancing economic growth and conservation. Each park is located in the mountainous, rural south of the province, and sits adjacent to a relatively small, traditionally natural resource-dependent, community (Figure 2.1). The Parks were once extensively logged, but since the imposition of a logging ban on the Island in 1993 now protect a mix of primary and secondary tropical forest.

Fig. 2.1 Location of Hainan Province and the Study Sites

In exploring the existing relationships, this study is intended to provide planning direction to park managers/directors that will enhance the capacity of ecotourism at the destinations to generate benefits for both the local communities and the parks, and thus contribute to the sustainable development of the region more generally. A case study approach has the capacity not only to produce specific recommendations for the area under investigation, but also to generate broadly applicable results and strategies for allowing communities and destinations elsewhere to improve their capacity to benefit from ecotourism.

Methodology

In order to be able to comment on the tourism-park-community relationships, input from the various stakeholders—park managers, community residents, hotel managers and tourists—at each site was required. Interviews, observations and secondary sources (pamphlets, newspaper articles, reports, etc.) were employed to gather information on park management, facilities and attractions, community perceptions of the park and tourism, and levels of tourism spending. Wherever possible multiple sources of data/ information were used (triangulation) to confirm findings and limit personal and methodological biases.

A total of 100 community residents and business owners (65 at JNFP and 35 at DNFP) were interviewed between May and August 2001. Senior park directors and hotel managers were also interviewed at each site. An additional 13 supporting interviews were conducted with a variety of tourism and environment government officials, park managers, academics and researchers that were not directly associated with either park.

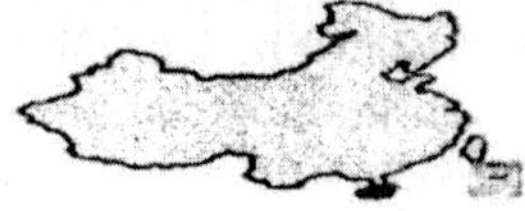

Fig. 2.2 Framework for Conceptualizing and Evaluating Ecotourism

Source: Ross and Wall, 1999

An evaluative framework developed by Ross and Wall (1999a) was adopted to help guide each case study evaluation (Figure 2.2). The framework considers ecotourism in terms of synergistic links, and uses a variety of indicators to determine if existing relationships are operating in a manner that allows each to make positive contributions to the other.

Results

Diaoluoshan National Forest Park (DNFP) Case Study

Ecotourism, strictly defined and assessed under the adopted framework, does not currently exist at DNFP. There is widespread understanding that the Park was created to protect the forest and to develop tourism. All community members interviewed believe that forest protection is important, with water resources and ecology being the most common reasons given. The vast majority of respondents see the Park as a good thing overall, and close to half of respondents perceive the Park as having had only positive effects, mainly in terms of increased incomes and jobs in the local economy. However, in reality, socio-economic benefits for the community and Park have been limited. Indeed, close to one-quarter of respondents indicated that the Park has had no effects whatsoever on their lives (Table—2.1). At the same time, residents are trying to cope with reduced access to resources. Limited numbers of tourists, the absence of park entrance fees the failure of the Park owned hotels to earn a significant profit has meant that tourism has not generated revenues to be put towards conservation activities.

Table—2.1 Selected Community Interview Responses at JNFP and DNFP

Interview Question	Response	Residents **JNFP**			
DNFP ents **DNFP**	Business Owners **DNFP** nessers **DNFP** **JNFP**				
Why do you think it was designated a Park?	Protect forest/ animals 80%	63%	57%	58%	
	Develop tourism	28	57	50	80

(Contd...)

Has Park establishment impacted your livelihood in a positive &/or negative way?	Positive only	38	50	74	40
	Negative only	28	7	0	20
	Neither	18	23	22	40
Positive effects cited	Local economy	36	14		
	Jobs	5	14		
	Increased incomes	0	29		
	Roads	27	14		
	Water resources	9	19		
Negative effects cited	Lost jobs	78	13		
	Only officials benefit	28	25		
	Forced to move/ lost land		22	0	
Is Park designation a good or bad thing overall?	Good	58	70	76	100
What are your feelings about possible future increases in tourism to this area?	Welcome more—no reservations	70	83	84	100
Is Protecting the forest/resources important to you?	Yes	100	100	100	
	100				
Why?	Nature/ecology/ protection	18	41	12	40
	Water resources	36	55	52	40
	Climate	47	17	44	40
Do you see any benefits or negatives if tourism was to increase (A) To yourself?	Benefits only	63	37	92	100
	Neither	37	63	8	0

(Contd...)

Personal benefits cited	Indirect-community				
	benefits therefore I do	41	45		
	Jobs	50	27		
(B) To the community?	Benefits only	66	67	88	80
	Both	23	30	8	0
	Neither	11	3	4	20
Community benefits cited	Local economy/ business	90	86	42	50
Community negatives cited	Environmental concern	25	22		
	Drugs/safety	38	22		
Have the Park staff involved you or the	Yes-given information	47	90	48	100
community in any way—planning, education, information, etc.?	No	45	10	36	0
Can you estimate the % of total sales/ revenues that come from tourists?	10% or less	82	80		

Table—2.2 Summary of the Relationships Between the Community and DNFP

Indicator	**Assessment**
Greater town population	~21,700
Local resident dependency on natural resources	High
Access to park resources	Restricted; some land for agriculture; fishing rental

(Contd...)

Access to resources in Buffer area	Not determined if a buffer zone exists
Illegal resource use	Minimal
Enforcement capacity	Not determined
Benefits from resource protection	Water resources, ecological protection, climate and disaster/food prevention (perceived)
Conservation attitude	Positive
Potential for stewardship	Good
Staff-local relations	Variable
Participation in planning	None; provided with information only

Although the majority of residents (not including business owners) did not think that tourism growth would yield personal benefits, most interviewed—residents, business owners and Park officials—were optimistic that tourism will bring local economic benefits to the broader community. A very limited number of respondents expressed concern over the potential for environmental damage, drugs, that there were initially some problems (like job loss) or that only officials are benefiting. Widespread optimism is not surprising given the early stage of development at DNFP, which likely reflects Doxey's 'Stage of Tourist Euphoria' (Doxey, 1976), early tourist-resident relationships under D'Amore's model (D'Amore, 1983) and Butler's 'Exploration Stage' (Butler, 1980) of a tourism development.

A number of key weaknesses in the existing tourism-park community relationships were identified that will limit the ability of ecotourism to generate benefits should it expand in the future. Very limited tourist traffic in Diaoluo, coupled with few spending opportunities (limited tourist infrastructure/ services) and the prospect of an increase in joint development ventures all suggest that the leakage of economic benefits to areas outside of Diaoluo will potentially be substantial. Community members have not had an active voice in Park or tourism planning processes. Information on DNFP tourists has not been collected and monitoring programs to provide current data on biophysical conditions are not in place. Additionally, the Park (Diaoluoshan Forest Bureau) staff has very limited experience in park or tourism management. Nevertheless, a variety of planning and management strategies can help to overcome these weaknesses. The potential for ecotourism to develop so that it provides a diversity of benefits for both the community and the Park is strengthened by recent funding increases under the National Natural Forest Protection Project (NNFPP) and fairly widespread community support and optimism. Tables—2 to 4 summarize the existing relationships at DNFP.

Table—2.3 Summary of the Relationships Between the Community and Tourism

Indicator	Assessment
Number of tourists	>30,000 (in 2000)
Tourism employment	Very limited
Tourism income for local community	Very limited
Tourism related entrepreneurship	None
Host attitudes towards tourism's impact	Positive; optimistic; some concern for environment, safety and potential for only government to benefit
Social welfare benefits	New roads; building improvements; water resources
Intercultural exchange opportunities	Very limited
Potential for positive intercultural exchange	Good

Table—2.4 Summary of the Relationships Between Tourism and DNFP

Indicator	Assessment
Park entrance fee	None
Tourism's financial contribution to conservation at JNFP	None
Availability of educational materials/opportunities	Limited; Pamphlet; Guides
Quality of educational materials/opportunities	Needs to be evaluated

The opportunities and constraints that have been identified in this case study could potentially be used to provide the framework for the development of a park (eco) tourism plan. The creation of such a plan will be essential in ecotourism is to develop in a manner that provides broad-based benefits at DNFP. Appendix A outlines potential planning responses and strategies for some of the main opportunities and constraints identified in this case study.

The JNFP can study yielded very similar results to that for DNFP. A summary discussion of the JNFP case is available in Chinese from the author or the park managers at JNFP. A complete discussion of both case studies and their planning and management implications is available in English from the author.

Interpretations of Ecotourism in Hainan

This Study also undertook to determine how Park managers and other key decision-makers in Hainan interpret ecotourism and what their expectations in developing it are. Hainan's Eco Province initiative, the Provincial Governments sustainable development strategy, identifies ecotourism as a tourism development strategy for the Island, nothing that ecotourism destinations are to be developed and marked nationwide (Department of Lands, Environment and Resources, 1999). Although no clear definition is provided in the documentation, there are excerpts that suggest that ecotourism is intended to be a sustainable form of tourism that allows people to enjoy nature, while at the same time protecting some of the Island's more precious natural resources. While it does stress protection, the Proposal does not specifically call upon ecotourism to improve the conditions of people living in close proximity to ecotourism sites. However, ecotourism is, more generally, identified as one of the main strategies under the EcoProvince initiative, the Island's policy framework for "improving the ecological environment, accelerating economic development, raising people's living standards and achieving modernization" (p. 3).

With a little reading between the lines, it appears as though most of the key elements of a strict definition of ecotourism, like that adopted for this study, are recognized by the Provincial Government (at least by the Department of Lands, Environment and Resources). However, the EcoProvince proposal goes on to subdivide ecotourism into marine ecological tourism, equatorial rainforest tourism and tourism for exploring/investigating plants, animals and mountains. Under this division, a number of sites are identified for the development of ecotourism, ranging from undeveloped, fairly remote wilderness areas and parks (consistent with a strict definition of ecotourism) to botanical gardens, beaches, and facility-intensive wildlife/ocean and cultural theme parks (more commonly associated with other forms of tourism). This suggests that perhaps there is some confusion over what exactly ecotourism is or what ecotourists would be attracted to.

Based on 16 interviews with site-level managers and key officials from Provincial Government and research agencies, it appears that overall there is fairly broad consensus that ecotourism involves travel in natural areas, resource protection and benefits for local population (Table—2.5). Less noted overall were cultural aspects and that ecotourism is a form of responsible/low-impact travel that, unlike mass tourism, may

Table—2.5 Interviewees' Interpretations of Ecotourism

Response	**Provincial officials n = 7**	**As a %**	**Site level officials n = 9**	**As a %**	**Total n = 16**	**As a %**
Nature focused travel	2	29%	6	67%	8	50%
Learn about/enjoy nature	1	14%	5	56%	6	38%
Environmental education	2	29%	4	44%	6	38%
Low impact/responsible travel	0	0%	2	22%	2	13%
Cultural attractions	2	29%	1	11%	3	19%
Local economic benefits	7	100%	2	22%	9	56%
Tourism $ for conservation	2	29%	1	11%	3	19%
Protects nature/good for park	4	57%	4	44%	8	50%
Form of sustainable development	4	57%	1	11%	5	31%
Limits # of tourists	0	0%	2	22%	2	13%
Planning/management important	6	86%	1	11%	7	44%
Increasingly popular trend	1	14%	2	22%	3	19%
Is a buzz-word	2	29%	0	0%	2	13%
Cited potential negative impacts	3	43%	3	33%	6	38%

involve limiting the number of tourists an area receives. Although half of the respondents associated nature protection with ecotourism, less than one-fifth overall specifically noted that tourism-generated dollars can be put back into conservation efforts. Only one-third of site level officials, and two-fifths of outside agency officials, noted that ecotourism has the potential also to generate negative impacts. However, those that did suggest potential negative impacts generally felt that the potential benefits would outweigh any associated costs. Indeed, the predominant feeling among those interviewed was optimism—the belief that ecotourism will generate broad-based benefits for Hainan. As under the Ecoprovince document, a variety of sites were identified by officials—forest parks/ reserves, a cultural botanical garden, and a monkey reserve/ zoo—as good examples of, or potential sites for, ecotourism, again suggesting some degree of confusion.

Discussion: Implications for Planning and Management

Some proponents of ecotourism have suggested that it can provide high quality tourism experiences, while stimulating socio-economic development, promoting environmental awareness and generating funds for resource management and conservation activities. The promise of broad-based benefits has prompted many developing regions to adopt ecotourism as a sustainable development strategy for balancing economic and conservation objectives. Although there are success stories, the reality is that ecotourism's impact has been highly variable. Fortunately, two decades of experience has resulted in the promulgation of a variety of planning and management strategies that may help to promote the development of positive tourism-park (resource)-community relationships and, as a result, the generation of benefits at an ecotourism destination.

According to a strict definition, DNFP can not currently be considered a successfully operating ecotourism destination—community benefits are very limited, tourism-generated funds for conservation are absent and educational opportunities for tourists are few. Nevertheless, government officials and community members are optimistic that tourism will bring benefits. Limited benefits, optimism and positive attitudes are characteristic of an early stage of tourism development (D'Amore, 1983; Butler, 1980; Doxey, 1976). Most officials interviewed recognize that development is at an early stage. A smaller group, to their credit, is also cognizant of some of the existing weaknesses and barriers that the development of ecotourism faces. The researcher is also very aware that tourism development is in its infancy and that neither site can realistically be expected to be operating without flaws. The comments, critical and supportive, offered in this study should be received in the cooperative spirit in which they are intended—to provide officials with planning direction that will help them to find a path of development that promotes synergistic tourism-park-community relationships and, ultimately, the generation of broad-based local benefits.

Relationships Between the Local Community and Park

Forms of nature-based tourism, such as ecotourism, have emerged in recent years as a popular means for integrating parks and people in rural developing regions (Place, 1991). However, park establishment alters the local economic base, and has often resulted in reduced access to resources for local people)Lindberg et al., 1996). This has been the case at DNFP. Where residents face pressures due to resource use restrictions, compensation should be provided (Sherman et al., 1991). This is especially important recognizing that many of the threats protected areas face arise from the needs of local communities to use resources to survive (Norris, 1992). Dependence on natural resources is high, especially for the ethnic minority groups (the Li people) in the Diaoluo region. Although opinion is divided as to severity, illegal resource harvesting does occur at the Park. Some residents also noted that they had lost jobs or land, and that it is now harder to make a living, highlighting the need for compensation. Some compensation has been provided to residents for lost land/resource access in the form of monthly payments, free electricity, water and education fees. However, interviews revealed differing interpretations of what compensation was provided, with some contesting it was provided at all or complaining that it was insufficient. Park managers are also hoping that compensation will come in the form of increased employment opportunities from the development of ecotourism. However, for now, such opportunities have yet to materalize and other strategies are needed. For example, a portion of the Park's revenues or budget could be earmarked to go towards community development projects (Sherman et al., 1991). However, the Parks themselves have in the past, been short of funds so that the potential to do this is limited unless Park incomes can be put on a more stable basis, perhaps through increased ecotourism. The provision of alternative resource supplies and land for agriculture, plantations, etc., outside of the Parks would also be very valuable. The creation of a buffer, multi-use, zone at JNFP is a positive step in this direction. It was not determined if a similar zone exists at DNFP. In the Jianfeng region it has been noted that there appears to be a direct correlation between poverty, subsistence farming and resource exploitation, and that progressive, diversified farming, including the sale of cash crops, may help to reduce pressures on natural resources (Associates in Rural Development, 1998). The same observation could also likely be made for the Diaoluo region.

Although Park staff has made an effort to educate community members, providing them with information about the reasons behind Park establishment and the importance of protecting the forest, residents have not had the opportunity to participate actively in planning processes and decision making. This problem is not unique to DNFP. Communities adjacent to protected areas have frequently been overlooked (Ceballos-Lascurian, 1996). This is significant, recognizing that the generation of community benefits and positive attitudes towards tourism is to a large degree dependent on local people's ability to participate effectively in decision making (Campbell, 1999; Lindberg et al., 1996). The failure to involve local people can lead to poorly integrated conservation-development projects that damage the resource base and reduce tourism's potential to generate benefits (Cresswell et al., 2000). Effective local participation can be defined as "the ability of local communities to influence the outcome of development projects such as ecotourism that have an impact on them." (Drake, 1991, p. 132). Participation opportunities exist at all stages of a development—planning, implementation, monitoring—and may take a wide variety of forms depending on the particular socio-cultural circumstances. At DNFP opportunities to participate could be provided using public forums to allow residents to voice their concerns and make suggestions on key issues. It might also be feasible to establish committees, comprised of local residents and business owners, which provide input in Park planning processes and decision making. If community members have a vested interest in such processes they are more likely to become advocates for the Park and support the continued development of ecotourism. Although participation can be a time consuming and difficult process, with some also cautioning that residents may not be in a position to make appropriate decisions (Byod, 2000), the risks associated with not providing such opportunities would seem to outweigh any potential costs.

Relationships Between the Local Community and Tourism

Ecotourism is at an early stage of development at DNFP. As such, there have been relatively few impacts to date. Some perceive improvements in water resources, climate, roads, incomes and the local economy (Table—2.1). This is important, recognizing that attitudes towards tourism are largely based on perceived costs and benefits (Lindberg et al., 1996). Although road improvements were observed, climate and water resource effects are difficult to confirm and, in reality, tourism-related employment, entrepreneurship and income have been limited. Aside from employment in the Park hotels, Travel Company, or as a guide, and occasional small shop sales to tourists (water, fruit, snacks, etc.), employment and income from tourism have yet to materialize on a significant scale at either site. Should ecotourism grow and employment opportunities expand, it will be important that local residents have the necessary skills to be able to fill positions. Park managers should consider developing training programs for local people before employing workers from more distant regions, who may already possess the necessary skills, but will add to the loss of economic benefits from the local community (Sherman et al., 1991). In the future, earmarking a portion of tourism revenues on the Park's budget for small loans for local people wishing to start a tourism venture may also help to generate and retain community benefits (Lindberg, 1991). Stimulating entrepreneurial activity may also require that training—how to start a business, how the tourism industry operates, etc.—be made available to local community members.

Given the prospect for future foreign investment/joint ventures at the Park, managers will want to ensure that they retain some control over the development of the industry. Foreign investment increases the potential for economic leakage (profits generated by foreign-owned businesses will not necessarily remain in the Diaoluo community) and can limit opportunities for locals to get involved in tourism if outside investment outpaces local capacities to accumulate capital or acquire training (Place, 1991). Local control will allow the flexibility to impose conditions on projects that will maximize community benefits (Loon et al., 2001; Sherman et al., 1991). For example, if the Park was to lease management rights of a facility to a private investor, they could require that investor, to train and employ local residents (Lindberg, 1991), or perhaps require them to purchase locally produced goods. The use of locally made goods and services, and the employment of community members whenever possible are absolutely critical to generating and retaining benefits in the community.

Although the lack of benefits can be attributed, in part, to the relatively low levels of visitation at the Park, it is also due to the location of tourism activity (at the hotel in the Park) and the absence of spending opportunities for tourists in the town of Diaoluo. While tourist volumes can be influenced to some extent, managers have much greater control over where tourism infrastructure is located. The capacity of ecotourism to generate benefits in the future will, to a large degree, depend upon the ability of managers to encourage tourists to spend larger sums of money in desired locations (*i.e.* in both the Park and the town). It is inherently difficult to spend money in the wilderness, where facilities are typically limited (Wall, 1994). Simply, providing tourists with opportunities to spend money locally, through the development of tourism facilities and services—interpretive media, food concessions, souvenirs, etc.—can help in this respect and also encourage tourists to return in the future (Lindberg, 1991). Encouraging tourists to lengthen their stay at the Park (one night is in the current average length of stay at DNFP) would also help in increase spending levels (Hvenegaard et al., 1998). This might be accomplished by offering reduced room rates for extended stay and publishing, multi-day, suggested sightseeing itineraries. Interpretation facilities, programs and guides may also help.

Spending opportunities are not only important for tourists, but also for local residents. In small, rural economies like that at DNFP, aside from food and basic supplies there are few goods or services available. This results in local people travelling to larger centres—Sanya, Haikou, etc.—to purchase clothing, major appliances, electronics and other 'big ticket' items. If tourism grows, much of the money that will be spent on accommodations, food and other items by tourists, will ultimately leave the community in the absence of locally available goods and services. Hotel managers will purchase appliances in Haikou and employees may spend their tourism-generated wages in Sanya on clothing or 'luxury' items. Although tourists' direct expenditures are important, it is also important that a portion of those expenditures be kept in the community through local secondary (indirect) and tertiary (induced) spending. The flow of tourism dollars through an economy is known as the multiplier effect, and, in considering overall economic impact it is important to consider both the volume of initial spending and the re-circulation and retention of money in the local economy.

Assuming that more tourists visit DNFP in the future, that they spend larger sums of money, in both the Park and in the town of Diaoluo, and the socio-economic benefits begin to increase, there are still a number of important points managers will want to consider. First, the employment opportunities arising from ecotourism are often limited due to the low variety of jobs created—guides, guards, cooks, porters, drivers, etc. (Brandon, 1996). Second, tourism, of any form, is an unstable source of revenue, one that is subject to seasonal fluctuations and many external (locally uncontrollable) forces, including weather and political factors (Norris, 1992). Third, tourism benefits are often inequitably distributed among community members (Hummel, 1994; Lee et al., 1992) and typically reflect disparities that existed prior to tourism's development (Nepal, 2000). At DNFP, where substantial income gaps exist between (and within) the Li ethnic minority and the Han Chinese, some have expressed concern that only the government will gain from ecotourism. Strategies may be required to ensure an equitable distribution of benefits within the community. These considerations suggest that ecotourism should not be depended on as the only strategy for improving conditions for community members.

Relationships Between Tourism and the Park

Protected are use fees, especially in developing countries, are often nominal (Wall, 1994; Lee et al., 1992) or missing altogether (Lindberg, 1991). At DNFP no use fees have ever been charged. Furthermore, the Park operated hotels and Travel Company have generated little, if any profit. As a result, tourism has yet to raise funds for management or conservation activities. Although levels of visitation have been relatively low, even a small fee, such as the 50 RMB ($9.60 CDN) that management is considering implementing at DNFP, could have raised substantial funds. A fee of 50 RMB, times the approximately 20,000 visitors that have apparently visited DNFP annually in recent years, would have raised about 1 million RMB ($192,300 CDN). This highlights the importance of charging tourists, even nominal amounts, for the privilege of visiting a park. It is quite possible that tourists would be willing to pay more than the 50 RMB that managers at DNFP are considering implementing in 2002. A survey of park tourists, asking what they would be willing to pay to enter the Park could help to determine appropriate use fees. The same survey could be designed to collect information on tourist demographics, spending patterns and satisfaction levels—information that is missing at DNFP. There is also a need to adopt a set of rigorous, standardized, guidelines for measuring, collecting and reporting on public use (tourism) in the Parks (see Hornback and Eagles (1999) for example, available in Chinese from the International Union on the Conservation of Nature (IUCN).

Some have also suggested that donation mechanisms should be put in place in order to capitalize on the documented willingness of nature-oriented tourists to contribute financially to conservation (Hvenegaard et al., 1998). Opportunities to contribute to conservation might be provided in the form of donation boxes at visitor centres. Management could also consider providing tourists with a letter, explaining current conservation projects, and an envelope that could be left at the visitor centre or hotel reception should they wish to make a contribution. If tourists were found to be reluctant to donate, management could consider imposing a special forest-protection tax on the sale of tourist-related goods, hotel rooms, or popular attractions for example (Sherman et al., 1991), to raise funds for conservation activities.

Higher use fees than those currently being considered could potentially be charged if a high quality tourism experience is provided at the Park. DNFP offers spectacular tropical scenery, but accommodations are basic and educational opportunities few. Although ecotourists may be content with basic accommodations (Eagles, 1998), they do demand high quality experiences (Eagles, 1992). DNFP does not currently offer such an experience given the lack of educational opportunities and interpretive media. Park authorities need to consider how educational opportunities could be expanded and attractions more easily accessed. For example, the abandoned timber mill that sits on the river immediately outside of Diaoluo could potentially be developed into a visitor centre, housing interpretive media on the Park's biophysical and cultural history and resources. The Park is in need of a Nature Interpretation Plan, similar to the one that has been developed for JNFP by a consultant team from Associates in Rural Development Inc. in 1997. Recent funding increases may help to begin this process. On a positive note, thc Park has provided some training for a small number of Chinese-speaking guides. It would also be beneficial to ask tourists how satisfied they are with their Park experience, the guide they had the educational materials they used or wish had been available, etc. Visitors' opinions can help management to develop suitable educational/interpretive programs.

Many of the tourism-park-community relationship weaknesses identified in this study have been aggravated, if not caused, by funding shortages and limited, or inappropriate, staff education. Senior officials at both the Park and Provincial Government have identified each of these as key problems. Careful planning and management are required if ecotourism is to develop successfully (Boo, 1991). This in turn, requires a properly trained, interdisciplinary staff (Boyd, 2000) and the presence of sufficient funds. Under the NNFPP, DNFP is to receive 6 million RMB ($1.15 million CDN) annually until 2010, suggesting the potential for enhanced management effectiveness. An official at Diaoluoshan National Forest Park indicated that they are trying to establish a special university training program to prepare students to fill key park management positions. Aside from this, on-going training seems to be limited to occasional seminars/visits from experts and self-directed study. The effectiveness with which funding increases and training initiatives can be used to strengthen the tourism-park-community relationships will be critical to the successful development of ecotourism at DNFP.

The opportunities, constraints and recommendations that have been identified at DNFP, considered within the broader framework of the soon-to-be-released World Tourism Organisation Tourism Master Plan for Hainan, potentially provides the necessary information for the creation of site-level park tourism plans (Appendix A). The creation of such plans will be critical to the successful development and management of tourism at DNFP.

Ecotourism in Hainan

If ecotourism is to develop successfully at a destination there should be some consensus among decision-makers on what the term means and what the objectives are in promoting its development. Overall, interviews revealed that most interpret ecotourism as a form of nature-oriented travel that balances resource conservation and human use (Table—2.5). Although less noted among site-level managers, officials also see tourism as a means for producing economic benefits for the Province, protected area agencies (the Forest Bureaus) and local communities. However, interviews and secondary sources also revealed that diversity of sites, ranging from undeveloped, wilderness areas to botanical gardens, beaches and facility-intensive wildlife and cultural theme parks, have been identified as good examples of, or potential sites for, ecotourism. This suggests that some degree of confusion exists, between and among different levels of jurisdiction, over what exactly constitutes ecotourism, what ecotourists are motivated by, and what tourism market the Province is aiming to attract.

If the Hainan Government is trying to appeal to ecotourists, they may need to reconsider some of the sites they are promoting/considering as ecotourism destinations. Failure to do so may result in low satisfaction levels among visitors who arrive in Hainan expecting ecotourism sites, which do potentially exist, but are lured to inappropriate destinations as a result of indiscriminate marketing. If, on the other hand, the Province adopts a loose interpretation of ecotourism, one that might be better described as general nature tourism or park tourism, then the marketing of a diversity of sites becomes more appropriate. Although Hainan possesses a wealth of natural resources and attractions, not all will be equally appealing to potential visitors. Those that would enjoy the luxurious resorts and beaches of Yalong Bay may not appreciate the basic accommodations, limited facilities and generally more rustic conditions that exist at places like DNFP. Similarly, those attracted to an environment like that provided at DNFP might be disappointed by the experience provided at a facility-intensive, highly manicured, but still arguably 'nature' site such as Nanshan Buddhist Cultural Park on Nanwan Monkey Island Reserve. The important point here is that the marketing of specific destinations needs to be tailored to the appropriate tourist segments.

Appropriate marketing will also be critically important for distinguishing Hainan from other competing destinations in China. The Province faces stiff competition from other, mainland locations in China. Yunnan Province, Like Hainan, offers tourists tropical forests, hot weather and ethnic minority culture. Indeed, beautiful scenery and culture abound throughout China. Hainan is also an island with a peripheral location, which may make it less appealing to some tourists (but attractive to others). Careful marketing is needed in order to establish a niche for Hainan in the tourism market for China, especially in the international markets.

Forest, park and tourism management in Hainan involves multiple management bodies, including the Hainan Tourism Bureau, Hainan Department of Lands, Environment and Resources, local Forest Bureaus (such as the Diaoluoshan Forest Bureau) and their parent body, the Hainan Forest Bureau. Different agencies are also responsible for Parks and Nature Reserves. Although some tensions have apparently surfaced between Park and Reserve managers in the past, interviews revealed that cooperation and relations among the diversity of agencies involved have generally been good. Nevertheless, if tourism grows, the management of visitors, and the areas they visit, will become increasingly more complex. It will be imperative that clear lines of responsibility and accountability be defined among the numerous bodies that are involved in the management and administration of tourism and protected areas (Boyd, 2000).

Conclusion

Although time, language and funding constraints prevented an in-depth examination of all relationships, the broad overview of ecotourism conducted at DNFP has identified a number of important opportunities and shortcomings. Recommendations based on these findings are intended to help promote the successful development of ecotourism at the case study site and, more generally, throughout Hainan. This study has potential practical value, in that it would be feasible to use the opportunities, constraints and recommendations identified to develop park tourism plans for the study site (Appendix A). In distributing results to interested parties at the Hainan Forest Bureau, Department of Lands, Environment and Resources and Diaoluoshan National Forest Park, it is hoped that this study will contribute to ecotourism planning on the island.

Along with the results from the JNFP case study, this research also contributes to the growing body of tourism literature by providing site-specific assessments of ecotourism at two destinations in Hainan Province, China and, by demonstrating how an evaluative framework can be applied to site-level assessments. Furthermore, the case-study approach has not only produced case-specific recommendations, but has also identified a number of more broadly applicable findings, issues and strategies that may help destinations elsewhere to improve their capacity to benefit from ecotourism. Research designed to improve the efficiency, with which ecotourism operates will be increasingly important as regional and national governments, especially in developing nations, continue to look to ecotourism as a sustainable development strategy.

Acknowledgements

This research was undertaken with the support of the Canadian International Development Agency through the support of the Canada-China Higher Education Program.

REFERENCES

Associates in Rural Development. (1998). *Jianfengling Park Management and Biological Diversity Protection Project: Final Report, Technical Assistance Project 2394-PRC.* Burlington, VT: Associates in Rural Development. Technical Assistance Project 2394-PRC.

Boo, E. 1990. Ecotourism: The Potentials and Pitfalls. Washington, D.C.: World Wildlife Fund.

Byod, S.W. 2000. Tourism, National Parks and Sustainability. In Tourism and National Parks: Issues and Implications. R. Butler and S. Boyd (eds). London: John Wiley and Sons Ltd. 161-186.

Brandon, K. 1996. Ecotourism and Conservation: A Review of Key Issues. Biodiversity Series. Washington, D.C.: The World Bank. Paper #33.

Butler, R.W. (1980). The Concept of a Tourist Area Cycle of Evolution: Implications for Management of Resources. *The Canadian Geographer*, *xxiv* (1), 5-12.

Campbell, L.M. (1999). Ecotourism in Rural Developing Countries. *Annals of Tourism Research*, 26(3), 531-553.

Ceballos-Lascurian, H. 1996. Tourism, Ecotourism and Protected Areas: The State of Nature-Based Tourism Around the World and Guidelines for its Development. Gland: IUCN.

Cresswell, C., and MacLaren, F. 2000. Tourism and National Parks in Emerging Tourism Countries. In Tourism and National Parks: Issues and Implications. R. Butler and S. Boyd (eds). London: John Wiley and Sons Ltd., 283-299.

D'Amore, L.J. (1983). Guidelines to Planning in Harmony with the Host Community. In Murphy, P.E. (Ed.), *Tourism in Canada: Selected Issues and Options*. (pp. 135-159). Victoria: University of Victoria.

Department of Lands, Environment and Resources. (1999). *Proposal for the Creation of An Eco-Province in Hainan.* Haikou, China: Hainan Provincial Government.

Doxey, G.V. (1976). When Enough's Enough: The Natives are Restless in Old Naigara. *Heritage Canada*, 2(2), 26-29.

Drake, S.P. (1991). Local Participation in Ecotourism Projects. In Whelan, T. (Ed.), *Nature Tourism: Managing for the Environment*. (pp. 132-163). Washington, D.C.: Island Press.

Eagles, P.F.J. 1992. The Travel Motivations of Canadian Ecotourists. Journal of Travel Research. 31(2): 3-7.

Eagles, P.F.J. (1998). International Trends in Park Tourism and Economics: Implications for Ontario. Paper Prepared For: Parks Research Forum for Ontario, Peterborough, ON, February 5-6, 1998.

Eagles, P.F.J., McCool, S.F., and Haynes, C. 2002. Sustainable Tourism in National Parks and Protected Areas: Guidelines for Planning and Management. Gland: World Tourism Organisation.

Hatton, M.J. 1999. Community-Based Tourism in the Asia-Pacific. Toronto: Humber College. APEC Publication # 99-TO-01.1.

Hornback, K.E, and Eagles, P.F.J. (1999). *Guidelines for Public Use Measurement and Reporting at Parks and Protected Areas*. Gland: IUCN.

Hummel, J. 1994. Ecotourism Development in Protected Areas of Developing Countries. World Leisure and Recreation. 36(2): 17-23.

Hvenegaard, G.T., and Dearden, P. 1998. Ecotourism Versus Tourism in a Thai National Park. Annals of Tourism Research. 25(3): 700-720.

Lee, D.N.B., and Snepenger, D.J. (1992). An Ecotourism Assessment of Tortuguero, Costa Rica. *Annals of Tourism Research*, 19(2), 367-370.

Lee, V.J. (2000). Assessing Ecotourism's Abilities To Generate Community Benefits: Bunaken National Park, Indonesia. M.E.S. Thesis. University of Waterloo.

Lindberg, K. 1991. Policies for Maximizing Nature Tourisms Ecological and Economic Benefits. International Conservation Financing Project Working Paper. USA: World Resources Institute.

Lindberg, K., Enriquez, J., and Sproule, K. 1996. Ecotourism Questioned: Case Studies from Belize. Annals of Tourism Research. 23(3): 543-562.

Loon, R.M., and Polakow, D. 2001. Ecotourism Ventures: Rags or Riches? Annals of Tourism Research. 28(4): 892-907.

Mitchell, R.E., and Reid, D.G. 2001. Community Integration: Island Tourism in Peru. Annals of Tourism Research. 28(1): 113-139.

Nenon, J. and Durst, P.B. 1993. Nature Tourism in Asia: Opportunities and Constraints for Conservation and Economic Development. Washington, D.C.: Forestry Support Program, U.S. Department of Agriculture and Office of International Cooperation and Development.

Nepal, S.K. 2000. Tourism, National Parks and Local Communities. In Tourism and National Parks: Issues and Implications. R. Butler and S. Boyd (eds). London: John Wiley and Sons Ltd., 73-94.

Norris, R. 1992. Can Ecotourism Save National Areas? National Parks (January): 33-34.

Place, S. 1991. Nature Tourism and Rural Development in Tortuguero. Annals of Tourism Research. 18: 186-201.

Ross, S., and Wall, G. 1999a. Ecotourism: Towards Congruence between Theory and Practice. Tourism Management. 20(1): 123-132.

Ross, S., and Wall, G. 1999b, Ecotourism: Towards Congruence between Theory and Practice. Tourism Management. 20(1): 123-132.

Sherman, P.B., and Dixton, J.A. 1991. The Economics of Nature Tourism: Determining If It Pays. In Nature Tourism: Managing for the Environment. T. Whelan (ed). Washington, D.C.: Island Press, 89-131.

Slinger, V. (2000). Ecotourism in the Last Indigenous Caribbean Community. *Annals of Tourism Research*, 27(2), 520-523.

Wall, G. 1994. Ecotourism: Old Wine in New Bottles? Trends. 31(2): 4-9.

Walpole, M.J., and Goodwin, H.J. 2000. Local Economic Impacts of Dragon Tourism in Indonesia. Annals of Tourism Research. 27(3): 559-576.

Weaver, D.B. 1998. Ecotourism in the Less Developed World. New York: CAB International.

Wells, M.P. (1997). *Economic Perspectives on Nature Tourism, Conservation and Development.* Environmental Economics Series. The World Bank. Paper #55.

Western, D. (1993). Defining Ecotourism. In Lindberg, K. and Hawkins, D.E. (Eds.), *Ecotourism: A Guide for Planners and Managers.* (pp. 7-12). North Bennington: The Ecotourism Society.

Ziffer, K. (1989) *Ecotourism. An Uneasy Alliance.* Washington, D.C.: Conservation International. Working Paper No. 1.

APPENDIX A

Potential Framework for the Development of a Park Tourism Plan at DNFP

Opportunity/Constraint

Opportunities

- The Park's tropical setting, features and attractions
- The DFB has a large number of Staff
- The NNFPP will increase funding, providing a stable source of funds over the next 10 years
- Existing jurisdictional responsibilities requires coordination with other government bodies
- The government controls the Park and tourism
- There is broad community support for the Park, tourism development and forest protection
- Community residents perceive social welfare benefits-water resources, ecological protection, roads
- The presence of Li and Miao culture

Constraints

- Staff have limited and/or inappropriate training
- Resources inventories are outdated
- The Park and its attractions are difficult to access
- Educational opportunities for tourists are very limited
- Little is known about Park tourists
- Tourism has not contributed funds to conservation
- Tourism-related employment and income are very limited, and the potential for economic leakage is high
- Local dependency on natural resources remains high, illegal harvesting continues to occur and some community residents are unhappy over lost jobs, reduced incomes and/or with the government in general

Potential Planning Response/Action

Opportunities

- Formulate and implement a marketing strategy based on the Park's unique features and desired tourism market (clientele)
- Provide training opportunities, incentives and, rewards for dedication and outstanding work
- Develop a detailed budget that allocates funds for investment in conservation, facility/amenity expansion, community development projects, biodiversity research and staff education
- Ensure clear lines of responsibility and accountability, so as to make the most efficient use of institutional capacities and resources
- Ensure future developments are located in areas that minimize environmental damage and maximize community benefits through the imposition of conditions on foreign investment that requires the use of local labour and goods
- Renew and maintain community outreach efforts re. the benefits of forest protection, current initiatives, etc.
- Foster community stewardship through public involvement in planning and decision making—resident advisory committees, participation in conservation activities, etc.
- Highlight benefits through outreach efforts to demonstrate the value of forest protection
- Work with the Li and Miao people to develop cultural attractions, over which they have substantial control, that will enhance tourist experiences and provide minority groups with an alternative source of income/compensation for reduced access to resources

Constraints

- Provide (re)training opportunities for management, security and interpretive staff
- Continue to pursue the development of a special training program at Hainan University for future Park staff

- Work with research agencies (CAF, HFRI, ITTO) and universities to update inventories
- Develop and implement a resource monitoring program
- Investigate the opportunity to apply for a biodiversity conservation grant from the Global Environment Facility (GEF)
- Continue with recent road improvements
- Work with travel agencies and bus companies to establish regular transport links to and from Diaoluo
- Consider constructing a backpacking trail network with camping facilities that would allow tourists to access Park attractions without an automobile
- Construct a Park entrance gate to provide a central location for tourists to register, obtain information on accommodations and attractions, hire a guide, etc.
- Develop and implement an interpretive plan, perhaps learning from the existing interpretive plan at JNFP
- Construct a visitor/interpretive centre
- Support (second) language training for interpretive staff
- Design and conduct a tourist survey to collect information on demographics, activities undertaken, spending patterns and satisfaction levels
- Analyze survey information and prepare a marketing strategy
- Adopt and implement a set of guidelines for the measurement and reporting of visitor statistics (e.g. Hornback and Eagles, 1999)
- Implement a Park user fee based on an analysis of budgets, the desired level of visitation and willingness-to-pay information from tourists
- Establish donation mechanisms and consider implementing a special conservation tax on the sale of tourist-related goods

- Expand the amenities available in the Town of Diaoluo, thereby providing more spending opportunities for tourists and community residents
- Provide training opportunities and hire preferentially from the community for Park/tourism positions
- Provide information on how to start/operate a tourism business and consider developing a small grant/loan program to help community residents to do so
- Impose conditions on new/foreign-invested developments that require the use of local labour and goods
- Encourage tourists to stay longer at the Park through reduced room rates for extended stays, multi-day sightseeing itineraries and the provision of interpretive facilities/programs
- Work with community members to develop satisfactory compensation arrangements for reduced access to Park resources
- Renew and maintain community outreach efforts that explain and document the benefits of forest protection
- Support diversified, not purely subsistence based, agriculture and invest in research that experiments with alternative livelihood strategies
- Provide training and skills development opportunities for community residents
- Encourage community stewardship for the Park through public involvement in planning and decision making
- Develop a monitoring program and investigate security staff's capacity to enforce regulations

3

Regional Tourism Information Centres: A Case for Community Involvement in Tourism Promotion: An Australian Model for Indian Consideration

Dr. Robert Inbakaran and Prem Chhetri***

Abstract

Community participation in regional/rural tourism development has become an established norm in regional Australia. Main tourism development bodies at federal and state levels have taken steps to promote rural tourism in so many imaginative ways. One of them is the voluntary involvement of talented and willing local elders of the community in managing the regional (rural) tourism information centres all across Australia. This paper endeavours to highlight the significance of regional tourism information

* Hospitality, Tourism and Leisure, School of Marketing, Faculty of Business RMIT University, Melbourne–3001
E-mail: robert.inbakaran@rmit.edu.au

** Dept. of Geospatial Science, RMIT Universsity, Melbourne–3001

centres as beacons of diffusing necessary tourist information to the needy visitor and at the same time, increasing the visitation levels gradually in the region concerned.

Introduction

Regional tourism[1] has gained a paramount significance in the development of rural areas, and established a new paradigm of 'alternative development' focussed on community participation, decentralisation and self-sustainable tourism based on local resources with global perspective. Rural tourism is a multi-dimensional process of attracting people visitation in rural ambience outside the urbanished areas and characterised by predominance of agricultural pursuits, forestry or natural areas (Lane, 1994, Page, S.J. and Getz D., 1997, NRTS, 1994). These rural attractions/activities can be segmented into various categories such as natural based ecotourism: sightseeing, hiking in national parks, rafting, skiing, abseiling and caving; cultural and religious tourism: travelling to heritage sites of cultural significance, visiting museum and art galleries and attending religious festivals or events; country town, rural resorts and other styles of country accommodations (NRTS, 1994). Rural tourism is not restricted to the activities in the ultimate destination but it is a cognitive/mental experience that gain through travelling in the serenity existing in the country and exotic places.

The development of tourism is often seen as a panacea for the underdevelopment of a rural community in the developing world. But underdevelopment can only be alleviated when a planning emphasised a strategy that focuses on identifying the host community goals and desires for and its capacity to absorb tourism. (Murphy P.E., 1985). He further explained that each community is supposed to identify its own goals and pursue tourism to the extent that it satisfies local needs (Ibid). Hence, as rural communities develop tourism, a process model that delineates the process exclusively for rural areas should be developed. Lewis has identified four different stages of rural tourism development process. The first stage involves the identification of resources in the community/area that would be of interest to tourists. Second stage involves 'formalising' the tourism process. Formal organisations would be started, local businesses would get involved, and the beginning of a plan to market tourism would start. In the third stage, development has begun, and marketing is in full swing. Finally, communities have begin to work together to establish regional tourism and tourism development becomes a centralised process in the rural community. (Lewis, J.B., 1998). The proper collaboration with Local government and community involvement in the tourism promotion can generate regional employment opportunities, an increased non-agricultural income; diversification of the region's economic base and global outlook.

An integration of local community participation is a vital component of rural tourism development process that can be viewed from at least two perspectives: in the decision-making process and in the benefits of tourism development (McIntosh and Goeldner 1986, Wall 1995, Timothy D.J., 1999). The first perspective involves the local community and other stakeholder in the planning process and decision making. "*Participation in the benefits of tourism includes allowing and encouraging residents to gain economically from the industry, and engaging local community in awareness-building efforts and other form of education*" (Timothy J.D., 1999). Participation generally refers "*to empowering local residents to determine their own goals for development, and consulting with locals to determine their hopes and concerns for tourism*" (Ibid). The concept also incorporates the involvement of other stakeholders and interest groups in tourism developmental process. Increasing incomes, employment, and education of locals are the most apparent ways of involving community members in the benefits of tourism development (Pearce et al., 1996). The adequate development of tourism is feasible only when the government industries and community involve in the decision making process and appropriately establish the adequate structures and linkages between the visitors and the information. The representation of this triangular relationship is best expressed in the form of rural information centres in regional Victoria. These information centres stimulate the tourist instinct for visiting a certain location by anticipated mapping of the regional attractions. The cognitive mechanism that affects consumers' decision system consists of stimulus and response to available information. (Goossens Cees, 2000). An effective information system is, therefore, a crucial element in strategic marketing planning. "*An effective marketing information system can be of great value to a regional organisation, particularly in its potential role as influencer and guide to the tourist business units*". (Heath and Wall, 1992). The merchandising material available in these information centres facilitates image marketing, establishing intimate interaction between locals and tourists with multi-directional feedback loops, and provide other services to the visitors like toilets, telephone services and shopping. Availability of visual and vivid information on pleasure destination attributes will enhance both the visitors' involvement and their ability to perceive more differences in service supply. Eventually this will increase their determination in making the right travel destination decision. Travel information had a significant impact on their travel decision, duration, expected expenditure in the region. According to Fesenmaier forty per cent of the respondents obtaining travel information reported they would increase the length of their stay as the direct result of this information (Fesenmaier, D.R., 1994). More than 75 per cent of the same respondents said the travel information would influence their choice concerning places they would visit (Ibid).

Triangular Model[2] for Rural Tourism Development

The triangular model of regional tourism with industries, local government and local community forming three corners shows interactive relationships and interdependency in the process of effective and efficient communication and dissemination of tourist information. Proper coordination and establishment of association are essential practice for maintaining rural tourist information centres (RTIC) in regional Victoria.

Industries are the immediate beneficiary of the tourist travelling in the destination. Private operators have prime responsibilities for supplying rural tourism product. Operators range from the large in-bound tourism businesses to the smaller specialist agriculture tour groups; the rural accommodations sector which includes farm-host, bed and breakfast, country motel, hotel, caravan park and rural resort operators; the rural tourism attraction and adventure tour operations; and organisers of country events and festivals. (National Rural Tourism Strategy, 1994). Tourism industry bodies and associations that operate at various functional levels at local, regional, State and National are important decision-makers. Issues such as industry leadership and organisation, product development, education and training, marketing, accreditation and standards are best managed and driven by them. (National Rural Tourism Strategy, 1994)

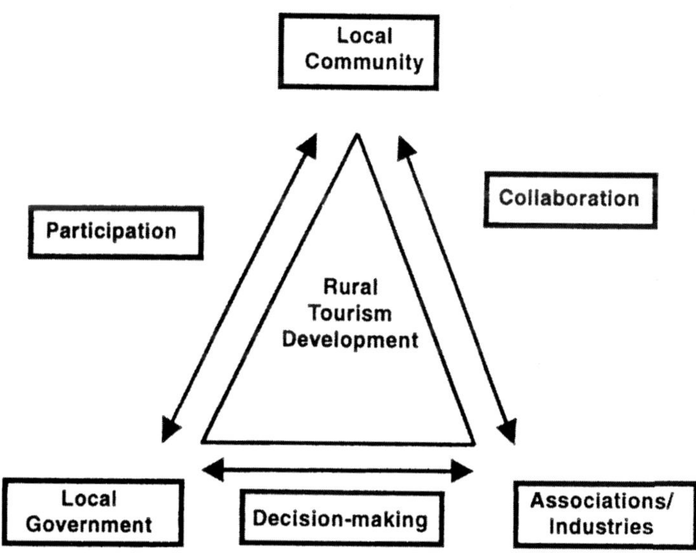

Fig. 3. 1 The Triangular Model of Rural Tourism Development

The support of Local communities can be essential in the successful operation of any RIC in the rural areas. Community involvement is seen as particularly important with the integration of tourism into local and regional development programs becoming essential components of an area's overall economic development. Also important is that the host community's itself is often a vital part of the rural tourism Product and act as rural attraction for the visitors by offering them hospitality and comfort in rural environment. The primary responsibilities for maintaining RTIC lies mainly with industries/associations and local communities, although it is recognised that the liabilities in many areas are shared with other stakeholders, including local government.

The support of local government has been particularly important for a number of regions that have sought to implement expanded tourism activities, both in terms of infrastructure provision and marking campaigns. Local government provides and maintains infrastructure and public facilities; often being the major funding sources for tourist associations, visitor centres and caravan parks. The Country Victoria Tourism (CVTC) has coordinated a Visitor Information Centre Development program, which has resulted in the preparation of guidelines for the establishment, management and general operation of visitor information centres (Business Plan, Country Victoria Tourism Councils INC). Outcomes of the new program include a consistent standard of excellence programs for staff and volunteers and improved credibility of information centres in Victoria.

The functional components that bring the stakeholders together are the most significant in managing and planning rural tourism. These functional components are participation, collaboration and decision making which determine the overall framework for organising and marketing tourism products of the region.

Regional Tourism Information Centre (RTIC)—Locational and Operational Parameters as Perceived by Visitors

"RTIC are often located near state borders, contain brochures and displays and are staffed with trained travel

counsellors who offer information and advice on attractions, special events, travel routes and lodging alternatives" (Tierney T et al, 1993). According to Tierney and Hass the information obtained at Welcome Centre resulted in a 25 per cent increase in visitor's average daily expenditures (Ibid). The establishment of RTIC in the rural areas is quite different than the urban environment because of the multifaceted nature of criteria. The attractions of stopping at information centre involves reasons for stopping at the centre, trip type, how far in advance visitors planned the current trip, the overall length of the trip, amount of the time spent, the type and amount of information obtained, the perceived usefulness of this information. A study done by Bureau of Tourism, Illinios, had identified six major attributes:

1. ease of highway access (ie., on the frontage road to the interstate versus within one-third mile of the interstate);
2. service setting (ie., the number of services nearby including gas stations and restaurants);
3. whether the tourist information centre stand alone or physically part of another type of service;
4. format with which travel information is made available (ie., tourist brochures versus interactive computer without paper printout);
5. availability of travel counsellors; and
6. whether the tourist information centre is publicly or privately owned and operated. (Fesenmaier, D.R., 1994).

Establishing RTIC in the state is a costly affair and alternative strategies for meeting the information needs of tourists must be considered due to budgetary constraints. Location factor of the RTIC is a vital component in establishing and maintaining tourist information centre. Fesenmaier findings support that tourist information centres located at interstate rest areas are one of the most effective means for providing tourism information (Ibid). This conclusion is based upon the relatively high-perceived importance of easy access, availability of public rest rooms and perceived safety of tourist information centres. However, the findings of the study also indicate that a relatively large segment of travellers (52 per cent) would consider stopping at off interstate locations (Ibid). Services provided by the information centre are the main reasons for stopping at the centre for this group.

Operational Structure of Regional Tourism Information Centre

The operational structure of RTIC is an important factor in the efficient and effective delivery of the information for the tourist. Its design and structural arrangements consideration facilitates adequate operational paraphernalia in managing, marketing and organising the RTIC operations and building congenial customer interface. The basic layout of the centre should create an image, which the centre wishes to deliver, promote and market. The outer design should be accessible, welcoming and identifiable for its unique local theme, feature and product that facilitates maximum efficiency and minimum staffing.

According to Rob Tong and Myott Don E. (1993) mentioned the following main components in any tourism information centre of reasonable size are:

1. Public lounge and information area
2. Static Displays: freestanding and on walls
3. Manager's office
4. Staff/workroom
5. Public toilets (Tong R. Myott E., 1993)

Depending on the type, size and location of the centre, the following additional components should be included where practicable.

- Theatrette
- Large display areas for local products

- Hot showers
- Facilities for nursing mothers
- Refreshments: drinks and meals (Ibid)

Signposting is an important component of destination marketing. Tourists tend to be reluctant to turn around if they miss the centre, and may bypass the facility and the town. If visitors cannot easily find their way around an area, it is likely many will not make the efforts and will move on.

Two types of strategically placed signs are required (Rob Tonge et al., 1993):

- *Advance Warning Sign*: Prior to the centre in each direction, placed at an adequate distance to allow ample time for drivers to react.
- *Directional Signs*: These should be located on all roads entering the town and in the other appropriate local government authority (Ibid).

Another important place of interaction is the public area where tourists interact with the staff. The area should provide an ambience that is friendly, accessible, open and self-driven. The set up should be able to navigate the customer with the tourism products of the region and stimulate the tourist to spend more time than they planned. The wall poster and display (tourism products) should not only be attractive but also provides adequate information, which the visitor seeks. The maps in the counter and wall should be comprehensible and deliver sufficient information about the area.

Due to shortage of space in the RTIC, the positioning for the information counter as recommended by Rob Tong and Myott, should be as a island facilitates easy access for staff to move from behind the counter to service and mix with visitors. The provision for the refreshment counter in the RTIC generates additional revenue for the maintenance of the centre and enhances the customer levels of satisfaction. It can also be deliver through vending machine. One of the vital components of the RTIC structure is public toilet that could be one of the major causes of tourist visit in the information centre. The public toilet as far as possible should be well maintain, clean, and preferably open 24 hours with a running water tap and power point. It should have facilities for handicapped; separate female toilets and baby changing bench (Tong R et al, 1993).

Visitor Information Centre Accreditation Program: Government Participation in Tourism Development

The success of establishing RTIC in the regional Victoria not only relay on its performance in attracting tourists/visitors but also attaining recognition and accreditation from government bodies and delivering quality products and reliable information to the visitors. Primary goal of all Visitors Information Centres must be excellence in the provision of information services irrespective of location and resources. It is essential that if a region or community is to operate productively and economically in a manner that maximises the benefits of tourism, appropriate tourism structures must be put in place. The Government took initiative in this direction by establishing local tourism associations, which is primarily an inward focused organisation concerned with product development issues and meeting the visitors needs at a local community level. "*Local tourism associations act as important catalysts for encouraging facilities and infrastructure development in cooperation with regional tourism associations*" (Local Government and Partnership, 1997). There are three models recommended by Tourism Victoria (1997) based on the local conditions and priorities. In all the models, RTIC is considered an important component for the tourism development planning except Regional Tourism Development Model.

Tourism advisory board model shows the place of Visitor Information Centre in the organisational structure designed for integrating both local government and the private sector involved in the tourism development decision-making process (Local Government and Tourism—The Partnerships 1997). The Regional Economic Development Board Model where "*local governments provide funding for tourism staff, and services such as information centres, marketing, facilities and administration and tourist officers through a regional economic development board"* (Local Government and Tourism—The Partnerships 1997). In this model tourism officer, who manage the information centre and other event marketing reports to the local government's economics development manager who is directly accountable to Tourism Advisory Board. On the Regional Economic Development Model where the Visitor Information Centre is manage by Regional Tourism Association that is formed by local tourism associations in the region (as shown in the Fig. 2). Therefore the information is playing a dual role of coordination between local council and local tourism association in the region. Technically it is a smallest unit that provides various functions and services to government operations and other regional association.

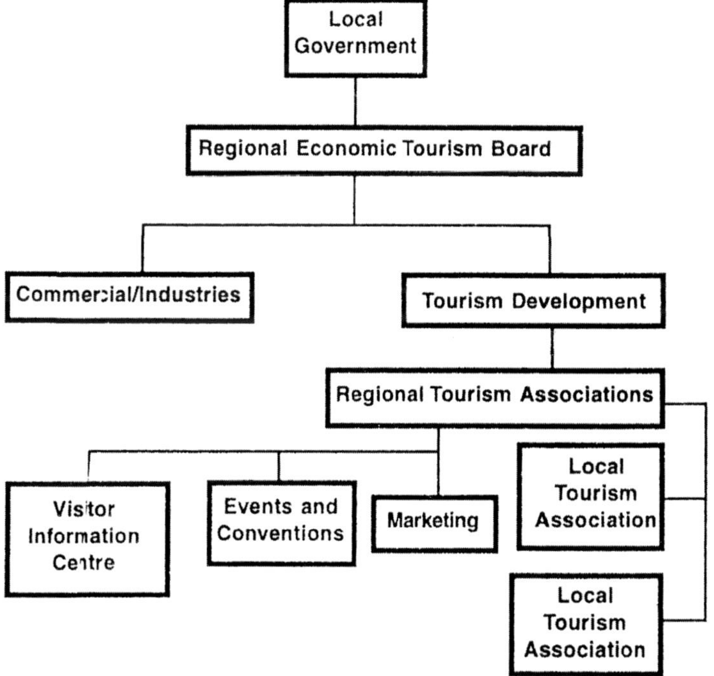

Fig. 3.2 Regional Economic Development Model, (Local Government and Tourism—the Partnerships 1997).

According to Country Victoria Tourism Council's view that the *most effective method of achieving a high standard of excellence is to produce an industry developed and approved accreditation program (Ibid).* Visitor Information Centre Accreditation Program (VICAP) is a tiered network of certified information centres, which will evolve and be marketed under the promotional name "Visitor Information Network Victoria. (Country Victoria Tourism Council Inc, Business Plan, 1977).

Major objectives of the VICAP are:

- The provision of quality Visitor Information Centre and services throughout regional Victoria.
- To improve the standards of professionalism within Victoria Visitor Information Centres.
- Develop a network of accredited Visitor Information Centres all meeting a set of best practice guidelines.
- To increase the length of stay, expenditure and yield of visitors to regional Victoria through the provision of quality visitor specific services.
- To promote and encourage accreditation of Visitor Information Centres (Country Victoria Tourism Councils INC, Business Plan, 1997).

To achieve these objectives the following strategies will be implemented: (Country Victoria Tourism Council Inc. Business Plan, 1977)

- "To develop, implement and promote an industry approved accreditation scheme for Visitor Information Centres. The scheme will be known as the Visitor Information Centre Accreditation Program.
- To develop and implement a range of training initiatives designed to Co-ordinate existing tourism industry courses and integrate the national competency standards for visitor services.

- To develop a plan to Co-ordinate other government agencies and tourism related organisations offering visitor services.
- To introduce a new i-sign as part of the State Tourism Signing Program to clearly identify the accredited Information Centres.
- To investigate all available avenues for additional funding be they grants, sponsorship or co-operative commercial opportunities.
- To provide leadership and direction thereby increasing the recognition, overall efficiency and professionalism of Visitor Information Centres.
- To continually develop and deliver tangible benefits to accredited Visitor Information Centres" (Country Victoria Tourism Councils INC, Business Plan, 1997).

Business and Management Structures Criteria

These are core requirements and all levels are required to meet these criteria.

- Business Registration
- Insurance
- Work Care
- Occupational Health and Safety—First Aid and Emergency Procedures
- Operational Manual
- Business Plan
- Hours of Opening
- Funding (Country Victoria Tourism Councils INC, Business Plan, 1997)

Business name of the Visitor Information Centre must meet all formal statutory and regulatory requirements and must be registered. The centre must also have insurance cover to protect staff, management, public liability and consumer

Level One	*This is the highest level. Generally Centres reaching this level run a Centre with a high volume of visitors per year (Approx 40,000 +)*	*The information provided in the Centres covers every region across Victoria*	*These Centres would be eligible to become involved in any state-wide promotional activities*
Level Two	*As the second level, Centre reaching this status will have a moderate volume visitor per year (Approx 20,000 +)*	*The information provided in these Centres often covers several regions*	*Centres reaching may also be eligible to because involved in state-wide promotional activities as advised.*
Level Three	*The last level caters for the smaller Centre, which is often run by volunteers or a private company and has small numbers of visitors per year*	*These Centres usually provide information on their local town only*	*Centres in this level would not eligible to become involved in any statewide promotional activities*

Fig. 3 Three Tier Hierarchy Model designed in VICAP (Country Victoria Tourism Councils INC, Business Plan, 1997)

protection (*Country Victoria Tourism Councils INC, Business Plan, 199)*. Work care agreement must cover all staff under operation in the centre and must meets Occupational Health and Safety standards. Another important criteria for accreditation program are operational manual and business plan. Business plan outlines the direction and broad objectives of the business and operation manual provides the written operational policies and procedures which each centre need to follow. Apart from these the centre must be financially supported by local government and in addition funded by tourism associations, a community organisation or a combination of sources (*Country Victoria Tourism Councils, INC, Business Plan, 199*).

There are three levels of accreditation available. All are eligible to receive the accreditation *i*-sign. A general indication of the difference between the three levels is indicated in the above Fig. 3.3.

In this three-tier hierarchy model develop by VICAP shows three levels of information centres in Victoria. Level one shows the highest level with a very high volume of visitors and provides information for every region across Victoria. Level two information centre covers regional information and visited by moderate volume approximately 20,000 plus. The lowest level of centre receives only small number of visitors and distributes information regarding local attractions in the area. The regional information centre normally falls within the level 2 and 3, due to their non-metropolitan locations.

Other Criteria for Accreditation in Victoria

According to the Business Plan of Country victoria Tourism Councils INC, the following criteria must meet by centre for the level of accreditation for which they have applied.

Premises

Level One	Level Two	Level Three
• Purpose built or stand alone building or premises occupied independently or other tenants	• May be purpose built or stand alone but may also have shared tenancy with the main use of the building dedicated to the Information Centre	• Is part of a shared tenancy with only a small area dedicated to the Information Centre This may be a private business

Parking

Level One	Level Two	Level Three
• The centre must have adequate car parking to meet demand	• The Centre must have adequate car parking to meet demand	• The centre can have car parking in close proximity

Equipment

Level One	Level Two	Level Three
• Toll free telephone line	• Dedicated telephone line	• Dedicated telephone line
• Dedicated telephone line after hours answering machine	• Dedicated after hours answering machine	• Dedicated after hours answering machine
• Dedicated personal computer with capacity for e-mail address and Internet address and Internet connection	• Dedicated personal computer with capacity for e-mail address and Internet connection	• Dedicated personal computer with capacity for e-mail address and Internet connection
	• Dedicated facsimile machine	• Dedicated facsimile machine

Staffing

Level One	Level Two	Level Three
• Minimum two permanent paid staff on site, one with a minimum of three years experience as a Tourism Officer/ VIC Manager or Management experience	• Minimum one permanent paid staff member on site with a minimum of two years as a Tourism Officer/VIC Manager or management experience	• Can be part time or volunteer staff with overall management from a tourism association within the region

Networking

Level One	Level Two	Level Three
• Effective networking with all Visitor Information Centres state wide and with travel trade	• Effective networking with all Visitor Information Centres state wide and with travel trade	• Effective networking with all Visitor Information Centres state wide and with travel trade
• Effective networking with other Visitor Information Centres in the product region/s and adjacent region	• Effective networking with other Visitor Information Centres in the product region/s and adjacent region	• Effective networking with other Visitor Information Centres in the product region/s and adjacent region
• Provide appropriate regular information support to Level 2 & 3 Centres within the regions	• Provide appropriate regular information support to Level 1 Centres within the regions	• Provide local area information support to Level 1 & 2 Centres

Source: Country Victoria Councils INC, Business Plan, 1997

Community Involved Regional Tourism Information Centres

The benefits of Regional Tourism development in any region can only be effectively disseminate when the process is collaborative with all stakeholders. A stokeholder is defined here to be "*any person, group, or organisation that is affected by the causes or consequences of an issue*" (Bryson and Crosby, 1992, p. 65). In tourism development the group can be homogeneous interest group such as any travel agency with specific business focus, or it can be heterogeneous such as local community living in the destination. The local community can be important human resources for tourism development when it is integrated in planning decision about the community based local resources whether it is own by government or by other business entity. It should be able to "*motivate and encourage participation in community groups, create opportunities for training and technical assistance, develop communities' ability to manage financial resources or establish community development funds, and lead the establishment of well-managed reserves, educational facilities and other attractions*" (Ruth Noris et al). There are two approaches involve in the community based regional tourism, firstly, privately sponsored ecotourism/regional tourism which seeks to preserve the resources by benefiting the local people, whereas community based regional tourism seeks to benefits local people by preserving the resources (Ruth Noris et al.,).

The operation of Regional Tourism Information Centres in Victoria is an exemplary of community based regional tourism. It is collaboration among local government, industries, and local community in the region. It is difficult to assess what might be a representative balance among the relevant stakeholder groups and generally it is experience that some stakeholders seek to collaborate only with those who share compatible goals and resources while others are ignored or marginalised (Stoker 1995). Hence a rationale and systematic balancing is required in power sharing and decision-making about destination marketing for sustainable harnessing of local attractions for rural tourism development.

Voluntary Community Participation in Regional Tourism Development

Tourism development should engross local community in a consultative role to recognise and fulfilled locally defined aims. Regional Tourism Centre in regional Victoria is a manifestation of this collaborative relationship whereby community gets involved in decision making regarding local attractions in destination by participating through Information Centre. As discussed earlier that tourism development can be initiated with two approaches: firstly by delivering the benefits to the local community by making them extrinsic part in the regional tourism, with their external support. Another approach to involves local community in decision making process, by incorporating them as an intrinsic element of the tourism structure. Victorian RTIC is reflection of second approach whereby the community participate in the decision making process with the collaboration of local government and regional tourism association. The information centre incorporates the interest of various stakeholders such as local government representative such as Tourism Development Officers, Representative of Regional Tourism Association, and volunteer from local community. This collaborative approach facilitates a common decision making platform where various interest groups share their ideas and coordinate for achieving community goals and regional self-reliance. Various focus groups such as retired people, teachers, tourism tertiary students, and non-government organisations participate in the planned and systematic rostering system for proper delivery of information to the visitors. Local Government facilitates infrastructure and financial support, regional tourism monitors and managers RTIC functions directly and indirectly, and local commune delivers the information to the potential visitors in the region and promotes local attractions and maintains regional culture and values.

Community participates in the tourism development as voluntary workers, with no immediate benefits, but long-term community prosperity by promoting regional tourism products.

The local community gains benefits in terms of local employment in the ancillary industries, fostered as a result of regional tourism. The volunteers in the RTIC roster their working hours with their convenience and demand. This flexible arrangement of hours whether once in a week, or four hours in a day are planned with community consensus and congenial environment in the RTIC. Apart from volunteers involvement in delivering information services to the visitors, their skills in making various items can establish cottage industry, to make quality handmade items which can be used as souvenirs. Their services can be used as guides for local tours and hospitality people for functions and special events.

According to Tonge R. and Myott D.E., apart from cost savings, there are other benefits by inviting senior citizens to staff information centres on a voluntary basis:

- It involves a sector of the community, which is traditionally reluctant to accept growth in tourism.
- Many long-time residents have extensive local knowledge—particularly of the local history and can often provide the information in a manner, which enhances the visitor experience.
- It provides retires with a challenging and interesting activity, and the opportunities to communicate with a wide range of people (Rob Tonge et al., 1993).

The probable shortcoming in involving retirees in the operations can be less adaptability with new technology, adamant and stubborn attitude, and less energetic in marketing the product. DEET, Skill share and TAFE College are other sources for volunteers, all require workplace to train their student.

The operations of regional tourism Information Centre (RTIC) in the regional Victoria function with the support of various organisation and government bodies. Local government and association (local and regional association) provide decision support and determine the immediate goals, and policies,

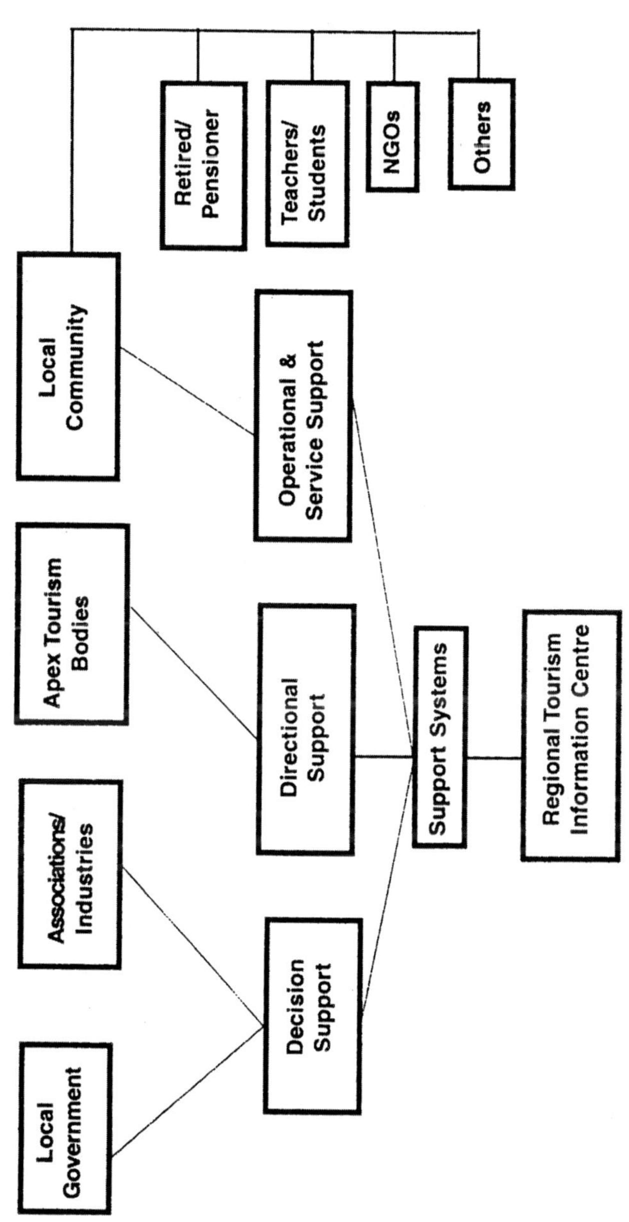

Fig. 3.4 Regional Tourism Information Centre Support System

examine financial resources and manage human resource of the RTIC. The apex bodies such as Tourism Victoria formulate overall objectives and directions of the RTIC and conduct accreditation program. The operational and service support is managed by local community such as retired persons, students, teachers and NGO etc. Collaboration among these components of support systems is imperative for the maximising the quality of service delivery and optimising the levels of satisfaction.

Levels of Visitor Satisfaction with RTIC—A Case Study of Dunkeld Information Centre in Regional Victoria

The research survey conducted was focussed on two different geographical areas; the core region which supply visitors and the periphery region which received visitors. The pre-test survey was conducted in Melbourne city to test a sample of ten persons to review the data collection plan so that the questionnaire could be checked for errors due to improper design elements such as semantic structure, sequences and flow of questions, and its relevance to the research. Data collection for both the surveys was based on random, sampling techniques. The target groups for the Melbourne survey included people in the CBD area, around City Visitors Information Centre, Australian Pacific Tours along Swanston Street, and the Spencer Street coach terminal and train station. The survey was designed to comprehend the tourist awareness and recognition about Southern Grampian tourist region and Dunkeld RTIC and to analyse Visitors perception about the region. The survey also tried to investigate multi dimensional nature of travel behaviour and decision making by looking at various aspects such as influence of distance, quality of attractions offered, level of services, provided, quality of the information and perceived usefulness of this information, duration of the visit and levels of Visitor's satisfaction. A personal interview with the Shire Council Tourism Officer was conducted to gain information in organising and maintaining Regional Tourism Information Centre (RTIC).

The Melbourne questionnaire consisted of 12 prudentially selected questions, which would enable research to deduce the respondents' receptiveness and their knowledge about Dunkeld and Dunkeld RTIC. The majority of the respondents in the Melbourne City survey already visited regional Victoria (84 per cent) and the rest of the respondents (16 per cent) have no immediate plan/intension to visit the region.

Eighty five per cent of the respondents have been the Southern Grampian region but majority of them did not visit Dunkeld. Remaining 15 per cent who visited Dunkeld associate the place mainly with National parks, serenity and cultural heritage in the area and they used Dunkeld as a Southern Gateway to Grampians. Most of the respondents shows not desire to know about Dunkeld (71.3 per cent) a high proportion had little experience in Dunkeld. Among those who already visited Dunkeld, 92 per cent indicated that was their first trip in Dunkeld while an additional 7 per cent visited twice. The result indicates that the main purpose of visiting Dunkeld was primarily to collect information (60.7 per cent) and using the facilities as a rest room (28 per cent). Sixty per cent of the respondents would like to recommend Dunkeld to an overseas visitor and also believe Dunkeld has potential as a tourist destination. Majority of the respondents associate and identify Dunkeld with Grampian National Parks (89 per cent) as a tourist attraction, followed by scenery and winery in the region. Since the Dunkeld is known as a Gateway to Southern Grampian, therefore most of the visitors recommend the place as a rest point (69 per cent).

The quality of the information and services can only be judge rationally when one can compare the Regional Tourism Information Centre with the other Centres existing in the region. The last part of this section of the survey focussed on respondent assessment of the relative importance of Dunkeld RTIC in the region.

The result of the study provides substantial information, concerning the relative rating of Dunkeld RTIC with other

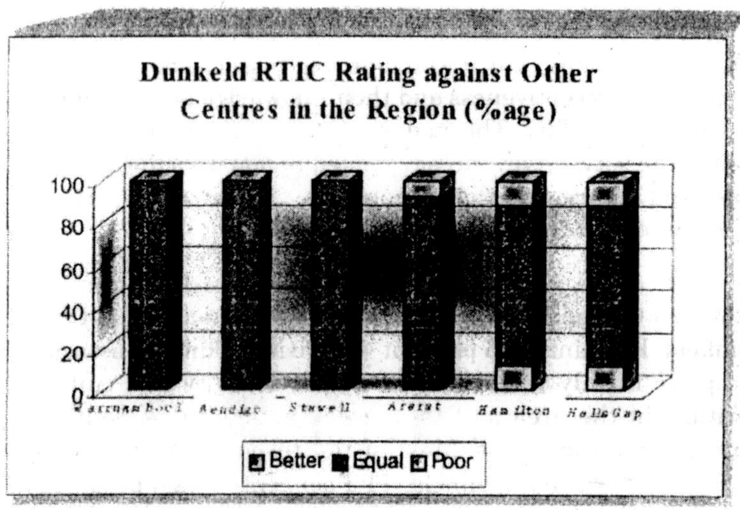

Fig. 3.5 Dunkeld Rating against other centres in the regional Victoria

Tourism Information Centres in the region. As shown in the figure 3.5 (as shown above) that Visitors rated Dunkeld RTIC at par with other important Information Centres in terms of quality of information and services. The Information Centres that are in close proximity with Dunkeld shows a variation with 12 per cent rate Dunkeld better than Hamilton and Halls Gap, while 12 per cent rate vice versa.

Eighty nine per cent of the respondent who travelled Dunkeld, also visited Dunkeld Information Centre (83 per cent), and believed that the information gathered from the centre was very informative (72 per cent), very helpful (84 per cent) and highly tourism oriented (64 per cent). Respondents who visited the Dunkeld RTIC rate the information good (64 per cent) and thirty-two percentages rate it average. Visitors mainly consider Dunkeld as a linking point to Grampian and visited the town mainly for the purpose of refreshment (32 per cent) rest room (18 per cent), and accommodation (15 per cent) as shown in the figure 3.6.

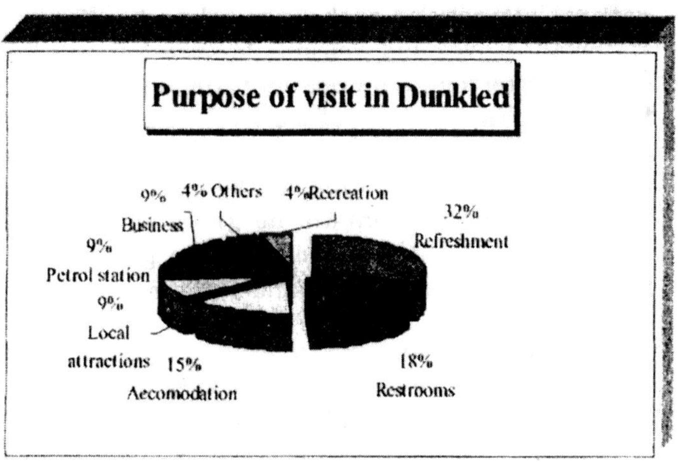

Fig. 3.6 Purpose of Visit in Dunkeld Rural Tourism Information Centre

Overall scenario in the Melbourne City survey provides relevant information pertaining to travel behaviour and perception. Dunkeld as a town and Information Centre in not very known to large number of respondents, but the Centre facilitates and delivered a large range of services the Visitors and is considered an important node linking Southern Grampian with the other places. Notwithstanding of its less popularity as compare to other Information Centres such as Halls Gap, Hamilton and Bendigo, Visitors still ranked it at par with these Centres.

Primary surveys become most successful when they are conducted in real time scenario because in that ambience the responses from the Visitors provide an instantaneous reflection of experiences and meticulous evaluation of perceived landscape. Visitors immediately assess the quality of information, levels of services and overall facilities provide in the RTIC, which stimulate in situ prudential judgement/

decision about any question. The study reveals that the Southern Grampian is mainly known National Parks and natural attractions such as peculiar landforms such as Waterfall, Caves and Volcanic features (figure 3.7). These natural attractions comprise approximately 70 per cent of the Visitors purpose of travelling in the region. Other tourist attractions are cultural heritage mainly aborigine arts, Wine region, recreational boating and fishing etc. This indicates a higher importance should be given to these perceived attractions by visitor and must be given priorities in formulating tourism policies and planning in region.

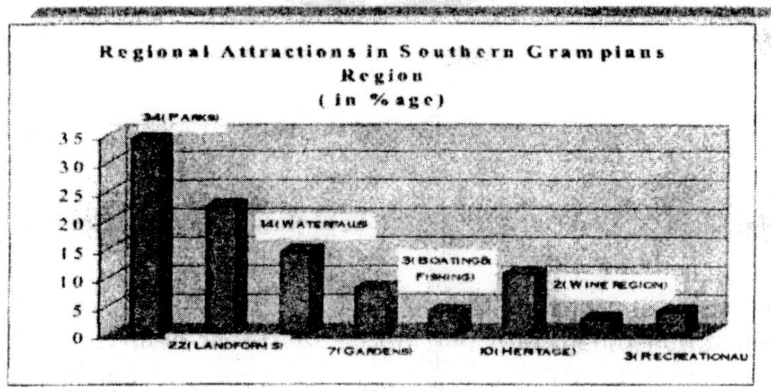

Fig. 3.7 Regional attractions in Southern Grampians Region (Dunkeld Survey)

Location of the RTIC is another vital factor that influence Visitors' decision making. Large number of the respondents surveyed believed that the location of the Dunkeld Information Centre is conveniently situated (82 per cent). Geographically also Dunkeld location is strategically favourable to both Southern and Northern Grampians. Therefore it is known as "Gateway to Southern Grampian." The spatial flow of traffic networks depicts a discernible pattern of high volume and concentration from Warrnambool, which comprised 59 per cent of the total respondents, followed by Penhurst (26 per cent),

Port Fairy (21 per cent). These pattern shows that the majority of the Visitors to Dunkeld are presumably coming from the Great Ocean Road and part of the Great Southern Touring Route.

The duration of the trip to Dunkeld RTIC is usually very short less than 1 hour (62 per cent). This reveals that the Visitors intend to use the RTIC as a source of getting the information or using it only for refreshment purposes. Only three per cent stayed in the place for more than one day.

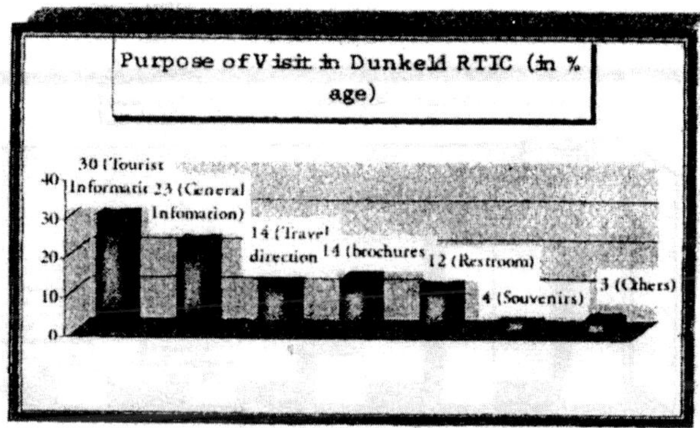

Fig. 3.8 Purpose of Visit in Dunkeld RTIC

Respondents were asked to identify the reasons they visit to Dunkeld RTIC. The majority (30 per cent) of the visitors stopped for travel information, 23 per cent general information, 14 per cent travel direction etc. The purpose of visiting Dunkeld and Tourist Information Centre varies, where most of the respondents visited Dunkeld for information, followed by rest stop (refreshments), rest stop (restrooms) accommodation, and local attractions (figure 3.8). Although most of the options given to the visitors in Dunkeld RTIC are pertaining to tourism, but it further investigate the precise reasons for visiting the centre. For example the centre should not only distribute the tourism-related information, but also be able to deliver other general information.

Another part of the survey focussed on respondents' assessments of the importance of travel information they received at the tourist Information Centre. The result indicates that a large proportion of the respondents considered the travel information very important. Travel information had a significance impact on their travel. More than 47 per cent of the Visitors are very satisfied with the visit in the RTIC, followed by Satisfied 32 per cent, 9 per cent poorer, and only 6 per cent very unsatisfied. This shows that a large amount of the visitors are satisfied with the services and information provided.

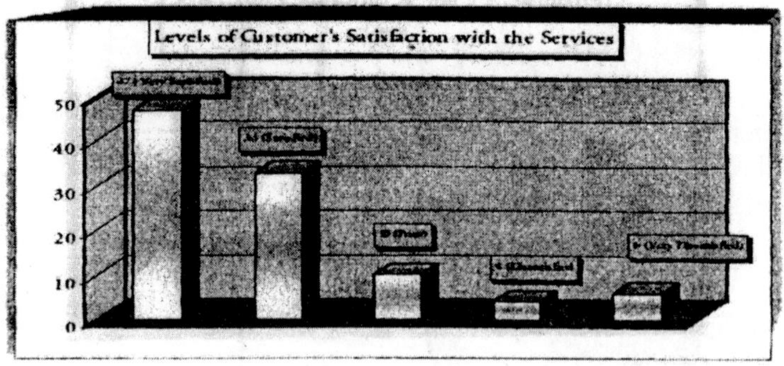

Fig. 3.9 **Levels of Customer's satisfaction with the Dunkeld RTIC's Services**

Ninety per cent of the Visitors believed that the information provided in the Center was useful and adequate, but they expect more information on National parks, Local events, Accommodations in the region. Seventy nine per cent Visitors think that the staff in the RTIC was knowledgeable, but they also expect additional services such as tour booking, accommodation bookings, and transport booking. This is another avenue of enhancing revenue and resource base by involving industries into this venture. Seventy nine per cent of the visitors rated the standard of the services provided by staff at the Centre as satisfactory and 9 per cent rated it as unsatisfied.

Socio-Demographic Characteristics of Visitors

Analysis of data provided interesting information describing the demographic characteristics of Dunkeld Regional Tourist Information Centre Visitors, Sixty per cent of the Visitors in the Centre were females, which shows that females are more keen in information gathering and search that there counterparts. Majority of the respondents belong the adult age group, mainly 30-39 years (24 per cent), followed by 20-29 years (18 per cent), and 40-49 years (18 per cent) as depicted in the age structure of the respondents. The diagram shows that the 53 per cent respondents were from Australia, followed by Singapore (12 per cent), United States (9 per cent), and Germany (6 per cent). The visitors in Dunkeld RTIC were belonged to multi-cultural background, therefore demanding information and services in wider context, which is easily comprehensible and legible. The economic profile of the Visitors was also diversified which comprise 21 per cent self employed, followed by students (18 per cent), and businessman (6 per cent).

The overall scenario reveals in the case study is that the community driven and operated regional tourism information centre in regional Victoria is quite successful in achieving basic objective of rural tourism. It successfully establishes the effective and efficient tourist information delivery system with quality and high levels of Visitors satisfaction. Customer's feedback regarding the quality of services and information may give a chance to improve the existing operation through adequate training and learning. In the whole process the community played a vital role by actively participating in the decision-making and shows proactive attitude. The success could only be attained when the information delivery system collaborates and coordinates with triangular forces of regional tourism development.

Interoperability of RTIC Model in Indian Scenario

The interoperability of this prescriptive model in the Indian Scenario would essentially be difficult to accommodate due to complex and intricate socio-economic and political conditions. It appears that local participation in the tourism development is regional India is essentially resistive in nature and there is no linkages and collaboration among various components of tourism development. Lack of integrated planning and rigid bureaucratic structure are other hindrances in the initiation of community based regional tourism.

The major constraints in the establishment and operation of RTIC in India are multi-dimensional in nature. These constraints can be listed as:

1. ***Socio-cultural Traditions:*** Indian history and culture has evolved in an imbalance in power sharing and decision making. It is always concentrated in the hands of few urban elites and local landlords who resist local community involvement in power sharing and keep the community deprive of their right of participation. Perhaps one of the most apparent traditions is that of authority and reverence toward people in positions of power or of otherwise high social standing (Timothy D.J., 1999). Although Government policies of allocating power to Panchayats to activity participate in the planning process enhanced the chances of involving community in the decision making.
2. ***Political Economy of the Region:*** Another dimension which hinders tourism development in the rural areas is vicious circle of poverty, whereby the community is enmeshed in their day to day livelihood and get no time to participate in any short term benefits.
3. ***Government Negligence of Rural Tourism and Lack of Direction and Strategies:*** Although the importance of rural tourism has been identified in the planning, but no effort has been taken to define

objectives and strategies to attained them. Desai (1995) argued that "*there is a lack of political will to implement participation because of the implication for the distribution of power and resources*".

4. ***Lack of Education and Training:*** This is a key to success in establishing RTIC because the information can only be deliver when the service providers are educated and trained. In India there is no mechanism through which the local community can be train and educate for the promotion of regional tourism.

5. ***Lack of Tourism Infrastructure Development:*** Inadequate tourism infrastructure is clearly one of the main reasons behind India's inability to attract tourists (Raguraman K., 1998). According to Choudhury, Lack of positive image mainly on the infrastructure and safety fronts is a main cause for poor image formation in promoting tourism, regardless of its strong cultural image (Chaudhary, M., 2000). Tourism infrastructure is a range of tangible and non-tangible services and facilities provided which enhance the quality of tourism experience. These physical facilities in the urban areas are very poor, such as Airport, Hotel rooms, transport network, railway station and other public facilities (toilets, post offices, etc.). These facilities are almost negligible in the rural area or ecotourism destination.

6. ***Lack of Coordination among Governing Bodies:*** The primary step for the successful establishment of RTIC in India is efficient coordination among governing agencies. As Raguraman said that the Department of Tourism is the overall coordinating agency for tourism, but several of the tourism related tasks are in the heads of a diverse range of agencies and there is little coordination between them (Raguraman, K., 1998).

Notwithstanding of these constraints existing in the establishment of rural tourism information centre in India, the governing bodies at local level should take initiation in that direction with the collaboration with local community. The first task is to identify various existing tangible and non-tangible components of tourism infrastructures and interest groups. These interest groups can be identified as Panchayats, temple committee, and local cultural events/festivals committee and non-government organisation in the region. The tangible components of tourism infrastructure should be identified which can be any focal/nodal point of high social interaction such as Panchayat office, any historical building (in operational conditions), and temple/church/mosque etc. The interest groups in the region should mobilised local community to participate in the tourism development by educating and involving them into decision making process.

Conclusion

This paper has presented a normative model of regional tourism information centre based on the principle and concept evolved in developed world. The model transferability in developing countries seems to be not feasible due to complex socio-economic structure and uncertainty in political decision making. The only approach of establishing an effective regional tourism information centre in rural India is to amalgamate and accommodate western model into oriental reality by incorporating existing regional structures and process in planning. As argued by Tosun, "*it may be naive to suppose that participatory tourism development approach will change existing structure of a local tourism industry in a developing country without changing dominant socio-economic and political structure of that locality*". (Tosun C., 2000) The focus of the paper was to comprehend the process of regional tourism development with the involvement of three triangular forces of local government, local community and the industries. The successful RTIC should collaborate with these components for the effective information delivery system. The paper also provides the analytical framework that intended to assist tourism planner and designer by explaining the VICAP model and it's various objectives and strategies. Design consideration is a vital aspect for a successful RTIC in a region. The essential structural components of RTIC were analysed, keeping in mind the volume, needs, intensity of the tourist, and resources available. The tiered/hierarchy structure of RTIC adopted by Country Tourism Victoria keeps the standard and motivates the Centre to compete for higher order.

A case study on Dunkeld RTIC substantiated that fact that collaboration among local government, community and industries can not only generate benefits and an additional income for the local community in the region but also established an effective information delivery system with high levels of Visitor's satisfaction. The Dunkeld RTIC has increased the length of stay and therefore also enhanced their expected expenditure. Location, regional attractions, quality of services and information are pertinent elements in tourism perception for their level of satisfaction.

The successful operation of the model in the Indian domain could only be feasible when the local conditions are kept in mind. Complex socio-cultural structure, political uncertainty, regional disparities, inadequate tourism infrastructure, lack of tourism education and inefficient outlook of local community toward tourism are some of the important constraints in the establishment of RTIC in regional/rural environment. The effective and efficient functioning of RTIC in Regional India can only be possible when the local amenities/infrastructure and local interest groups are identified and collaborate among one another.

NOTES

1. Regional tourism is the study is assumed to carry similar meaning as rural tourism, which characterised by as multifaceted activities of attracting visitors in a rural environment.
2. Triangular model is basically develops to reveals the functional components in regional tourism development with various interaction dimensions.

REFERENCES

1. Adams, K.M., (fall 1997), "Ethnic Tourism and the Renegotiation of Tradition in Tana Toraja (Sulawesi, Indonesia)", in *Ethnology*, Pittsburgh, Vol. 36, Issue 4, pages 309-320.

2. Bramwell, B. and Sharman A., (April 1999), "Collaboration in Local Tourism Policymaking" in *Annals of Tourism Research*, Vol. 26, Issue 2, Pages 392-415.

3. Bryson, J.M., and Crosby B.C. (1992), Leadership for the Common Good: Tackling Public Problems in a Shared-Power World, San, Jossey-Bass, Francisco.

4. Chaudhary, M., (2000), India's Image as a Tourist Destination—a Perspective of Foreign Tourists, In Tourism Management, 21, pp. 293-297.

5. Connell Jo and Reynolds P., (1999), "The Implication of Technological Development on Tourist Information Centres" in *Tourism Management*, Vol. 20, pages 501-509.

6. Country Connection, The Quarterly Newsletter of Country Victoria Tourism Council, November, 1998, Country Victoria Tourism Councils INC.

7. Country Victoria Tourism Councils INC., Business Plan.

8. Desia, V., (1995), "Community Participation and Slum Housing: A Study of Bombay", New Delhi Publication.

9. Edgell, David L. and Staìger, Lee, (April 20, 1992), "A Small Community Adopts as a Development Tool", in *Business America*, Washington, Vol. 113, issue 8, p. 16.

10. Fesemaier, D.R., (summer, 1994), "Traveller Use of Visitor Information Centres: Implications for Development in Illinois" in Journal of Travel Research, Vol. 31, Issue 1, page 44.

11. Fesenmaier, D.R., Vogt, C.A., (1993), "Evaluating the Economic Impact of Travel Information Provided at

Indiana Welcome Centres" in ***Journal of Travel Research***, Vol. 31, Issues 3, pages 33.

12. Goossens, Cees, (April 2000), "Tourism Information and Pleasure Motivation" in ***Annals of Tourism Research***, Vol. 27, issue 2, pages 301-321.

13. Gunn, C.A., (1988), Tourism Planning (2nd ed.), New York, Taylor and Francis.

14. Health, E., Wall G., (1992), Marketing Tourism Destinations—A Strategic Planning Approach, John Wiley and Sons, INC., New York.

15. Huang, Yueh-Huang. and William P., (1996), "Rural Tourism Development: Shifting basis of Community Solidarity", in *Journal of Travel Research*, Vol. 34, issue 4, p 26.

16. Landon, Philip J., (1999), "Inventing New England: Regional Tourism in the Nineteenth Century" in *Journal of Popular Culture,* Vol. 33, issue 2, pages 165-169.

17. Lewis, James B., (Sept. 1998), "The Development of Rural Tourism", in *Parks and Recreation*, Vol. 33, Issue 9, pp 99-107.

18. Local Government And Tourism—The Partnerships, Country Victoria Tourism Councils INC., 1997, Hampton Press.

19. Marcouiller, D.W., (Feb 1997), "Toward Integrative Tourism Planning in Rural America" in *Journal of Planning Literature*, Columbous, Vol. 11, Issue 3, pages 337-357.

20. McCool, S.F. and Martin S.R. (winter 1994), "Community Attachment and Attitudes toward Tourism Development" in *Journal of Travel Research*, Vol. 32, Issues 3, page 29.

21. McIntosh, R.W., Goeldner, C.R., (1984), Tourism: Principles, Practices and Philosophies, (5th edi.) New York, Wiley.

22. Murphy, P.E., (1985), Tourism: A Community Approach, London, Methuen.

23. Nakazawa, A.T., Patricia La Caila J., (spring 1993), "The Rural Information Centre: *A Resources for Economic Development*", in *Economic Development Review*, Vol. 11, Issue 2, page 62.

24. National Rural Tourism Strategy, (1994), Commonwealth Department of Tourism, Canberra.

25. Norris Ruth et al., (199), "Community-Based Ecotourism in the Maya Forest: Problems and Potentials" *http://www.2.planeta.com*

26. Page S.J., and Getz D., (1997), The Business of Rural Tourism—International Perspectives, International Thompson Business Press, London.

27. Pearce, D.G., Moscardo G., and Ross, G.F., (1996), Tourism Community Relationships, Oxford, Pergamon.

28. Raguraman, K., (1998), "Troubled Passage to India" in *Tourism Management,* Vol. 19, No. 6. pp. 533-543.

29. Singh, Shalini, (1997), "Developing Human Resources for the Tourism Industry with Reference to India", in *Tourism Management,* Vol. 18, No. 5, pp. 299-306.

30. Stewart, W.P., Anderson, B.S. Fesenmaier D.R., and Lue, Chi-Chuan, (winter, 1993), "Highway Welcome Centre Surveys: Problems with Nonresponse Bias" in *Journal of Travel Research,* Vol. 31, Issue 3, page 53.

31. Stewart, W.P., Lue, C. and Fesenmaeir, D.R., (winter, 1993), "A Comparison Between Welcome Centre Visitors and General Highway Auto Travellers", in Journal of *Travel Research*, Vol. 31, Issue 3, page 30.

32. Stoker, G., (1995), Regime Theory and Urban Politics, in Judge, D. et al (eds.), Theories of Urban Politics, pp. 54-71, Sage, London.

33. Tierney, P. and Hass G., (1988), "Colorado Welcome Centres: Their Users and Influence on Length of Stay and Expenditures", Unpublished Report, Department of Recreational Resources and Landscape Architecture, Colorado State University.

34. Tierney, P.T. (1993), "The Influence of State Traveller Information Centres on Tourist Length of Stay and Expenditures", Journal of Travel Research, 31, (Winter), pp. 28-31.

35. Timothy, D.J., (1 April 1999), "Participatory Planning View of Tourism in Indonesia" in Annals of *Tourism Research*, Vol. 26, Issue 2, pages 371-391.

36. Tonge R. and Myott D.E., (1993), How to Plan, Develop and Market Local and Regional Tourism, Coolum Beach, Gull Publishing Pvt. Ltd.

37. Tosun, C., (2000), "Limit to Community Participation in the Tourism Development Process in Development Process in Developing Countries", in Tourism Management, 21, pp 613-633.

38. Tourist Signing Guidelines—Guidelines for Tourist and Services Signing on Roads in Victoria, (1999), Prepared by Tourism and VicRoad.

39. Wall, G. (August 1995), People Outside the Plans, Paper Presented at the ICCT Conference, Yogyakarta, Indonesia.

40. Wilkenrson, M.L. (spring 1996), "Information for Developer" Developing a Rural Tourism Plan: The Major Publications" in *Economic Development Review*, Vol. 14, issue 2, page 79.

4

Tourist Motivation: Past, Present and Future

James Murdy

For the past four decades, scholars and tourism industry professionals studied the motivation of tourists. These works focused on three main areas: activities as motivation (e.g.,), psychological needs (Ryan, 1991, 1998; Gibson and Yiannakis, 2002; Pearce, 1993), or a lifecycle approach (Hill, McDonald, and Uysal, 1990; Plog, 1972, 1974; Rapoport and Rapoport, 1975; Yiannakis and Gibson, 1992). These studies provided a sound theoretical basis for understanding why leisure travellers leave home for unusual, often remote and exotic destinations. By understanding these fundamental drives of tourists, we are better able to predict what behaviours they enjoy while travelling and at the destination. The likelihood of satisfying our customer also increases with the knowledge of why they chose this destination, excursion, or pursuit.

Because an understanding of tourist motivation is vital to the success of any tourism-based business, the purpose of this chapter is to provide a tripartite perspective of the reasons for leisure travel. The first section, *A History of Tourist Motivation*, discusses the origins and major theories of tourist motivation. In *Current Concepts and Applications*, an exploration of new applications and extensions of existing theories are presented. The final section, *Into the New Millennium*, explores exciting possibilities in tourist motivation research and practical usages of it in the field.

Introduction

For Several decades, scholars and tourism industry professionals studied the motivation of tourists. These works focused on three main areas: activities as motivation (Dunn Ross and Iso-Ahola, 1991; Figler, Weinstein, Sollers, and Devan, 1992; Fodness, 1994), psychological needs (Ryan, 1991, 1998, Gibson and Yiannakis, 2002; Pearce, 1993), or a lifecycle approach (Hill, McDonald, and Uysal, 1990; Plog, 1972, 1974; Rapoport and Rapoport, 1975; Yiannakis and Gibson, 1992). These works provide a sound theoretical basis for understanding why leisure travels leave home for unusual, often remote and exotic destinations. By understanding these fundamental drives of tourists we are better able to predict what behaviours they will enjoy while travelling and at the destination. The likelihood of satisfying our customers also increases with the knowledge of why they chose this destination, excursion, or pursuit.

Because an understanding of tourist motivation is vital to the success of any tourism-based business, the purpose of this chapter is to provide a tripartite perspective of the reasons for leisure travel. The first section, *Approaches to Tourist Motivation*, discusses the origins and major theories of tourist motivation. In *Current Concepts and Applications*, an exploration of new applications and extensions of existing theories are presented. The final section, *Into the New Millennium*, explores exciting possibilities in tourist motivation research and practical usages of it in the field.

Approaches to Tourist Motivation

Phychological Needs

During the 1970s and 1980s, the several models using psychological needs as tourist motivations were developed. In order to better understand these models, we first must define the term "psychological needs". According to Lounsbury and Polik (1992), a need is a state of arousal or activation caused by lack or change in a desired level of homeostasis or balance (p. 106). In simpler terms, a tourist develops a need when something within themselves or their environment triggers a response, either physical (e.g., hunger stimulating a need for food) for psychological (loneliness stimulating a need for companionship), which (s)he then attempts to fulfil. For example, a person may realize that she is hungry, which activates her to find something to eat. It deciding what she wants to eat, she recognizes that she is alone and would like some company during her meal. Two needs are identified here: the need for food and the need for companionship.

One of the first models of needs to be adopted in the study of tourists was Maslow's hierarchy of needs (1943, 1970). According to this theory, there are five levels of needs; physiological needs, safety needs, needs for love and affection, esteem needs, and self actualization (Fig. 4.1). It is important to note that before advancing to higher levels of needs, the lower level needs must be fulfilled. Therefore, if a person wishes to address a need for safety, it is necessary to satisfy physiological needs first.

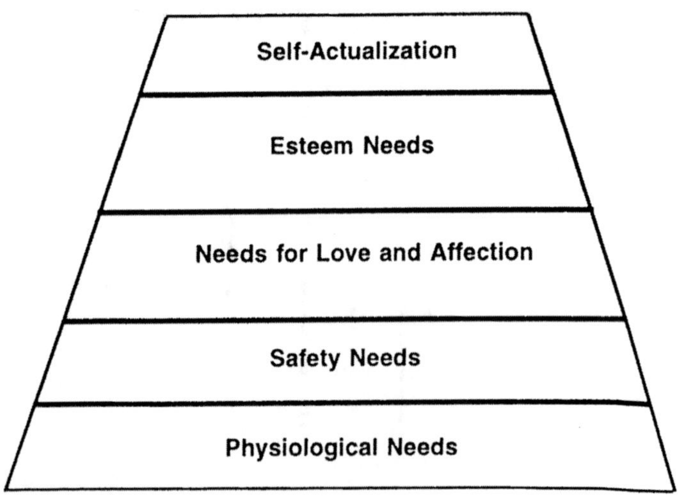

Fig. 4.1 Maslow's Hierarchy of Needs (1970)

Fodness (1994) found support for Maslow's work in his study concerning tourist motivation. Using a multi-dimensional approach, the author identified four distinct constructs that represented the behaviours associated with vacation motives based on the hierarchy of needs. The first component, escape, is bipolar, indicating that the need for escape, represents two distinct functions, a knowledge function and a punishment avoidance function. The knowledge function represents the need to escape mundane routines by attaining some goal or state. The punishment avoidance function is associated with escaping daily pressures and responsibilities. In terms of Maslow's theory, these needs to escape and avoid punitive situations are similar to the first two levels of hierarchy. As argued by Pearce (1996), escape represents a biological need to relax and re-create the self. Avoiding punishment combines with escape to suggest that the home environment may be over stimulating, triggering an imbalance that a vacation may fulfil. The second dimension shows the need for social interaction. In this context, tourists are motivated by the need to visit or vacation with family and/or friends, which may enhance these relationships or even create new ones. The third dimension indicates the ego-enhancement and self esteem needs of the tourist. The final dimension measures another aspect of escape. While the first dimension is associated with escape from daily life and pressures, the fourth dimension represents a form of escape to the fun world awaiting the tourist at the destination. By using these four unique, need based categories of tourist motivation, market segments may then be developed, supporting the managerial and marketing value of such a model.

Escape is a commonly identified tourist motivation. Dann (1977) integrated escape into his now famous 'push' and 'pull' model of tourist motivation. Based on a survey of visitors to Barbados, he developed a continuum with anomie at one extreme and ego-enhancement at the other, where anomie is the desire to escape from the isolation of daily life and "get away from it all". At the other end of the continuum is recognition and status achieved from travelling. Underlying this continuum, however, is the fantasy component of the vacation. Ego-enhancement and fantasy are united during a vacation by the possibility for the tourist to experience a temporary but alternate model of existence. In relating fantasy to anomie, Dann states that tourists attempt to overcome the ordinary, 'normlessness' and hollowness of life by escaping from the home environment. From this work, we see that tourists not only seek to fulfil lower order needs from their travels, but they also attempt to add meaning and value to their lives, thereby contributing to their overall sense of worth and potentially to their self-actualization or highest levels of personal attainment. A vacation then becomes more than a break from reality; it allows people to explore new and unusual environments during a break from the vagaries of the work a day world.

Push and pull factors may also be integrated with tourists' needs and destination attributes. Like Dann, Crompton (1979) found that vacationers may be encouraged, or pushed, to leave home by socio-psychological needs. These included escape from a perceived mundane environment, personal exploration and evaluation of the self, relaxation, prestige, regression, improving family relationships, and promoting social encounters. Most of these motivations are self-explanatory, with the exception of regression, which refers to efforts to engage in adolescent or childhood behaviours while on vacation. Clearly, escape from both adult responsibilities and the everyday environment are important motivations for some tourists. Pull factors are the attractions at the destination that draw the tourist to it. These features may include the culture or people living there, the climate, a theme park or museum, the natural environment or a host of other qualities unique to the location.

This search for unusual or different destination attributes is also a predominant theory employed in tourist motivation. Cohen (1972) created a tourist typology based on the need for novelty and familiarity. That is, tourists seek destinations outside their home and work environments because of an interest in places and people different from those at home. He identified four tourist roles; the drifter, individual mass tourist, organised mass tourist, and explorer, arguing that tourists engaging in these roles are motivated by a search for novelty while maintaining some degree of familiarity within the vacation environment. To achieve this sense of novelty in a foreign environment without becoming overwhelmed, the individual and organised mass tourists operate within an 'environmental bubble' of the familiar at the destination and confine themselves to amenities such as transportation, hotels, and food that are similar to those found at home. The explorer ventures out of the environmental bubble, but retains some of the routines present in his/her everyday life. The drifter is immersed in the host culture, living with the indigenous population, eating their foods, and avoiding the typical tourist route.

Activities

Cohen was among the first to relate tourist activities with motivation, and other scholars have used this premise as a basis for their work. For example, Fodness (1994) developed a functionalist approach. From this perspective, needs are the underlying causes of tensions that a potential tourist experiences. These tensions then affect attitudes, which in turn, influence the actions taken. The outcome should be actions that satisfy the needs of the tourist. Thus, the vacation activity is an expression of the tension resolution. Therefore, engaging in diversions during pleasure trips may reflect certain unfulfilled needs.

Using the functionalist approach, four categories of need-based activities have been identified (Fodness, 1994). The knowledge function includes activities such as seeing works of arts, learning about current events, and visiting historical sites. At the other end of this bipolar category is the utilitarian-punishment avoidance dimension, which suggest that tourists seek a break from the mundane activities of life such as washing dishes, going to work, and civic duties. The utilitarian function refers to pursuits such as shopping, romantic encounters, and new, adventuresome, and fun activities in general. The social-adjustive category typically involves interpersonal interactions. For example, a business person may use vacations to spend time with family members or friends. The fourth category is the value-expressive function, which is slightly different from the others previously discussed. Although activities such as fine dining are associated with this dimension, it mostly represents the tourist's desire to have vacation destinations that are reflective of their personal values. That is, it is important that the vacation be indicative of the wealth, sophistication, and 'bragging rights' of the person who took it.

Dunn Ross and Iso-Ahola (1991) adopted a different approach to using activities as vacation motivations. In a study of tourists visiting Washington, D.C., they found that educational activities were an important motivation. Additionally, social interaction, escape, impulsive decision-making, specific knowledge, and shopping for souveniers played a role in motivating study participants to take sightseeing tours. The education factor, called 'general knowledge' by the authors, and the social interaction, specific knowledge, and shopping for souvenirs factor constitute seeking motivations, supporting Iso-Ahola's (1982, 1983) position that seeking is a primary motive for leisure and tourism. The seeking of knowledge may be related to the underlying need to learn about one's past or roots, to growth as an individual, self-discovery, self actualization, and other needs associated with tourist roles (Gibson, 1994). As stated above, however, seeking of any kind is an expression of latent needs.

Figler, Weinstein, Sollers, and Devan (1992) undertook a similar approach to tourist motivation. Using Figler's Travel Motivation Survey, five factors were identified: anomie/ authenticity-seeking, culture/education, escape/regression, wanderlust/exploring, and jetsetting/prestige-seeking. The presence of an anomie/authenticity-seeking component lends support to idea that vacation activities serve to satisfy tourists' needs. In this case, the tourists are seeking out new social contacts, which is also found in the hierarchy of needs discussed above, as well as opportunities to have more 'real' or meaningful experiences while on holiday. The culture/ education dimension involves visiting historical sites, learning, and 'seeing new things'. Clearly, these endeavours help tourists to restore themselves psychologically (or escape), which is again indicative of the physiological need for rest and relaxation.

Similarly, the motivation of escape is also found in the third factor. Regression in this instance refers to an adult's ability to act like a child. This group of activities indicates that tourists not only want to escape from their mundane, anomic lives, but also from their adult roles and responsibilities. The fourth group of activities includes items concerned with roaming, being on the move, danger and exploring the unknown that may be termed wanderlust or exploring. Here, the need for novelty again becomes apparent in their selection of these behaviours. The final activities factor, jetsetting/ prestige-seeking, is similar of Fodness's value-expresive function. However, this new group of activities integrates a number of tourist pastimes, including participating in sports, experiencing sexual liberation and visiting exotic locations as well as meeting needs for social prestige *Motivation and Lifecycle Models*.

Certainly, not all activities are consistently pursued across an adult's life, just as not all needs are simultaneously out of balance. The use of lifecycle or life course models is particularly helpful in explaining why tourists with similar lifestyle characteristics, family and marital status, and demographic characteristics choose specific types of vacations. To better understand which needs may be prevalent, and therefore which activities preferred by tourists, our attention now turns to the adult life course.

Levinson et al. (1978) developed a theory of adult development, which states that there are three eras through which adults pass. The initial era is Early Adulthood, occurring in persons between the ages of about 17-45 years, during which an adult identity and 'dream' (preferred life goals) are created and tested. The second era of the adult life course is Middle Adulthood, which lasts from approximately 40-65 years. In these years, men and women evaluate the life structure they developed during early adulthood, with the creation of a stable and satisfying life structure the goal. The final era, starting around 60 years of age is Late Adulthood. The goals associated with it are adjusting to one's new role in society while maintaining some form of youthful vitality. Each of these stages consists of periods of relative stability and of transition. Typically, the former last between 6 and 8 years and have specific tasks associated with them (see Table—4.1). For example, between the ages of 22-28 years, a young adult is expected to make critical life decisions concerning occupation, love relationships, and life style, and establish a life structure. The transitional periods, which typically last between 4 to 5 years, usually terminate one life structure and begins another. These transitional periods often compel an individual to examine the previous life structure before attempting to modify it or to develop a new one.

Table—4.1 The Adult Life Course as Identified by Levinson et al. (1978) and Levinson (1996)

Developmental Period (age in years)	**Period Tasks**
Early Adult Transition (17-22)	Move out of the pre-adult world; Begin life as an adult (consolidate adult id., make choices for adult living
Entering the Adult World (23-27)	Explore potential adult life alternatives; Create a stable adult life structure and 'dream'
Age Thirty Transition (28-33)	Evaluate current adult life structure and make changes as deemed necessary

(Contd...)

Settling Down (34-39)	Establish self in society; Build a better life and be affirmed by society
Mid-life Transition (40-45)	Reevaluate adult life structure: explore and test alternatives, create new life structure or modify old structure
Entering Middle Adulthood (46-49)	Construction of a stable and satisfying life structure
Age Fifty Transition (50-55)	Evaluate life structure established by end mid-life transition and modify as necessary
Culmination of Middle Adulthood (56-59)	Adapt to biological, social and psychological changes
Late Adult Transition (60-65)	Maintain some form of previous youthful vitality
Late Adulthood (66-80)	Establish a new relationship in/to society with primary importance placed on the self

The tourism literature using Levinson et al.'s model of the adult life course is sparse. Anderson and Littrell (1995, 1996) investigated souvenir-buying behaviours of women in the Early and Middle Adulthood eras. Women in the early adulthood era shopped with their children, made spontaneous purchases, and bought souvenirs that represented local places and events. The older women in the middle adulthood era frequented seasonal and speciality shops, often shopped with spouses or friends, and made planned purchases of high quality souvenirs for personal satisfaction. These women also enjoyed watching artisans at work. The differences between the two groups of women reflect their different eras in the life course. The younger women are focused on purchasing souvenirs reflecting specific destinations and memories. This may be related to the major task of this era: building and establishing a dream. The older women, having most likely established their dreams, now focus on buying souvenirs that reflect their task of building and maintaining stable life structures. Therefore, they know their own tastes better and pursue them in how, where, and with whom they shop.

The work of Gibson (1989, 1994) demonstrated that tourist role preferences vary over the adult life course, and between men and women. By examining the tasks associated with each life course stages, Gibson discovered a relationship between tourist role preference by life stage and specific developmental tasks. She concluded that tourists engage in specific roles at different stages of the adult life course to meet the underlying needs associated with that life stage. For example, the Action Seeker is interested in partying, going to night clubs and meeting others for sexual gratification. This role is most associated with men and women in the Early Adulthood era, during which they focus on such tasks as the exploration of the adult world, breaking away from the family of origin, and gaining more personal freedom. The logical conclusion is that the Action Seeker role is most associated with needs for freedom, variety, excitement, stimulation, exploration, novelty, discovery, change, and sexual gratification.

A significant contribution of these works in tourist behaviour and adult psychological development is that we know have a better understanding of tourists' motivations. That is, there is now a theoretical framework combining tourist role theory and adult development that results in a better understanding of the leisure travel customer. Furthermore, the evidence suggests that selection of vacation behaviours (tourist roles) may contribute the fulfilment of needs necessary to move up Maslow's hierarchy. Finally, as will be discussed later in this chapter, this work may contribute to service providers' ability to create customer satisfaction and loyalty.

Current Concepts and Applications

Motives and Motivations

Of primary importance to any discussion of tourist motivation is the relationship between motivations and motives. Until recently, the two terms had been used interchangeably, with both referring to the reasons for engaging in a behaviour. Recently, however, a clear distinction between the two terms has been made. According to Gnoth (1997), motives are broad-based, genetic causes for behaviour, 'tend[ing] to be more global and less situation—specific' (p. 291). In other words, motives are enduring over time, setting the parameters for fulfilling needs. Motivations, on the other hand, are situation specific to an individual's interactions with their surroundings. In the context of tourism, motivations are cognitive and more easily accessible than motives. Therefore, tourists stating that they went to the mountains for the solitude found there are giving their motivation for selecting the destination. The motive, however is deeper, possibly relating to their need for psychological restoration.

Travel Career Ladder

Maslow's hierarchy of needs is one of the predominant models currently used in studying tourist motivation. In developing the Travel Career Ladder (TCL), Pearce (1991, 1996) adapted it to tourist behaviour (Fig. 4.2). Because tourism is a discretionary activity, Pearce modified the names for each of the levels and divided them into intrinsic and extrinsic needs. The first level then becomes the need for relaxation, with self directed needs such as relaxation and other directed needs like lack of demands on the tourist. A similar pattern emerges for the next three levels addressing stimulation, relationship, and self-esteem and development needs. Tourists control their own need for stimulation by regulating their levels of excitement and safety while also being concerned for these needs in their travel companions. Tourists address relationship needs by the giving and receiving of love and affection. This may be accomplished by maintaining existing relationships or by initiating new ones while touring. At the self-esteem and development level, tourists seek to improve skills, knowledge, and/or abilities. The other directed component of this level deals with how other people view the tourists. Key to fulfilling self-esteem needs is being perceived as competent and respected in one's endeavours. The highest level of tourist needs, fulfilling, is not divided because of the intrinsic nature motivations exhibited at this point in the travel career. At this level, tourists pursue feelings of peace, happiness, and spirituality while becoming immersed in the destination.

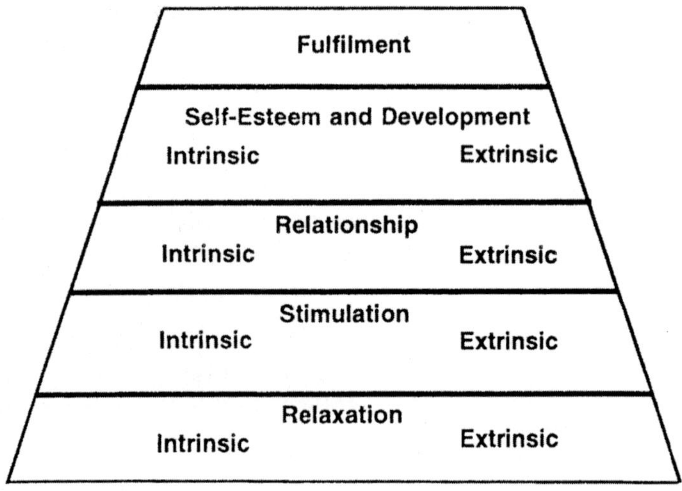

Fig. 4.2 Pearce's Travel Career Ladder (1996)

One of the benefits of the ladder concept is the opportunity for individuals to move both vertically and horizontally through the hierarchy, with any move across or up seen as a progressive step. Therefore, unlike, Maslow's model, advances may be made within a level as well as between levels. Another benefit of the ladder is that tourists may enter the hierarchy at any point and progress at different rates as experiences are acquired. Pearce speculated that by using the travel career ladder, a tourist-environment fit could be created for individuals at each stage of development. He proposed self-actualized vacationers seek authentic, independent destinations, allowing for introspection and self-development. Tourists meeting other needs, such as those associated with love and belongingness, might choose environments that foster group experiences and the building of relationships.

Pearce found support for the travel careers concept and tourist-environment fit. In a study at the Timbertown theme park, the author found those travellers at the love and belongingness level reporting lower satisfaction with the resort than visitors at other need levels. Additionally, this same group of tourists rated the destination lowest in terms of authenticity. This finding supports the theory that tourists at various need levels will find different destinations more or less appealing. Additional support for the travel career concept and tourist-environment fit is found in Pearce and Moscardo's (1985) work, who found that a tourist's location in their travel career influenced satisfaction with specific destination attributes. For example, they found that travellers higher on the TCL reported lower satisfaction with in authentic destination settings, while satisfaction with the same locals increased among those who were at lower levels of their travel careers. These results indicate that tourists' needs influence the type of vacation they pursue as well as their vacation satisfaction. It should be noted, however, that the two-dimensional nature (intrinsic and extrinsic) of the need levels hypothesized to exist was not empirically supported.

A recent study (Holden, 1999) provided more conclusive empirical support for the travel career model. A sample of 490 skiers was divided into four groups: beginner, intermediate, advanced, and snowboarder. Each of these groups rated stimulation level needs as the most important reasons for participating in skiing. With the exception of snowboarders, skiers reported relationship needs as the least important. The general trend found in the data indicated higher level needs become more important as skill increases. To support this conclusion, beginners rated four of the five levels of needs as less important than every other group participating in the study. Holden concluded "The research illustrates that Pearce's concept has the ability to demonstrate changing need priorities through time and to add a dynamic element to motivational assessment" (p. 437).

The value of the travel career ladder model is evident. As tourists travel and gain experiences, they move from one level or aspect of motivation to another. However, before progressing from a lower to higher level, they must first meet the needs of the lower level(s). Because need levels vary by persons, entry into the ladder may be at any step, depending on the life history of the traveller. Furthermore, the ladder concept also permits the incorporation of multiple and dynamic motivations into the study of tourist behaviour.

Into the New Millennium

The above discussion of the theories of tourist motivation provides a comprehensive review of the current knowledge on this issue. Maslow's work has been expended by Pearce's Travel Career Ladder model. Even scholars who are critical of the TCL, such as Ryan (1998), agree that a needs-based, hierarchical approach offers valuable insights into tourist behaviour. When added to the adult life course as put forth by Levinson et al. (1978) and Levinson (1996), a more complete framework is provided, enabling both researchers and tourism industry professionals alike to better serve their customers. Tourist roles also contribute to this framework by providing an essential, behavioural like to needs-based motivational models and the adult life course. The integration of all three concepts (needs, the adult life course, and tourist roles) facilitates the following theory: as adults progress through the life course, different needs become the motivations for engaging in specific vacation behaviours, which in turn may act to satisfy or fulfil the aforementioned needs.

Lending empirical evidence to this theory, Gibson and Yiannakis (2002) found that needs are associated with adults' places in the life course and do underlie preference for specific behaviours, or tourist roles. They also found that these behaviours exhibit three distinct patterns over the adult life course: roles that generally decrease in preference; roles for which selection generally increase; and roles demonstrating variability over the life course. For example, they reported that both men and women choose vacations during which they pursued sporting activities less often as they progress across life course stages. Men choosing this role are motivated by satisfied needs for play, control, and sex and an unsatisfied need for family and home, while women are driven by unsatisfied needs for control and sex and satisfied needs for family and home, health, and escape. In contrast, as men and women aged, their preference for holidays involving meeting the locals, trying the food, and staying off the beaten tourist path increased. Additionally, unique sets of needs predicted selection of this set of behaviours. For men, a combination of satisfied needs for companionship, escape, status, and feeling connected with their roots and an unsatisfied need for health indicated preference for this role. Among women, satisfied needs for financial security, personal growth, and safety and unsatisfied needs for stimulation and feeling connected with their roots are associated with it. In selecting specific types of vacation activities, men and women may be acting to restore their psychological balance in the liminal and ludic (see Lett, 1983) environments found at tourist destinations.

By integrating Levinson et al.'s work on adult psychological development with tourist role theory, Gibson and Yiannakis demonstrated a link between the tasks associated with each stage of the adult life course, tourist behaviours, and the needs predicting specific tourist behaviours. This type of work offers valuable insights to tourism marketers and managers. Not only does it foster more effective market segmentation, but it may also assist managers identification of potential new markets. For example, men and women interested in sports-based vacations are associated with specific sets of needs, demographics, and psychographics at different eras of the life course. However, a sports tourism supplier may not commonly target all segments of this market, choosing to focus exclusively on young adults. With this new model, managers may effectively broaden their customer base.

Tourism suppliers may also find need-and life course-based models helpful in creating customer loyalty. One method for creating loyalty is increasing service satisfaction (Noe, 1999). In order to do this, the provider must deliver services whose value exceeds tourists exceptions. By satisfying the needs associated with specific tourist roles or behaviours, we are more likely to meet customers' expectations. Furthermore, being able to satisfy customers needs through activities adds value to any business. Knowing your customers satisfied and unsatisfied needs empowers marketers, managers, and tourism developers to effectively design, develop, promote and manage tourism resources that may fulfil these needs (or aid in keeping them satisfied). The important lesson here is that to increase customer loyalty, satisfying the underlying needs of tourists should be the penultimate objective.

One possible means for accomplishing this goal is found in the work of Gnoth (1997). Her discussion of motives and motivations has broad implications for the understanding of tourist behaviour. First, a clear distinction is made between two seemingly synonymous terms. By differentiating between them, researchers and managers alike now have a better understanding of the situation specific solutions to unsatisfied expressed needs (motivations) and the more lasting and less specific counterparts (motives). Second, a new model of tourist behaviour is available for testing. Specially, Gnoth proposes a schema integrating needs, motives, values, perceptions, motivations, attitudes, expectations, and the actual behaviour with both general (objective) and specific (subjective) situations. The benefits of such a model range from increasing customer satisfaction to improved travel counselling. Next, this work is a necessary step toward a complete model of tourist behaviour. While the relationship between all of the attributes offers valuable insights into the long-term and circumstantial reasons for conduct, a model including information search, decision making, and recall processes must be developed to complete our understanding of tourist behaviour. Finally, the relationship between motives and motivation is suggestive of the relationship between expressed and latent needs. In order to understand tourists better, researchers must develop methods for assessing both types of needs.

Conclusion

In this new millennium, the challenges confronting the tourism and hospitality industry are complex and numerous. We begin it with a global economic recession that is further dividing the industrialized worlds. Tourism and other crimes against tourists are, and will continue to be, an ongoing challenge to both tourists and management of hotels, restaurants, attractions, and other tourism resources. Before tourism and tourists can become agents of peace, a better understanding of the latter must be achieved. In order to complete this task, empirical support for an integrated model of tourist motives, motivations, attitudes, behaviours, information search, expectations and needs.

While the majority of the components for this model have been studies, and the relationship between some have been demonstrated, there exists a lack of a complete model of tourist behaviour. In order for the study of tourists to advance, methodological innovations must be developed to study drives, urges, latent needs, and motives. As suggested by the research reviewed in this chapter, such model may require advanced techniques to test the relationships among these constructs. For example, artificial neural networks may be helpful in deciphering the unique contribution and role of each to tourist behaviour. Such a network may used to develop a computer program that may aid travel counsellors advise tourists concerning which destination to visit, activities to engage in, and in developing a travel career.

REFERENCES

Anderson, L and Littrell, M. (1995). Souvenir-purchase Behaviour of Women Tourists. *Annals of Tourism Research, 22,* 328-348.

Anderson, L and Littrell, M. (1996). Group Profiles of Women as Tourists and Purchasers of Souvenirs. *Family and Consumer Services Research Journal, 25, 1,* 28-56.

Cohen, E. (1972). Toward a Sociology of International Tourism. *Sociological Research, 39, 1,* 164-182.

Crompton, J. (1979) Motivations for Pleasure Vacation. *Annals of Tourism Research, 6,* 408-424.

Dann, G. (1977). Anomie, Ego Enhancement and Tourism. *Annals of Tourism Research, 4,* 184-194.

Dann, G. (1981) Tourist Motivation: An Appraisal. *Annals of Tourism Research, 8, 2,* 187-219.

Dunn Ross, E. and Iso-Ahola, S. (1991). Sightseeing Tourists' Motivation and Satisfaction. *Annals of Tourism Research, 18,* 226-237.

Figler, M., Weinstein, A., Sollers, J., and Devan, B. (1992). Pleasure Travel (Tourist) Motivation: A Factor Analytic Approach. *Bulletin of the Psychonomic Society, 30,* 113-116.

Fodness, D. (1994). Measuring Tourist Motivation. *Annals of Tourism Research, 21, 3,* 555-581.

Gibson, H. (1989). *Tourist Roles: Stability and Change Over the Life Cycle.* Unpublished Masters Thesis, University of Connecticut.

Gibson, H. (1994). *Some Predictors of Tourist Role Preference for Men and Women Over the Adult Life Course.* Unpublished Doctoral Dissertation. University of Connecticut.

Gibson, H. and Yiannakis, A. (2002). Tourist Roles: Needs and the Life Course. *Annals of Tourism Research, 29*, 358-383.

Gnoth, J. (1997). Tourism Motivation and Expectation Formulation. *Annals of Tourism Research, 29*, 283-304.

Hill, B., McDonald, C., and Uysal, M. (1990). Resort Motivations for Different Family Life Cycle Stages. *Visions in Leisure and Business, 8*, 18-27.

Holden, A. (1999). Understanding Skiers' Motivation Using Pearce's 'Travel Career' Construct. *Annals of Tourism Research, 26*, 435-438.

Iso-Ahola, S. (1982). Toward a Social Psychological Theory of Tourism Motivation: A Rejoiner. *Annals of Tourism Research, 12.* 256-262.

Iso-Ahola, S. (1983). Toward a Social Psychology or Recreational Travel. *Leisure Studies, 2,* 45-56.

Lett, J. (1983). Ludic and Liminoid Aspects of Charter Yacht Tourism in the Caribbean. *Annals of Tourism Research, 10*, 35-56.

Levinson, D. (1996). *The Seasons of a Women's Life*. New York: Knopf.

Levinson, D., and Darrow, C., Klein, E., Levinson, M., and Mckee, B. (1978). *The Seasons of a Man's Life*. New York: Knopf.

Lounsbury, J and Polik, J. (1992). Leisure Needs and Vacation Satisfaction. *Leisure Sciences, 14*, 105-119.

Maslow, A. (1943). A Theory of Human Motivation. *Psychological Review, 50,* 370-396.

Maslow, A. (1970). *Personality and Motivation*. New York: Harper and Row.

Noe, F. 1999. *Tourist Service Satisfaction: Hotel, Transportation, and Recreation*, Campaign, IL: Sagamore.

Pearce, P. (1991) Analysing Tourist Attractions. *Journal of Tourism Studies, 2,* 46-55.

Pearce, P. (1993) Fundamentals of Tourism Motivation. *In Tourism Research: Critiques and Challenges,* D. Pearce, R. Butler, eds. pp. 113-134. London: Routledge.

Pearce, P. (1996). Recent Research in Tourist Behaviour. *Asian Pacific Journal of Tourism Research*, 1, 1, 7-17.

Pearce, P., and Moscardo, G. (1985). The Relationship Between Travellers' Career Levels and the Concept of Authenticity. *Australian Journal of Psychology, 37*, 157-174.

Plog, S. (1972). Developing the Family Travel Market. *In The Travel Research Association's Third Annual Conference Proceedings. The Values of Travel Research: Planning Techniques, Applications*. Quebec, Canada, 209-221.

Plog, S. (1974). Why Destination Areas Rise and Fall in Popularity. *Cornell Hotel and Restaurant Administration Quarterly, 14*, 55-58.

Rapoport, R., and Rapoport, R. (1975). *Leisure and the Family Life Cycle.* London; Routledge and Kegan Paul.

Ryan, C. (1991). *Recreational Tourism: A Social Science Perspective.* London: Routledge.

5

Integrating Tourism and Resources Sustainability: from Resource Economics to Eclectic Marketing

*Dr. Pascal Tremblay**

Introduction

This paper distinguishes between a number of interpretations of tourism sustainability. It also provides a collection of theoretical arguments for shifting from a conventional resource economics methodology to a broader systemic approach blending marketing, economics and evolutionary arguments when examining issues involving tourism and sustainability. The early sections of the paper show that the "public goods" attributes of tourism services production has been central to the conventional analysis of market failures in tourism leading to viewing tourism production as capable of outgrowing its ideal capacity and destroy its resource base. The paper suggests that when ecological or wildlife sustainability is concerned, a conceptual

* Faculty of Law, Business and Arts, Northern Territory University, Darwin, Northern Territory, Australia 0909, Tel. [08] 8946 6772 fax. [08] 8946 6777, e-mail: pascal.tremblay@ntu.edu.au

shift away from such conventional cost-benefit principles is required to consider jointly the sustainability of resources on which tourism is based as well as the sustainability of the tourism marketing base. The paper argues that this implies that sustainability ought to be associated with supporting multiple resources uses (including recreation and tourism) rather than attempting to identify one that is deemed to optimally support a unique objective. The case of wildlife-based tourism resources is examined in the final part.

Market Failures and the Economic Approach to Resources Management

Much tourism planning and management is concerned with ascertaining the benefits and costs derived from tourism activities with a view to contrast development scenarios with respect to their relative desirability. Economists have played a central role in identifying the opportunity costs of using natural, social and cultural amenities for the purpose of generating economic activity in various locations. The standard economic logic describes tourism's use of resources as alternatives to other forms of production capable of generating employment and income. In the process it must assess the opportunity costs of using human, capital, organizational and natural assets for the sake of servicing tourists rather than producing other goods and services. Total reliance on "the market" to coordinate tourism consumption and production activities is in general deemed deficient insofar as a number of tourism-related market failures can be identified which prevent the achievement of efficient outcomes . The most frequently identified type of market failure is associated with the absence (or incomplete nature) of property rights typical of a large proportion of what constitute tourism attractions and places. The socio-cultural and natural assets of a place are often by nature at least partially non-excludable and non-rival in the sense that it is impossible or undesirable to prevent their use by people not having acquired rights to that use (Randall 1986). For an economist, this can be expressed in a number of different ways. The core problem of economic coordination associated with tourism consumption and production can be presented as involving the following characteristics and difficulties:

— the most critical components of the tourism commodity (often the central attractions) have important *public goods* characteristics. These constitute a typical market failure which private market competition will fail to adequately supply and can serve as a justification for some form of intervention or policy.

— given many types of overlapping externalities linked with tourism supply in general, most businesses or organizations involved with tourism are likely to *free-ride* by appropriating tourism revenue whenever possible (indirectly generated from the public good attraction) and contributing as little as possible to the costs. Public costs include the marketing of attraction and destinations in general. More importantly in the context of the present paper, tourism stakeholders will typically fail to adequately participate in the sustainable management of the common resources for the sake of limiting impacts. This is deemed likely to lead to over-use, abuse, deterioration or even depletion of those common resources, be they linked with relatively tangible assets such as access to clean air and water or the more intangible ones such as scenic landscape, authentic culture or undisturbed ecosystems.

— often the argument is presented as if the absence of *property rights* is to blame insofar as it suggests that if scale economies allowed property rights to be established, efficient allocations of costs and benefits would necessarily ensue.

The latter point naively assumes that the "tourism commodity" is itself well delineated while only a few peripheral-environmental attributes are the source of externality. It is here suggested that the difficulty to connect tourism benefits with the existence of a stable and well-identified set of economic agents capable of appropriating tourism benefits and be held responsible for its costs constitutes one of the "core tourism problems" of tourism management. The fuzzy connection between tourists, tourism attractions, tourism businesses and what researchers study as the relevant "tourism system" points at the lack of a standard "tourism commodity".

The difficulties these issues raise can be traced back to the discussions of some early commentators on the tourism dilemma. The economist Mishan (1967) for instance predicted a gloomy future for tourism on the basis of accumulating externalities and argued that the process of commoditization in tourism is unsustainable as it ultimately destroys those primary tourism resources constituting the essential motivation or attraction for tourism demand. The public good nature of many tourism resources, and the congestion which occurs once tourism infrastructures are put in place, leads to over-investments in commercial amenities and under-investment in sustainable core attractions. Although not expressing the problem in terms of property rights, Mishan was referring to the inability of services providers to appropriate the benefits they would ideally derive from efficient levels of production or protection of those attractions. According to this common scenario, tourism trade would eventually decline when destinations become less attractive because their initially authentic and differentiated lifestyle, culture or natural environments become crowded, destroyed or simply over-commoditised. This could lead to a succession of destination cycles involving discovery, boom, maturity and decline phases (although the evidence on the existence of regular cycles is mixed) where the quality of experience in a destination disappears because its formerly unspoiled, natural environments become contaminated (Mishan, 1967).

Walter (1982) utilises a parallel argument by identifying limits to tourism growth related to consumption externalities (more akin to type [c] above). Positional goods, as opposed to material goods, give utility to the extent that they signal status. Utility is derived through the ability to signal an individual's relative social position or class. Access to prestigious tourism products and destinations might partially be subjected to non-excludability but their consumption involves an indirect form of rivalry as everyone imposes a marginal social costs on everyone else by reducing the prestige associated with that product. In the long run, the popularity of destination leads to the growing consumption of positional tourism goods, which in turn leads to increasing deterioration of the psychic benefits derived by tourists and might even on average, decrease social welfare. According to Walter, this can lead to ongoing attempts to re-position oneself by discovering new fashionable destinations with snob-like qualities, and force tourists to discover new grounds, consume them and eventually abandon them. As for many commodities, one can identify tourism markets playing the role of trend-setters as well as followers. The complex interaction between snob and Veblen effects in the case of tourism has been explored by Tisdell (1987).

Thus while tourists and the tourism industry seem to be "killing the goose that lays the egg", the nature, the location and the attributes of the goose seem to be forever shifting. Account of spiralling cycles of tourism self-destruction depend on debatable assumptions regarding the nature of tourist motivations as well as the ability of complex systems (social, cultural and natural) to transform and even sometimes regulate themselves. In the environmental externalities case, simplistic views of tourists as consumers-recreationists generally driven by relatively similar motivations, searching for the same sort of experiences and finding satisfaction in the same sorts of consumption activities are nowadays generally refuted (Ryan 1997). Mishan's pessimism towards the ability of tourism to survive self-destruction surely did not anticipate the growth and increasing importance of such developments as urban, cultural and heritage tourism as well as meetings and events and the resulting diversity of motivations-based market segments modern tourism would be attempting to satisfy.

Equally, extending the notion of market failures to tourism can itself be problematic if the economist's tool (developed for the sake of analysing in a partial equilibrium context a small manageable problem at the time) is taken too far out of context and too many overlapping failures are agglomerated. Our partial ignorance of tourist motivations and our very incomplete knowledge of the local impacts of tourists on the main socio-cultural and natural attractors they pursue make traditional price or quantity regulations of tourism consumption or production utterly unrealistic.

Alternatively, suggestions based on the establishment of property rights for the purpose of solving market failures might miss the point and the essence of tourism coordination challenges. It might well be the case that what makes tourists travel is the "public good" and intangible nature of many assets that do not belong to anyone in particular and that no one can seize or relocate. Major attractors retain in part their power and value because they are anchored in a place and can not be appropriated as commodities. It might well be useless to propose conventional policy solutions that affect the nature of these assets and it might prove essential for tourism research and strategy to consider whether tourists correlate many authentic tourism experiences with their "non-commercial" dimension. This prospect can be extended to argue that the experiences or values "tourists-to-be" lack in their everyday lives are those very same public good characteristics they seek away from home in time and place. If the view that modern life has robbed masses from meaningful social or spiritual that they seek to compensate for with tourism is to be adopted (Ryan 1997), it would seem pointless to attempt to attend to tourists' needs and values by constructing private economic commodities.

It seems sensible to hypothesize that incomplete property rights are at the core of tourism economic activity and that market failures will never be completely dealt with by privatizing tourism attractions. This is very much the case when wildlife or nature become major tourism attractions for historical and cultural or ethical reasons. Yet, there is room for many approaches to organizing the management of such complex amalgams of natural tourism resources. Nowadays tourism resources management entails more than considerations of the impact of the ownership resources on tourism failures, it also encompasses the notion that tourism might destroy the resource base (cultural, social or natural) and that longer-term considerations such as sustainable use of a resource ought to enter decision-making processes.

The general perception that tourism might destroy itself and many social, cultural and natural assets along the way drives much of the discussions between the supporters of "ecotourism" and those who see it as a marketing ploy. Whether it is presented as a philosophy, a political movement, a management policy or a marketing strategy, it constitutes a simple extension of Mishan's fears towards the impact of tourism on the natural environment.

Sustainability in Economics, Marketing and Beyond

The above discussion on the link between market failures and alternative views of tourism coordination is important for the sake of putting the examination of the concept of "sustainability" in context. This quite recent but already prevalent concept has seen its meaning spanning to apply to a large array of settings, ranging from that of resources conservation (for instance the sustainability of fishing activities on a stock of fish), to more multifarious economic activities such as tourism itself (as a commercially sustainable activity) and to very complex systems such as ecosystems or human communities (places or destinations in the context of tourism). While the term has become used in an increasingly large number of contexts, its meaning has also stretched beyond what a single word or expression ought to convey. This section suggests that some of the more basic interpretations of the term (based on resources economics for instance when applying to simple commodities) have limited applicability to the more complex contexts such as that of tourism. Also, the traditional policy implications derived ought not to be extended to the analysis of complex interactions between ecological and tourism systems, usually encountered when studying wildlife tourism.

The notion of sustainability is often associated with the renewability of an activity such as the exploitation of a resource, a marketing idea, a concept or even the attractiveness of a place. Early uses of the term were generally associated with clearly identified environmental amenities as found in resources economics. A conventional economic categorisation distinguishes between exhaustible and non-exhaustible resources and analyses principles behind the efficient exploitation of a resource when there is a fixed or depletable stock of that resource. Assuming complete technical knowledge of the conditions of exploitation and of renewability, it is possible to derive relatively simple rules to establish an optimal rate of use. To this day, some discussions of sustainability of various types of resources surrounding tourism production activities borrow from these same general principles and extend to address resource-use conflicts by considering alternative uses of given resources as done in economics. It is useful to consider three contexts in which sustainability principles have been formulated in the context of tourism.

[a] The Sustainability of Natural Resources Used by Tourism

The most traditional "applied economics" approach examines the sustainability of tourism as depending on contrasting various demands for a semi- renewable resource. The general principles of opportunity costs and benefits are called on to contrast the net benefits generated by alternative activities (or substitutable products) and establish decision-making criteria for preferred uses. Tourism can become unsustainable because externalities creep in which have a negative impact on the physical attractiveness of a place: due to environmental degradation or congestion or something along those lines (Tisdell 1987). A direct connection is established between tourist numbers and the degradation of attractiveness. In theory, growth-type models can be used to establish the ideal rate of exploitation and the economic value of various strategies. In that hypothetical scenario, price control mechanisms could be implemented to maintain attractiveness at an optimal level.

It is useful to consider the premises of a cost-benefit perspective which allows the valuation of such alternatives. First, the alternative uses of the resource are sufficiently well understood to constitute a restricted but enduring set of measurable alternatives. The latter are essentially rival uses and non-trivial capital and time requirements make the costs of shifting from one use to the other non-trivial for producers. Second, the rate of regeneration of a non-exhaustible resource is sufficiently predictable to derive the dynamics of stocks growth and potential regeneration. Thirdly, the different impacts of the various uses on the total stock (quantity or quality wise) are also known. This implies that a sustainable level of exploitation of the resource incorporates considerations of relative impact of various production processes on total stocks as well as relative end-use valuations.

Much thinking related to environmental sustainability in the context of tourism seems to endorse that approach by attempting to establish if tourism puts more or less pressure on the environment than alternative uses (see for instance Moulton and Sanderson 1999). This is most often the case when "the environment" is made of wild ecosystems or animal species which can be exploited for some utilitarian purpose; for their meat or for alternative recreation purposes such as wildlife-viewing and wildlife-hunting or fishing. Indirectly, ecotourism proponents also claim that green tourism constitutes a preferable alternative to other uses when both the value/to tourists, community and the pressures (negative impacts) put on the existing stock or living system are taken into account. This is based on the general methodology of cost-benefit analysis and it assumes that a given resource is assessed with respect to alternative-competing uses (see Kopp and Smith 1993 on various methods, and Nias 1995 for an example of arguments based on use strategies as substitutes).

Sustainability is then presented as a choice between alternative exploitation strategies and taking into account different degrees of pressure on the fragile resource base.

[b] The Sustainability of Tourism as an Tnvestment in the Appropriate Marketing Mix

A second quite different interpretation can be derived which considers the sustainability of tourism commercial activities and focusses on long-term business profitability from a marketing perspective. This version of the argument is usually directed towards the survival of a tourism destination or place rather than an individual businesses. Tourism business sustainability refers to the ability of a tourism business entity to retain a sufficient market share of a broad tourism market. The emphasis is usually on the marketing image or popularity of a resort or tourism location and the multiple potential causes of growth or decline.

Interestingly, the resource which needs to be sustained is a market share of the "tourism potential" (a bit like a proportion of the fish stock!) but the reasons for which that resource is threatened vary considerably. In the most simplistic scenario, the lifecycle effect applies because of the mix of bandwagon and snob effects characterizing tourist behaviour (Veblen 1899). Walter's (1982) argument described above stems directly from these older ideas. In that simpler form, the inherent instability of tourism is due to the nature of tourism motivations. This leads to resort-product lifecycle scenarios (Butler 1980). If sufficiently predictable, tourist destinations can only adapt by shifting from a market segment to the next and attempt to milk the various market segments as they replace each other until destination decline sets in. The lack of sustainability of tourist destinations in that case is assumed to be mainly demand-driven.

Perhaps destinations can counter the decline with suitable marketing strategies. It might be possible to address the eventual tourist arrivals slowdown by adjusting the amount and type of advertising and infrastructures and hope that this will sustain growth. In that case, the resource to be sustained is the marketing capital. It can take the form of reputation, destination images, channel efficiency or of the basic destination infrastructure required to maintain visitation. One can then portray tourist destinations as continually reinvesting their brand, image or marketing capital. This constitutes a reasonable scenario in the case of many sunlust destinations as they cater for sufficiently predictable tourist tastes and feature many substitutes. The strategy of investing in brand loyalty implies a belief that tourists hold sufficiently stable and predictable tastes otherwise brandnames and destination images can become rapidly obsolete. Efforts to maintain sustainability can then be described as supply-driven insofar as the ball is in the court of tourism destinations to control the required promotional mechanisms.

[c] The Sustainability of Tourism Product Innovations

A third less prevalent perspective on tourism commercial sustainability moves beyond the previous ones to examine how destination "product(s)" can be sustained. This is a much more fuzzy perspective because the connection between tourist arrivals and product innovation has been insufficiently investigated at the theoretical level. Yet, if markets do change quite rapidly and if the nature of motivations for undertaking leisure and travel activities unfold unpredictably, the possibility of transforming tourism destinations (modelled as bundles of attractions and services) might need to be considered more closely. The resource to be sustained in that context is even less tangible and less well understood than in the prior interpretations. It has to do with the ability to adapt the tourism product (again, the bundle of attractions and secondary amenities) by developing expertise in understanding and envisioning changing market needs and motivations. It also extends to local capabilities for innovation by modifying the bundle of attractions at the core of the tourism destination product. While involving novelty by definition, the capacity to produce attractions (as well as basic amenities and services, infrastructures, distribution channels but less critically so for the latter) can be seized and invested in for the sake of ensuring the future of a tourism place or resort.

This differs greatly from the previous interpretations because the threats to sustainability arise from the nature of the commodity and sit between supply and demand. Nor does it rely on the predictability of tourist behaviour or the design of routine marketing plans to affect the sustainability of tourist arrivals and expenditures in a specific location. In fact, contrarily to the foundations of the resources sustainability principles it does not assume the existence of a verifiable empirical relation between consumption or production activities nor does it depend on a given stock of resources that must be controlled. Instead, it envisions a qualitative connection between the renewal of the tourism commercial potential of a place and entrepreneurship. The latter is compatible with describing tourism operators as partially ignorant of tourist's true compulsions and recognises them as participants in the product innovation process.

[d] The systemic Approach: Combining Concerns of Tourism Commercial Viability with Multiple Uses of Natural Assets

The more complex and interesting issues surrounding tourism sustainability usually combine at least two dimensions: the commercial potential of tourism (as a localized source of economic growth, income and employment) and a critical resource with a number of alternative uses (including tourism) which can potentially suffer negatively from tourism. While tourism production or consumption activities might have greater or lesser impacts on the resource base, potential conflicts regarding the use of the resource usually need to be worked out, and the choice of a development strategy depends in part on the value of tourism relative to other industries, on the sustainability of tourism in general and on the impact of tourism on that resource relative to that of other industries. This delineates a much more complex set of interactions usually plagued by important gaps in both scientific and economic knowledge.

An excessively simplistic dual model could be formulated which would consist of an attempt to integrate the cost-benefit principles discussed in [a] above with the requirements of tourism commercial viability as depicted in [b]. This would involve for instance optimizing the net economic benefits from the suggested alternative uses of the resource (as in a typical cost-benefit analysis) while incorporating "exhaustibility constraints" arising from the negative impacts of every possible use on the resource base. This conceptually leads to choosing an optimal strategy for the long-run exploitation of the resource that incorporates tourism sustainability considerations. The rest of this section argues that this would constitute a misguided approach to joint tourism and resource management in general while the next section will apply the argument more specifically to a case study: the considerations of sustainable wildlife tourism.

The basic argument against the application of opportunity costs principles to the dual dynamics of tourism-resources relationships is both conceptual and empirical. It is partly based on the view that cost-benefit reasoning applied in the context of complex dynamic relationships between tourism evolution and resource degradation mistakenly ignores critical knowledge gaps. These non-trivial gaps easily compound and can not be simply brushed away by the belief that they can be filled with reliable surveys and integrated research.

Instead, it is argued here that the sustainable coordination of both tourism and complex multiple-use resources must emphasize the evolutionary nature of the system and the impossibility of full knowledge. The coordination mechanisms and the choice of decision-making tools appropriate when combining tourism development with composite sustainability issues (such as the survival of wild species or ecosystems which constitute a tourism attraction but which at the same time are threatened by tourism impacts) is often trivialised when represented as measurable and comparable alternatives which can be contrasted or even added up to evaluate the value of the resource. A number of difficulties associated with the characterization of choice as one of picking the best of a given number of measured alternatives (based on the tradition of short-term cost-benefit analysis) in the context of tourism follow:

(i) At one level, strategic decisions need to take into consideration the inherent unpredictability associated with tourist motivations and needs which make it a volatile socio-economic activity in both quantitative and qualitative terms (Tremblay 1999). This leads to recognising that relying on tourism alone as a development strategy is highly risky and that most realistic scenarios need to consider mixes of tourism and other industrial development alternatives as potential complements.

(ii) At an other level, it is also important to recognise that tourism development is made up of market segments which can be very highly differentiated and even more incompatible (when fixed in place and time) than are choices involving tourism against completely different alternative uses. Such diversity can be linked with marketing investments (such as the presentation of a place and its products, as much as the cultural values portrayed in its packaging) and it leads to heterogeneity with respect to the nature of tourism impacts on social, cultural and natural resources on which it depends.

It is nowadays not very meaningful to suggest that "tourism" as an aggregate can contribute to economic development more (or less) than another industry; what matters more is which sort of tourism is developed and what marketing approach is used. This includes the choice of images and representations of a destination to be developed as well as the market mix capable of using without depleting the resource base which supports its attractiveness. In other words, different market segments will generate very different impacts on the resource base and these need to be taken considered in the design of a sustainable development strategy, particularly the market mix aimed at.

(iii) At a less general level, it also probably the case that there exist important synergies (or scope economies) when undertaking multiple production activities; for the sake of sustaining multiple uses, industries or markets. This provides further support for the view that alternative uses of natural or other resources ought not necessarily be considered as substitutes but rather as complements (even in the shorter term). This will prove particularly relevant when considering wildlife tourism sustainability as a production process and as supporting a set of more or less complementary markets.

(iv) A different but critical argument must be made regarding the methodological suitability of representing long-term strategic strategies as choices between substitutes. Point (i) argued that when development strategies take into consideration the sustainability of a resource base, they must recognise the great amount of uncertainty regarding both the impact of the various use on the resource capital as well as the demand for each use. This must be connected with the realisation that the technological (human, financial, technical and organizational) knowledge required to engage competitively and locally in any of the alternative uses of a resource could be jeopardized if any of the activities ceased completely. In other words, the ability to undertake an economic activity is greatly connected with past investments in local technological knowledge which could be extinguished if development strategies suggested to specialise in only one use (due to and excessive short-term focus).

This last dimension is particularly important and can be supported theoretically by a large number of abstract arguments. Sustainability issues relate to a long-term perspective by definition. They must fundamentally be concerned with flexibility and the ability to maintain diversity and reasonable alternatives, rather than how to discriminate between them as the cost-benefit methodology suggests. In that context, sustainability becomes not the choice of an optimal development path believed to minimise the pressure on a resource (given adequate measurement of alternative uses' costs and benefits) but instead the ability to flexibly maintain multiple paths in a context of rapidly changing socio-economic and natural values and environments.

This means that ensuring the sustainability of resources with multiple usages must take into consideration the necessity of maintaining complementary social—and technological—knowledge assets. In the recent evolutionary approaches to economic choice, this is largely represented as choices between learning strategies (Tremblay 2000). If applied to tourism places or destinations, the choice between exploiting intensively a small number of resource uses or maintaining a broad array of resource utilisations and activities becomes the core dilemma for tourism sustainability. Sustainability principles ought to shift the focus towards the ability to maintain a sufficient amount of flexibility to adapt to unpredictable changes in the environment of tourism (new markets, new products and new competitors) and of the alternative resources uses (new technologies and new uses as such).

This is considerably different from methodologies attempting to strictly measure positive and negative effects of alternative activities and concentrate on the presumed best use of the resource. Instead, sustainability is about maintaining a balance between diverse uses and acknowledging the way in which they support each other. In particular, it must recognise the existence of production and marketing synergies associated with simultaneous uses (say between tourism and non-tourism), between differentiated markets as well as the critical role "diversity of uses" plays in ensuring the sustainability of the resource base.

A Case Study: Sustainable Wildlife Tourism

Wildlife tourism poses particularly difficult challenges for sustainable management for a number of reasons. First, it blends issues of sustainability for a tourism market poorly understood and difficult to delineate insofar as seeing or interacting with wildlife is usually combined with other essential tourist motivations. It is important for tourism research to concede that tourists themselves have difficulties conceptualising clearly their interest in wildlife and might not even be able to verbalise it clearly in the surveys the researchers impose on them (Shackley 1996, Ryan 1997, Tremblay 2002). The unavoidable lack of knowledge about wildlife tourists and the potential for a large diversity of motivations prevent planners and managers to adopt or rely on ready-made marketing strategies in the hope that commercial sustainability will be ensured.

At the same time, there are good grounds to believe that the marketing image of a destination is quite important for wildlife tourism and that complementarity is expected between natural, social and cultural attractions as well as between various types of tourism (Alberta Tourism 1990, Baker 1997). As for other types of tourism attractions, important symbols or icons and reputed places are created from a variety of cultural products and marketing channels which become the source of the tourist's imagined wildlife experience. The tourism industry must then satisfy the expectations that tourists have built on that basis, mainly with respect to the nature, format and environment of that wildlife experience. The extent to which the wildlife tourist experience takes place in a controlled, safe and comfortable environment (say a wildlife park) rather than a purely wild (as in a National park) context is just an example.

Also different markets with dissimilar values and interests are likely to be highly influenced by a variety of representations of wildlife, of their links to a community or culture and by its role in economic life. In terms of commercial sustainability, this means that wildlife tourism planners must be concerned with the sustainability of various wildlife images transmitted to appropriate tourist market segments. They must manage a number of such representations and maintain to a certain extent the separation (physical and marketing-based) of the various types of tourists. For instance, some market segments interested in wildlife-viewing activities would be negatively affected by being exposed to some aspects of industrial production using wildlife (as found in animal farms in some instances) or even by knowing that hunting and fishing tourism activities exist. This is usually managed by spatially separating the diversity of wildlife attractions and experiences sought by different tourists. It must also by supported by the use of differentiated marketing channels reaching the appropriate audiences.

This also has implications for the management of representations of the interaction between local communities and the wildlife in the general images created for tourists (and for the clients of the potential alternative uses). It means that wildlife tourism marketing must also manage the perceptions of tourists about destinations with respect to the latter's commitment to use, consume, preserve or protect wildlife in various contexts. It is for instance believed important for diverse wildlife tourism segments to feel comfortable with local wildlife politics when major tourists segments embrace certain views about ethics and about the nature of human-wildlife interactions. This is why natural reserves, parks or territories involving wildlife-based tourism tend to specialise in promoting images based on conservation, recreation or game usage when targeting wildlife tourists. This is in no way simple for broad territories (for instance in Eastern Africa), especially when dominant, minority, ethnic or indigenous local groups conflict in their values towards and economic relationships with wildlife. Such problems are compounded when tourists themselves have strong views about alternative uses of wildlife, for instance if they disagree with certain forms of consumptive uses or activities undertaken by other market segments; for instance hunting and fishing.

Yet the sustainability of wildlife tourism is not merely about commercial and marketing considerations revolving around tourism competitiveness. In the previous section it was argued that alternative uses of the resource base (here the wildlife as a potentially exhaustible resource) ought to be placed at the heart of the analysis. Nor should the analysis be restricted to the comparison of various and often arbitrary conservation strategies to safeguard a single level of natural capital (say a species, a local ecosystem or a broader abstract concept such as biodiversity...). Finding the optimal use strategy with a single level in mind could easily come at the expense of the others. This has been exemplified with the African elephant overpopulation crisis (Kiss 1990). By attempting to overemphasize this single very popular species (in the West where tourists come from), policies designed to preserve these African icons have led to uncontrolled expansion which in turn has damaged broader ecosystems and led to the need to eliminate large groups of animals. This has in turn led to the need to employ previously evicted local poachers to trim down the elephant population and ensure that tourists would not see the carnage. Such situations can arise when a single use is promoted and excessive dependence develops on that production activity.

The evolutionary approach to sustainability applied to tourism suggests rather it is important to maintain multiple uses for the resources and that this constitutes a core principle for economic and ecological strategies directed at maintaining the multi-use resource base sustainability. It is useful for a place or community to maintain a portfolio of uses and industries to develop and conserve human and organizational capital invested by prior generations in a diversity of wildlife uses. Not only is it not clear what uses of the wildlife will hold the greatest value in the long-term, there are also synergies between consumptive and non-consumptive uses of wildlife for instance (Tremblay 2001). Tourists are interested in wildlife-viewing beyond the pure pleasure of gazing at animals. They usually value a wildlife experience in a cultural and historical context and express the desire to learn how the environment has shaped culture and industry in specific places (Shackley 1996, chapter 5).

Industrial uses of wildlife can often become important tourism attractions in themselves (for instance crocodile farms). It is also clear that indigenous tourism products exhibit the relationship between local natural resources and indigenous lifestyles and value systems. Conflicting political positions about wildlife uses by conservationists, wildlife-based industries and indigenous communities can be viewed as problematic for those attempting to provide simplistic images to tourists. This can lead to avoiding the issue altogether or having whole regions specialising in one use or image. For sustainability's sake, it is critical to consider maintaining a diversity of uses and perhaps even capitalising on that diversity to reflect the nature of a destination or place. This can be done if tourism marketing and travellers' movements are planned accordingly.

From an ecological viewpoint, there is also value in maintaining the diversity of uses and industrial capital as the cost of preserving the wildlife is in some more or less direct way always associated with a human use or another. As was argued above, if the future of any number of uses or activities is uncertain, resources will retain their sustainability if the community is capable of holding and developing sufficient amounts of human and organizational capital to preserve these long-term economic values. It might of course be necessary to keep buffers in such a way as to preserve the diversity of uses. This will generally involve separating those uses or wildlife utilisations which are not compatible. This might involve attempting to sustain almost pristine environments as well as commercial exploitation (for meat or other uses when economical) as well as research into the conditions of sustainability for the species and its ecosystem.

Conclusion

This paper put forward a theoretical argument to suggest that the key to many types of tourism sustainability (for instance wildlife tourism) lies in maintaining a sufficient amount of diversity in uses and in market segmentation. It has been argued that sustainability in that sense must take into account the commercial viability of the tourism industry as well as the potential conflicts and/or synergies associated with multiple uses of a resource. When the complexity of jointly dealing with both aspects is fully appreciated, arguments that the sustainability of resources lie in the management of diversity rather than the measurement of single optimal uses can be deduced.

This applies to the mix of uses as much as to the portfolio of market segments, product development innovations and marketing strategies which are aimed at tourists. The argument for moving away from conventional approaches to economic choice based on a full analysis opportunity costs and benefits lies on a number of considerations detailed in the paper. In particular, the unpredictability of tourism demand and the changeability of core motivations, the need to preserve vulnerable forms of capital (other than natural capital) which sustain other forms of economic value associated with resources such as wildlife and importantly the synergies associated with maintaining a large array of objectives (existence value and preservation, research, recreational pursuits and tourism, consumptive uses...).

These fundamental synergies extend to the tourism sector and its marketing. Wildlife tourism for instance depends on the existence, use and representations that various species and their habitats have played in indigenous, industrial and community cultural and socio-economic developments. Through clever management and marketing, wildlife tourism can therefore gain from being considered a complement to other uses rather than a substitute.

BIBLIOGRAPHY

Alberta Tourism—Watchable Wildlife Program, Marketing watchable wildlife tourism, Edmonton 1990.

Baker, J.E., (1997), Trophy hunting as a sustainable use of wildlife resources in Southern and Eastern Africa, Journal of Sustainable Tourism, 5(4), 1997: 306-321.

Butler, R. (1980), The concept of a tourism area cycle of evolution, Canadian Geographer, 24, 5-12.

Gauthier, D.A. (1993), Sustainable development, tourism and wildlife, In J.-G. Nelson, R. Butler and G. Wall, Tourism and sustainable development: Monitoring, planning, managing, Department of Geography, University of Waterloo, Canada.

Kiss, A.(1990), Living with wildlife—wildlife resource management with local participation in Africa, World Bank technical paper number 130, Washington.

Kopp, R.J. and V.K. Smith (1993), Valuing natural assets, Rsources for the future, Washington.

Mishan, E.J. (1967), The costs of economic growth. Staples Press, London.

Mishan, E.J. (1982), Introduction to political economy, Hutchinson/Heinemann, London.

Moulton M.P. and J. Sanderson (1999), Wildlife issues in a changing world, 2nd edition, Lewis publishers, Boca Raton.

Nias, R. (1997), Using and losing it—the commercial exploitation of wildlife in Australia, In Diekman, B. (Ed.), Sustainable use of wildlife: Utopian dream or unrealistic nightmare, Proceedings of the seminar held at the University of Technology, Sydney 1995.

Randall, A. (1986), Human preferences, economics and the preservation of species, In B.G. Norton (ed.), The preservation of species—the value of biological diversity, Princeton University Press.

Ryan, C. (1997), The tourism experience—a new introduction, Cassell, London.

Ryan (1998), Saltwater crocodiles as tourist attractions, Journal of Sustainable Tourism, 6(4), 314-327.

Shackley, M. (1996), Wildlife tourism, International Thompson Business Press, London.

Shaw, W.W. (1984), Problems in wildlife valuation in natural resource management, In G.L. Peterson and A. Randall (eds.), Valuation of wildland resource benefits, Westview Press, London.

Tisdell, C.A. (1987) Tourism, the environment and profit, Economic Analysis and Policy, 17, pp. 13-30.

Tremblay, P. (1999), "The future of tourism: An evolutionary perspective," in Molloy, J. and Davies, J. (eds.), Tourism & Hospitality: Delighting the senses 1999—Part two,, Bureau of Tourism Research, Canberra, pp. 306-16.

Tremblay, P. (2000), "An evolutionary interpretation of the role of collaborative partnerships in sustainable tourism," in Bramwell, B. and Lane, B. (eds.), *Tourism collaboration and partnerships—politics, practice and sustainability*,, Channel View Publications, Clevedon, UK, pp. 314-32.

Tremblay, P. (2001) "Wildlife tourism consumption: consumptive or non-consumptive ?", International Journal of Tourism Research, 3, pp. 81-86.

Tremblay, P. (2002) "Tourism wildlife icons: Attractions or marketing symbols ?", *Journal of Hospitality and Tourism Management*, 9, pp. 164-80.

Urry, J. (1990), The tourist gaze. Sage, London.

Veblen, T. (1899), The theory of the leisure class: an economic study of institutions. Macmillan, New York.

Walter, J.A. (1982) Social limits to tourism, Leisure Sciences, 1, pp. 295-304.

6

Strategies for Ecotourism Development in Mountainous Environments

*Sanjay K. Nepal**

Abstract

Many mountain communities around the world have promoted ecotourism to ameliorate problems of environmental degradation and under development. Although there is no agreement on what ecotourism is or should be, it is generally believed that ecotourism in the moutains will foster responsible tourist behavior, conservation of important wildlife habitats and ecosystems, appreciation of local cultures and traditional life styles, and provision of sustainable forms of livelihood for people living in remote and communities. This paper provides an overview of the trends in mountain ecotourism and suggests that any attempts towards mountain ecotourism should focus on sustainbility; diversity; institutional reforms; gender equity; local, regional and global economic integration; local financial

* University of Northern British Columbia (UNBC) Prince George, British Columbia Canada. Assistant Professor in the Resource, Recreation and Tourism Program.

incentives; and peace and security. The paper concludes with the proposition for a framework for mountain ecotourism site designation.

Introduction

Ever since the term was coined in the mid 1980s, "ecotourism" has been of special interest to policy and decision-makers, academics, and the business communities both at local and international levels (Ceballos-Lascurain, 1996). Hector Ceballos-Lascurain, who is credited for introducing the term ecotourism defined it as "traveling to relatively undisturbed or uncontaminated natural areas with the specific objective of studying, admiring, and enjoying the scenery and its wild plants and animals, as well as any existing cultural manifestations (both past and present) found in these areas" (Ceballos-Lascurain, 1987). The definition provided by the International Ecotourism Society includes the welfare of local people: ecotourism is "responsible travel to natural areas which conserves the environment and improves well-being of local people (TES, 1991). However, it has been questioned on environmental, economic, and ethical grounds. Those in favour of ecotourism consider it as the only hope to save endangered species, ecosystems and culture. The debate however is not of a choice between mass and ecotourism, but is rather about the arguments made in favour of ecotourism that it protects biodiversity and provides benefits to local communities. Indeed, it is difficult to find successful examples of ecotourism (Buckley, 2001). Despite all the controversies, there is general agreement that ecotourism, if planned properly can change the fortunes of people and places in the remote, and less developed regions. It is no wonder that governments in countries where mountains constitute a major biological and cultural niche have envisioned ecotourism as the panacea to problems of underdevelopment, marginality, and fragility. Year 2002 is both the International Year of the Mountains and the Year of Ecotourism. This dual significance has increased the importance of mountain communities where ecotourism posits itself as a potential driving force for sustainable mountain development.

Any discussion on mountain ecotourism faces two problems: first is the lack of consensus among tourism practitioners as to what exactly ecotourism is and should be; and second, there is very little research on mountain ecotourism. Ecotourism has been subject to various interpretations. Criteria such as local benefits, support for conservation, low-scale development, low visitor volume, and educational experience suggest that many mountain tourism destinations may not qualify as ecotourism venues. Nevertheless, mountain destinations that exhibit signs of mass tourism increasingly use the prefix "eco" in their advertising.

Literature on mountain-specific ecotourism is lacking, partly because the focus of ecotourism research is limited to well-known tropical islands, rainforests, and national parks and protected areas, not all of which are located in the mountains (Weaver, 2001). There are hardly any comparable empirical studies on ecotourism impacts, while economic, ecological and social evaluations of the so-called ecotourism destinations do not exist (Fennell, 2001). Ecotourism, nature tourism, and sustainable tourism are often used interchangeably, even though these are distinct forms of tourism. For example, the term ecotourism is not as widely used in Europe as elsewhere in the world. The term sustainable tourism is preferred, and is applied by the EU as a concept, approach, and form of organization (Blangy and Vautier, 2001). The Mountain Agenda in 1999 published a small report citing various examples of mountain tourism (Mountain Agenda, 1999). Only some of the case study areas cited in that report could qualify as ecotourism destinations. Literature on ecotourism often includes the Nepalese Himalaya, particularly the Annapurna and Everest regions as adventure/ecotourism destinations. However, neither of the two regions are ecotourism destinations if one were to consider the volume of tourist traffic and the resultant socio-economic and environmental problems (Nepal, 1999). Thus, to expand the scope of the discussion here, mountain ecotourism is defined as "tourism which does not degrade the natural and cultural environment of the mountain regions, provides economic, environmental, and social benefits to mountain communities (local residents), and offers a high quality experience for the visitors to such areas." It is apparent that this definition could include many nature-based activities that are not strictly labelled as ecotourism.

The Potential for Ecotourism in the Mountains

Mountainous regions, in most cases, are inaccessible, fragile, marginalized by political and economic decision-making, and home to one of the poorest people in the world (Messerli and Ives, 1997). While steepness, fragility and marginality often remain as constraints, which expose mountains to pervasive degradation, there are also several opportunities to be tapped. Given the complexities of development in the mountains, tourism development is seen as an obvious choice and one of the means for achieving sustainable mountain development.

The World Tourism Organization (WTO) predicts that international tourism by the year 2010 will involve one billion visitors, and is expected to contribute 11.6 per cent to the global gross domestic product (WTTC). Similarly, it is estimated that by 2010, roughly 250 million people would be employed in the tourism industry and 10.6 per cent of total capital investments would be made in the tourism sector (WTTC, 1999). Although in light of recent international events such predictions are unreliable, the significant impacts and implications of global tourism cannot be understated.

The WTO has suggested that the global turnover of ecotourism in 1997 was US$ 20 billion (WTO, 1998). This estimate does not take into account the value of domestic tourism. For example, it is estimated that Canadians spend CDN$ 11 billion (roughly US$ 6.8 billion) annually on nature-related activities, and that birdwatchers in USA spend US$5.2 billion on bird-related products (Statistics Canada, 1988, and Foot and Stoffman, 1996 cited in Fennell, 2001). Not all nature tourism is ecotourism and not all money spent in outdoor-related gears may be used in ecotourism-type activities, nevertheless, the real economic value of ecotourism, both domestic and international combined is very high. Not all ecotourism destinations are in the mountains; indeed, only a few mountain destinations have been cited as ecotourism destinations (Williams et al, 2001; Table—6.1).

Table—6.1 Mountain regions with ecotourism potential

Geographic Region	Destinations
North America	Alaska (Denali, Katmai, Alexander Archipelago) Yukon (Dawson Range and Pelly Mountains) Northwest Territories (Mackenzie Mountains) British Columbia (Columbia Mountains, Pacific Ranges, Vancouver Island Ranges) USA (Pacific Northwest, Cascade Range, Rocky Mountains, Olympic Mountains, and Sierra Nevada Appalachian Mountains Mexico (Sierra Chincua)
Europe	Alps Pyrenees, Cantabrians, Taurus, Apennines, Balkans, Western Carpathians, Jotunheim, and the highlands of Scandinavia Altai Mountains in Russia
Asia	Himalaya, Hindu Kush, Karakoram and Pamir Main destinations include areas around Nanga Parbat (Pakistan), Ladakh, Kulu-Kangara, Garhwal, Har ki doon (India), Everest and Annpunrna (Nepal) Northern hills of Thailand (Chiangmai and Chiangrai provinces) Highlands of China (Yunnan and Fujian provinces) and Korea
South America	Upland massifs in Brazil and Venezuela Andean Cordillera (Argentina, Bolivia, Chile, Columbia, Ecuador, Peru, Venezuela)
Africa	Atlas Mountains (North Africa) Drakensberg Range (South Africa) Virunga Volcanoes (Central Africa)
Australia	Australian and New Zealand Alps

***Sources*:** **Mountain Agenda, 1999; Williams et al, 2001.**

The WTO estimate would indicate that the global volume of mountain ecotourism is small. However, when domestic figures are taken into account, the total volume of ecotourism would certainly be high. It is estimated that 20-25 per cent of tourism is based in the mountains (Mountain Agenda, 1999). Even if we assume that only 5-10 per cent of all mountain tourism may be considered as ecotourism-type, it is still one of the key economic stimulants in many remote mountain communities. As such, the potential impacts and implications of mountain ecotourism are interesting issues for discussions. However, as noted above, research and evaluation of mountain ecotourism is lacking significantly. This will surely change as there is increasing awareness and interests in ecotourism and mountain issues. Series of preparatory meetings both on ecotourism and mountains at regional and international levels were held last year and have been planned for this year. It is expected that the two culminating events of this year, the World Ecotourism Summit in May in Quebec City, Canada and the Bishkek Global Mountain Summit in October in Kyrgyzstan will decisively influence future policies on ecotourism and the mountains.

Trends in Mountain Ecotourism

When considering mountain ecotourism issues, the striking differences between mountain destinations in the developed countries (hereinafter referred to as developed mountains) and the developing countries (developing mountains) must be kept in mind. A generic description of mountain tourism characteristics in developed and developing countries is provided in Table—6.2.

Developed Countries

In developed countries, many mountain tourist destinations have become major players in the local economy. With a relatively high volume and value, they have the characteristics of mass tourism. However, recent trends indicate a surge in visitors to ecotourism destinations such as remote wilderness areas, where access is only possible on foot or by air. Hiking, camping, mountain and rock climbing, mountain biking, wildlife viewing, and other forms of non-

Table—6.2 Some Characteristics of Mountain Tourism: Developed and Developing Countries

Developed countries	Sectors	Developing countries
Restructuring, consolidation regulation, control, diverse tourism activities seasonality less pronounced highly developed tourist centres, sophisticated infrastructure growth potential limited	Tourism Characteristics	Haphazard planning less regulation and control tourism activity specialized Marked seasonal variation growth potential significant peripheral tourism
High volume, high value, little variability in income, economic integration, local and regional effects	Economics	Low volume, low value, localized effects, tourism-dominated economy, significant income differences between hosts and guest, leakage of tourism revenues/ local inflation, lack of regional integration, high variability in income from tourism
Visitor-wildlife conflict, air pollution, traffic, noise pollution solid waste disposal issues, expanding built-up areas, tourism-induced climatic effects, environmental regulations	Environment	Deforestation/biodiversity loss garbage disposal, soil erosion, Untreated sewage land-use changes Visitor-wildlife conflict
Resident-visitor conflicts User conflicts Overcrowding in critical areas Amenity migration	Social	Loss of social cohesion, disfranchised community Gender issues Attitude towards tourist generally favourable

consumptive recreation are in growing demand, particularly in North America. For instance, the 1994-1995 US National Survey on recreation and the Environment reported that between 1982/83 and 1994/95, number of bird-watchers had increased by 155 per cent, hikers by 94 per cent and backpackers by 73 per cent (US Federal Government, n.d. cited in Fennell, 2001). Frontier areas such as the Yukon and Northwest Territory in Canada, and Alaska, USA have experienced increased tourism, partly as a result of growing international demand for remote areas. Destinations in the Columbia Mountains in Northern British Columbia, and Yukon and Northewest Territories have recently seen more visitors from alpine countries of Germany, Austria, and Switzerland. Many guide and outfitters active in these regions see immense potential for ecotourism development. Although tourism destinations in the Canadian Rockies such as Jasper and Banff national parks are characteristics of mass tourism, several lesser-known sites in the Rockies are becoming ecotourism destinations. Mt. Robson Provincial Park, which shares the boundary with Jasper National Park and has the highest mountain in the Canadian Rockies (Mt. Robson, 3954m) within its boundary, is one such destination. There are many such examples in other parts of the mountain world where even amidst high levels of tourism development, one could find entities of ecotourism destinations.

In European countries such as UK and Germany, the trend is towards specialized and small travel fairs developing around "green," "nature," and "sustainable tourism" concepts (Blangy and Vautier, 2001) Recent reports show that 50 tour operators and travel agencies are involved in ecotourism operations. In Germany an association for alternative tourism (Forum Anders Reisen) has more than 40 small and medium tour operators and travel agencies catering to "ecotourists." The establishment of national parks and protected areas in several east European and central Asian countries will no doubt increase ecotourism-type activities in these regions, probably attracting a large number of visitors from western Europe. In fact, tourism is considered one of the rationales for establishing parks and protected areas in these regions. Within Europe, several protected area initiatives and related ecotourism activities, particularly in the UK, France, Italy, and Austria are the result of a new philosophy for European parks: encouraging development that is compatible with nature conservation, instead of simply forbidding development to maintain the pristine condition of an area (Blangy and Vautier, 2001). The French Natural Regional Parks have developed specific trademarks for environmentally friendly hotels, *Hôtel Nature* and *Gîtes Panda*. These gîtes (self-catering accommodation) provide visitors with information about the local fauna and flora, direct access by foot to nature sites, and provide materials intended to increase visitor awareness of the areas visited (Blangy and Vautier, 2001).

Mountain tourism destinations in developed countries are characterized by consolidation of businesses to increase profits and efficiency through reduced management costs and internal structural adjustments. But apart from these measures, strict regulations and control in the quality of services and facilities, implementation of environmental measures such as emission and pollution standards, minimization of energy costs, appropriate measures for solid waste disposal, and treatment of sewage have become focal concerns.

Developing Countries

In contrast with mountain areas in developed countries, mountains in developing countries are often influenced by the countries' high population growth rates and characterized by inaccessibility, marginal development, peripheral locations (from a global perspective) high levels of stress on natural resources, rampant poverty, and highly skewed distribution of wealth and property. Historical developments (former colonial rule), political systems (for example, in eastern European and Central Asian countries), and issues of governance (civil wars and conflicts such as those in Central and South America) have marred efforts in mountain development. However, developing mountains are also characterized by high biological and cultural diversity. National and international efforts to conserve biodivesity in these mountains have resulted in an impressive network of national parks and protected areas. The past few decades have seen a dramatic increase in visitor numbers to areas such as the world's highest national park the Sagarmatha (Mt. Everest) National Park in Nepal, Taman Negara National Park, a highland rainforest in West Malaysia, Simen Mountains National Park in northern Ethiopia, and Huascarán National Park in Peru. Similarly, several recently established national parks and protected areas in Central Asia hope to promote tourism.

With few exceptions, the developing mountains are in their early stages of tourism development, and many destinations are marketed and promoted as ecotourism destinations. If the WTO predictions hold true, Asia will experience the highest growth rate in visitor arrivals and receipts (WTO, 1998). A survey of mostly North American tour companies that offered ecotours to the Asia-Pacific region found that ecotourism had an overall growth of 20 per cent per year throughout the 1990s, at least prior to the Asian economic crisis (Lew 1998 cited in Lew 2001). 17 per cent of the North American-based ecotour providers reported that their clients were primarily interested in travelling to Asia-Pacific mountain regions (Yee, 1992 cited in Lew 2001). This clearly indicates a significant growth potential for mountain ecotourism in Asia. A potentially positive trend in the 1990s has been a growth in domestic and intra-Asian tourism, which might eventually lead to a surge in demand for ecotourism. Similar to Asia, a significant portion of tourism in Central America is directed to protected areas. The Andean highlands, notably in Ecuador, Peru, and Argentina are considered strong ecotourism destinations. Domestic ecotourism is also on the rise, for example, the majority of visitors to Glacier National Park in Argentina are locals. In the Nepalese Himalaya, despite some problems of environmental degradation, tourism has become a key factor in introducing positive changes in the environmental, social, and economic fronts (Nepal, 2002).

Tourism in the developing mountains is characterized by haphazard planning, lack of environmental standards and monitoring, price cutting resulting in high volume and low returns, stark seasonality, and domination of tourism in the overall economy. Some of the problems of tourism in developing mountains include competition between small-scale local operations and large international chains, alienation of local residents as a result of large number of visitors, sharp rises in property values, environmental damage, and native inhabitants being confronted with the values of post-industrial society (Stone, 1992; Nepal, 1999).

Strategies for Mountain Ecotourism Development

There are dangers in promoting mountain destinations for ecotourism, especially if there is no strategic focus on the type and intensity of activities to be promoted, the benefits and the beneficiaries, and the decisions related to governance, control and regulations. Some of the major environmental impacts with direct implications to local mountain communities include overcrowding, noise pollution, garbage pollution, extraction of valuable resources (for example, collection of firewood and rare plant specimens), pack stock grazing, fire hazard, introduction of non-native species, and sewage outflow.

In the developed countries the concern for environmental conservation has led to conflicts between tourism operators and public interest groups. The ski industries in the United States, Canada, Switzerland, and Austria illustrate this problem (Messerli, 1992; Zimmerman 1992; Goeldner, 1996). Goverenment representatives have begun to take action against some ski resorts that fail to comply with existing environmental laws. Tour operators in the European Alps face competition from overseas cheap destinations. Ecotourism desinations in the Canadian Rockies such as Mt. Robson Park are increasingly facing the complex challenges of maintaining the ecological integrity and providing high quality nature experiecne for visitors.

In the developing countries, the question is not how communities might respond to ecotourism-led development but rather how best to attract a critical mass of visitors who would stay longer pumping some cash into the local people economy. Sharma (2000) has identified six substantive issues that contribute to the unsustainability of mountain tourism in the Himalayas: exploitation of environmental resources and environmental pollution, lack of linkages with the local/ regional production systems, low retention of benefits, high degree of seasonality, socio-cultural impacts resulting from tourism, and policy and institutional development problems. These are also applicable to many other mountain destinations in the developing countries.

Müller (1996) states that mountain tourism must be characterized by a participatory planning process, efficiency, environmental friendliness, authenticity, slow development, a higher quality, and a humanistic (i.e, people-centered) philosophy and management. These requirements are particularly relevant to mountain ecotourism. More specifically, the following measures merit careful consideration:

1. ***Directing ecotourism towards the path of sustainability***: It is clear that mountain communities should decide for themselves which path they would like to take: one that moves towards sustainability or one which seeks to maximize profits in the short run but runs the risk of unsustainable development in the long run. Sustainble strategies might not yield immediate results, however, it ensures the long-term viability of ecotourism projects from all perspectives. Mountain communities should invest in mechanisms that allow them to monitor development over time in the environment, economy, and in social and cultural aspects. Strict regulation and controls for high environmental standards and realistic visitor use limits must be enforced.

2. ***Reducing dependency and increasing diversity:*** Tourism is known to develop dependency syndromes. Strategies should focus on diversifying local economy. As tourism matures, linkages must be established with other economic sectors such as agriculture and livestock herding, transport, communication, and small and medium business enterprises. As the local economy matures from a tourism-led to a tourism-driven development, strategic focus should change also.

3. ***Restructuring and reforming existing governmental and non-governmental institutions:*** Traditional hierarchical government structures that prefer top-down planning approach have been less successful in managing a complex and dynamic issue such as tourism. Experiences in some countries indicate that local control, autonomy, and decision-making at the grassroot-levels are the keys to successful ecotourism (Nepal, in press). Successful ecotourism will hinge on the implementation of national policies and strategies formulated in consultation with local stakeholders because it is the local stakeholders are the ones who implement the strategies in their respective areas. It is also necessary to examine the complexity and dynamics of power relations between local leaders, and traditionally accepted social hierarchical system in which people at the lowest tier have almost no say in the planning process. What village leaders might think is best for the community might disfranchise people from certain social and economic strata.

4. ***Focusing on gender equity:*** Gender issues have been considered significantly important in the discussions about mountain communities (Mountain Forum, 1997). Research has indicated that women-in-development (WID) models need to be tailored to a community-specific socio-economic and cultural context (Stoker, 2000). Projects and programs related

to ecotourism must consider equitable opportunities for both men and women as well as employment for young people.

5. ***Building global-local and local-local nexus***: In the current climate of global economic interdependency, there is a tendency to ignore local potential and development concerns. Ecological, economic, and social interdependency among and between local and regional units has not been satisfactory. Many tourism projects have developed out of local-global nexus, resulting in enclave development that does not allow local regions to link their development potential to the surrounding regions. There is a need to establish inter-dependent local economies; ecotourism projects should enhance this capability and not erode it. This means projects must take into account local as well as regional resources, and mechanisms should be sought to foster regional collaborations.

6 ***Funding incentives for enterprise and skill development***: Part of the reason why tourism has failed to benefit mountain communities, particularly in the developing countries is that there is very little opportunity for local-level enterprise and skill development. Ecotourism training must be comprehensive in that it should be able to instill responsible behaviour and professional attitudes among potential entrepreneurs. While village-level training in meal preparations, lodge management, etc. are appreciated, training should expand to include awareness of the potential harmful effects of tourism, and knowledge of ecotourism product development, product packaging, and marketing strategies. Access to modern means of communication such as the Internet is extremely important because not only it allows local entrepreneurs access to global markets, it also helps establish local and national alliances in raising awareness and sharing

knowledge. Support for funds to develop ecolodge operations, particularly by those entrepreneurs who have the skills but lack cash is crucial too.

7. ***Promoting peace, safety and security***: Recent political turmoils at the global level, and their likely impact on worldwide travel and tourism indicate that peace, safety, and security are the necessary conditions for tourism/ecotourism development. Hotbeds of conflict in mountain areas including Afghanistan, Bosnia, India-Pakistan, Nicaragua, Rwanda, Ethiopia, Yemen, and Peru have experienced declining tourist numbers in recent years (Godde et al, 2000). There are lessons to be learned from the virtual collapse of the tourism industry in the Indian-held territory of Kashmir, and the effects of kidnapping and murder of tourists on gorilla-watching expeditions in the highlands of Uganda. Even popular destinations such as the Khumbu and Annapurna in the Nepalese Himalaya have been recently impacted by the communist insurgency in the country. Internal conflicts, insurgency, political instability, and terrorism are very detrimental to current and future ecotourism destinations in the mountains.

Designating International Mountain Ecotourism Sites: A Proposal

Mountain ecotourism could greatly benefit from international collaboration, for example, by creating an international system to designate mountain ecotourism sites similar to the UNESCO World Heritage Site designation system. Such a program of Designation of International Mountain Ecotourism Sites (DIMES) would involve stakeholders in mountain ecotourism in developing a set of criteria and indicators to provide a basis for designating a mountain location as an ecotourism destination. The development of such criteria should involve policy makers, practitioners, local communities and the scientific community.

Each designated site should be required to go through periodic evaluation, perhaps every five years, to monitor whether or not ecotourism projects are implemented according to the principles laid out by DIMES. Destinations that adhere to the globally recognized principles should be rewarded financially and through other international forms of recognition and merit. Those that fail to adhere to established principles may be delisted.

Although the WTO has identified over 105 eco-labels and certification schemes for tourism, only 5,000 companies who have joined such schemes, mainly because they are voluntary, and offer no distinct benefits. With government involvement at the international level, DIMES could be truly instrumental in establishing standards, measures, and guidelines for managing ecotourism destinations. It would differ from the WTO eco-labeling in that it would not focus on a particular business or company but rather on all key ecotourism players in the destination area.

Conclusion

Mountain regions around the world are rich in biological and cultural diversity, and are home to ten per cent of all human population. Many mountain regions are increasingly under stress due to various forms of unsustainable economic development including tourism. As an alternative to mass tourism, ecotourism in the mountain regions seems to have a certain appeal for those concerned with mountain development and conservation. The global market for ecotourism (both domestic and international) has grown significantly, with a gradual shift in worldwide travel patterns and preferences. If mountain regions are to take advantage from ecotourism, then efforts must be focused on developing long-term plans and policies necessary for susccessul implementation. Key elements of such policies include sustainbility criteria; diversity; institutional reforms; gender equity; local, regional and global economic integration; local financial incentives; and peace and security.

Because the concept of mountain ecotourism tends to be used haphazardly, a clear definition must be developed and a set of criteria and indicators applied to the evaluation of ecotourism destinations. The international mountain community should cooperate to develop such criteria and indicators. Furthermore, the potential for a system of ecotourism site designation must also be explored. This will set the stage for increased compliance and adherence to ecotourism criteria and indicators by ecotour operators, establish monitoring mechanisms, and offer mountain ecotourism destinations a platform for raising their profiles at the international level.

REFERENCES

Blangey, S. and S. Vautier (2001) Europe *In* D.B. Weaver (ed) *The Encyclopaedia of Ecotourism*, Oxon, UK: CAB International, pp. 155-171.

Buckley, R. (2001) Environmental Impacts. *In* D.B. Weaver (ed) *The Encyclopaedia of Ecotourism*. Oxon, UK: CAB International, pp. 379-394.

Ceballos-Lascurain, H. (1996) *Tourism, Ecotourism and Protected Areas: the State of Nature-Based Tourism Around the World and Guidelines for its Development*. Gland and Cambridge: IUCN.

Ceballos-Lascurain, H. (1987) The future of ecotourism. *Mexico Journal* January, pp. 13-14.

Fennell, D. (2001). Anglo-America. *In* D.B. Weaver (ed) *The Encyclopaedia of cotourism*. Oxon, UK: CAB International, pp. 107-122.

Foot, D. K., and D. Stoofman, (1996) *Boom, Bust and Echo*. Toronto: Macfarlane Walter & Ross.

Godde P. M., M. F. Price, F. M. Zimmermann (2000) *Tourism and Development in Mountain Regions*. Oxon, UK: CAB International.

Goeldner, C. (1996) North American Alpine Tourism Development - competition, obstacles, strategies, consequences. *In* K. Weiermair (ed) *Proceedings—Alpine Tourism, Sustainability: Reconsidered and Redesigned.* Innsbruck: University of Innsbruck, pp. 95-114.

Lew, A. A. (1998) The Asia-Pacific ecotourism industry: Putting sustainble tourism into practice. In C.M. Hall and A.A. Lew (eds) *Sustainable Tourism: A Geographical Approach.* London: Routledge, pp. 92-106.

Lew, A. A. (2001) Asia. In D.B. Weaver (ed) *The Encyclopaedia of Ecotourism.* Oxon, UK: CAB International, pp. 123-137.

Messerli B., J. D. Ives (1997) *Mountains of the World: A Global Priority.* Carnforth: Parthenon.

Messerli, P. (1992) Integrated Development of Tourism—a Strategy to Cope with Environmental and Economic Uncertainities: Experience from the Swiss Alps. *In* A. Gill and R. Hartman (eds) *Mountain Resort Development: Proceedings of the Vail Conference.* 18-21 April 1991. Burnaby, BC: Centre for Tourism Policy and Research, Simon Fraser University.

Mountain Agenda (1999) *Mountains of the World—Tourism and Mountains.* Berne: Mountain Agenda.

Müller, H. (1996) Freizeittrends und Freizeitverhalten—Stellenwert des alpinen Bergurlaubs. *In* K. Weiermair (ed) *Proceedings—Alpine Tourism, Sustainability: Rconsidered and Redesigned.* Innsbruck: University of Innsbruck, pp.176-85.

Nepal, S. K. (1999). *Tourism-Induced Environmental Changes in the Nepalese Himalaya: A Comparative Analysis of the Everest, Annapurna, and Mustang regions.* Ph.D. Dissertation Submitted to the Faculty of Natural Sciences, University of Bern, Switzerland.

Nepal, S. K. (2002) Examining Tourism Impacts from an Interdisciplinary Perspective: The Himalayan Case Study. *Asiatische Studien* (Journal of the Swiss Geogrpahical Studies on Asia) LV 3.2001, pp.777-804.

Sharma, P. (2000) *Tourism as Development: Case Studies from the Himalaya*. Kathmandu and Innsbruck: Himal Books and STUDIEN Verlag.

Statistics Canada (1998) *The Importance of Nature to Canadians*. Ottawa: Ministry of Supply and Services.

Stocker, K. (1999) *Frauengruppen und deren Einfluss auf eine nachhaltige Dorfetwicklung in der Annapurna Region*, Nepal. Diplomarbeit, Universitàt Bern. Switzerland.

Stone, P. (ed) (1992) The State of the World's Mountains—A Global Report. New Jersey: Zed Books Ltd.

The Ecotourism Society (1991) *Ecotourism Guidelines for Nature-Based Tour Operators*. Vermont, USA: The Ecotourism Society.

The Mountain Institute/Food and Agriculture Organization of the United Nations (1997) *Investing in Mountains—Innovative Mechanisms and Promising Examples for Financing Conservation and Sustainable Development*. Franklin, WV: TMI/FAO.

United States Federal Government (n.d.) *The National Survey on Recreation and the Environment*. Washington, DC: US Federal Government.

Weaver, DB. 2001. The Encyclopaedia of Ecotourism. Oxon, UK: CABI Publishing

Williams, P.W., T.V. Singh and R. Schlüter (2001) Mountain Ecotourism: Creating a Sustainable future. *In* D.B. Weaver, ed. *The Encyclopaedia of Ecotourism*. Oxon, UK, CAB International, pp. 205- 218.

World Travel and Tourism Council (1999) *Travel and Tourism's Economic Impact. http://www.wttc.org*.

World Tourism Organisation (1998). *WTO News*. January/ February.

Yee, J. G. (1992) *Ecotourism Market Survey: A Survey of North American Tour Operators*. San Francisco: The Intelligence Center, Pacific Asia Travel Association.

Zimmermann, F. (1992) Issues, Problems and Future Trends in the Austrian Alps: the Changes within Traditional Tourism. *In* A. Gill and R. Hartman (eds) *Mountain Resort Development: Proceedings of the Vail Conference*. 18-21 April 1991. Burnaby, BC: Centre for Tourism Policy and Research, Simon Fraser University, pp 160-70.

7

Tourism and Information Technologies: Past, Present and Future

**Dr Dimitrios Buhalis*

Tourism and Information Iechnologies: a Revolution in Progress

The Information Technologies (ITs) revolution, experienced during the last decade, has had profound implications for the tourism industry management, mainly by altering the competitiveness of organisations and destinations, by enabling efficient co-operation and by offering tools for a real globalisation. Similarly with all other economic activities, *tourism is inevitably influenced by the business process re-engineering experienced* due to the technological revolution. As information is the life-blood of the travel industry, effective use of technology is fundamental to the tourism sector as we approach the 21st century. Therefore a whole system of ITs is being rapidly diffused throughout the tourism industry and no player will escape its impacts. ITs have undoubtedly become one of the most important elements of the tourism industry as in few other economic activities are the generation,

* Course Leader, MSc in eTourism, Director, Centre for eTourism Research (CeTR) School of Management, University of Surrey, Guildford GU2 7XH, England, UK.

gathering, processing, application and communication of information as important for day-to-day operations. The rapid development of both tourism supply and demand makes ITs an imperative partner of the industry, especially for the marketing, distribution, promotion and co-ordination of the industry. The re-engineering of these processes is particularly evident in the tourism product distribution, where a paradigm-shift is conspicuously experienced altering best practices and introducing new players.

In the late 1990s the proliferation of the Internet and the World Wide Web in particular revolutionised communications as it enabled organisations to demonstrate their offerings globally using multimedia interfaces. As a result, not only consumers felt empowered to search for more information and to undertake on-line reservation but also tourism providers had the opportunity to develop their global presence and to establish direct relationships with consumers. In addition, a wide range of new organisations emerged to capitalise on the electronic marketplace. As a result of the IT revolution experienced, the entire tourism industry is undergoing major changes and a wide range of opportunities and threats emerge.

The purpose of this paper is to examine and synthesise the technological change that has been experienced in the tourism industry in the last decade. The paper illustrates the different stages of ITs penetration in tourism and their implications for each sector of the industry. It aims to explain both the business practices that propel ITs in tourism, as well as the new opportunities they provide for innovative and dynamic players. The paper uses a comprehensive literature research on the topic as well as on going primary research with industry players. It illustrates that technologically advanced players will enhance their competitiveness in the future, whilst industry members who fail to take advantage of the emerging opportunities will lose market share and eventually will be driven out of the market. In order to compete, tourism organisations, destinations and enterprises will need to compute.

The Utilisation of ITs by the Tourism Industry Sectors and the Impacts on the Marketing Mix

Tourism has traditionally been a labour intensive industry. However, during the last decade ITs have been propelling a paradigm shift due to the new tools they provided for both operational marketing, and geographical expansion. ITs have been providing unprecedented opportunities for organisations to develop their market base and to enlarge their operations globally. Several major factors make ITs an integral part of the tourism industry, namely:

- economic necessity as global competition requires maximum efficiency;
- rapid advancements in technology;
- improvements in ITs' price/performance ratios which yield better productivity for capital employed in ITs; and finally
- rising consumer expectations, as consumers become used to advanced products and expect further improvements in customer service, personalisation and interaction.

As a result, the tourism industry becomes more flexible, quicker in responding to consumer requests and more efficient. ITs have also reduced the cost of operations by decreasing the number of people required for back office jobs. Some of these resources can be re-directed to consumer care and contact, whilst new tools emerge for understanding and servicing personal customer needs.

ITs also enable the redesign of the *marketing mix of tourism enterprises* by providing new tools. ITs provide unique opportunities to redesign tourism *products* to address individual needs and to satisfy consumer wants. Not only organisations can have a better understanding of their consumer by mining their data warehouses, but they can also pilot new products effectively by using different communication strategies. ITs also become part of the core product especially for business travellers who expect a certain degree of facilities available during their trip. Hence transportation, accommodation and conference facilities may incorporate mobile telephony as well as access to the Internet and data ports to their core product. Information offers value added to consumers and thus ITs provide the tools to differentiate and augment the tourism product. *Pricing* becomes a much more dynamic function with better informed managers through yield management systems. They have the tools to forecast and alter pricing almost instantly in order to maximise their profitability. Market intelligence also enables organisations to identify pricing strategies of competing organisations and offer flexible tools to respond with more flexible and dynamic fares. Auctions and the new practice of customers suggesting the prices that they would be willing to pay in order to purchase the product will enable tourism enterprises to reduce their distressed capacity as well as to generate interest for direct bookings and thus to save commissions to intermediaries.

In addition, *promotion* and communication are also revolutionised by developing personal marketing campaigns and one-to-one marketing by using the Internet. Instead of addressing broad audiences through mass media, such as Television and Radio, tourism organisations are empowered to develop personal relationships with their customers, to understand their needs and to make sure that they address them through personal communications. The new methods offer a much more cost-effective approach whilst at the same time they can improve customer satisfaction by offering tailor made packages of suitable products. Perhaps the most interesting change emerging as a result of the revolution of ITs is on the *Place-distribution* elements. ITs have revolutionised the entire channel of tourism by providing the tools for direct communications between principals and consumers. This enables tourism organisations to reduce their commission costs as well as to improve their relationship marketing. As a result, a wide spread disintermediation is expected to prevail the tourism distribution channel, as consumers increasingly bundle their itineraries alone. The new tools enabled a wide range of new players to emerge and to gain a significant market share. These are new Internet based companies, such as Expedia or the Internet Travel Network, which had no tourism background but still launched tourism products and demonstrated a spectacular growth in a limited period of time.

It is evident therefore that the rapid increase of the reliability, speed and capacity of ITs, in combination with the deduction of their cost, forced tourism organisations to adapt and use these new tools. Innovative tourism organisations take advantage of the new tools to enhance their value added and to gain competitive advantages. New players are increasingly attracted to take advantage of the electronic marketplace emerging and to serve the new wired customer. Location becomes much less significant in transactions and therefore global competition intensifies. In contrast, a large proportion of existing tourism organisations has been observing these trends passively and they have failed to address the requirements of the marketplace. These organisations increasingly lose market share and eventually will be forced out of the market as they will be unable to compete with the value added and interaction benefits offered in the new global market.

Information Technologies for Destination Management and Marketing

Destinations are recognised as the raison d'être for tourism as they satisfy the need for travelling, and the attractions at the destination generate the visit. Moreover, it is acknowledged that an amalgam of products, facilities and services at the destination level comprise the total tourism product. Traditionally planning, management and co-ordination of destinations have been undertaken by either the public sector (at national, regional or local level) or by partnerships between stakeholders of the local tourism industry. Although ITs have hitherto not been regarded as a critical instrument for the development and management of destinations, destination management organisations increasingly use technology in order to improve their organisational function and performance. In addition, Tourism Information Centres, which tend to promote destinations, provide information and help prospective customers to make reservations to local amenities, have been using ITs in order to facilitate their performance and enable consumers to match their requirements with the local supply. Despite the fact that studies on destination oriented CRSs have been traced back to as early as 1968, it was not until the late 1980s that the proliferation of *destination-oriented CRSs or Destination Management Systems (DMSs)* emerged. This delay is explained by:

- the lack of adequate and affordable technology at an earlier stage;
- the lack of ITs expertise by tourism professionals;
- the concentration of marketing efforts at the local markets;
- the relatively less intensive competition;
- the domination of small and independent tourism enterprises around the world;
- and the conflicting interests of different players in the tourism industry.

DMSs revolutionise destination marketing as they "combine a radically improved and rapidly evolving methodology [computing] with new or better communications [telecommunication networks] in order to satisfy a growing private sector market [tourism]", while it is estimated that 200 destination-oriented systems of various kinds emerged in the early 1990s. As these systems enable the dissemination of information and reservation functions for destinations, DMSs are emerging as a major promotion, distribution and operational tool for both destinations and SMTEs. Moreover, their contribution to strategic management and marketing, which is demonstrated by their ability to integrate destinations as well as increase the intra-channel power of principals within the distribution channel, elevates them to strategic tools.

Hitherto the majority of the DMS developments have been led by *public tourist organisations*. Public tourist organisations are traditionally involved in destinations' information provision and marketing. They undertake mass media advertising; provide advisory services for consumers and the travel trade; produce and distribute brochures, leaflets and guides both at destinations and at the places of origin of the tourists; and finally they have the strategic responsibility of the entire destination. DMSs facilitate this function by administrating a wide range of requests and by providing information to an ever-increasing tourism supply, in an efficient and appropriate way. Thus, ITs provide a way to improve the accessibility of, and the quantity and quality of information on the destination's facilities while they present travellers with options in minimising their search costs. Moreover, destinations take advantage of the database marketing techniques, in order to identify and target profitable market niches, by tailoring market-driven products for particular customers.

However, the majority of public tourism organisations' projects have exclusively supported the information-only side, excluding the most important part of the transaction, the sale/reservation. In addition a high failure rate has been observed as several DMSs failed to attract the support and commitment required from both the private and public sectors. DMSs have also failed to develop viable products which would be utilised from either the independent or institutional tourism demand. An exception to the rule are two systems, Gulliver, the Irish DMSs and the Austrian TIScover. Both systems have adopted their technological basis and their ownership status and remain as the few operational and successful systems in the world.

DMS concept can be taken a step forward, towards an ideal system. This systems will ultimately enable the strategic management and marketing of destinations and integrate both micro and macro functions at the destination level. This will support the achievement of long term prosperity for indigenous people, maximisation of returns of investments for tourism enterprises and also enhance the quality of products and satisfaction of consumers/tourists. *Destination Integrated Computerised Information Reservation Management Systems (DICIRMSs)*, are therefore proposed to undertake a wide range of strategic functions, aiming to provide advanced services to tourism enterprises, destinations and consumers. Acting at a *Destination or regional* level, these systems should incorporate and co-ordinate the entire range and population of tourism providers at the destination level. They should also be *multi-Integrated*, i.e utilise the entire range of available ITs, co-ordinate local SMTEs and integrate them with the local economy. *Computerisation* and networking of the entire population of enterprises at the destination would be essential for establishing an on-line network and enhance the function of these systems. *Information provision* is an integral part of DICIRMSs, as they need to provide information about everything related to a destination. Information for destinations should be classified in a 5A framework, namely: Amenities-Accessibility-Attractions-Activities-Ancillary Services.

Reservations and purchasing of tourism products should also be encouraged. It is vital that all required tourism products display their up-dated availability and price, and can be purchased via these systems. Prospective tourists can either use self-service kiosks and/or the Internet to make reservations, whilst they should also be able to make reservations through connected travel agencies. Provision of instant confirmation and easiness of payment are essential. DICIRMSs should also have a comprehensive *supply and demand Management function* which will facilitate the co-ordination as well as the strategic and operational management of both small and medium sized tourism enterprises and destinations. Therefore DICIRMSs emerge as the ideal tool to serve the new/sophisticated/experienced/ demanding tourists, while providing innovative methods to undertake strategic and operational management for the tourism industry. In addition, they provide an unprecedented strategic tool for SMTEs to take advantage of ITs, co-ordinate their marketing and management and establish their presence in the emerging global tourism market. This will help them strengthen their position in the distribution chain, identify and supply niche markets and make their unique features and character known to the tourism market. Hence DICIRMSs emerge as a *total System of wealth creation and value chain*, which facilitate both the competitiveness and sustainable development of destinations and small firms, while significantly enhance consumers' experience. In addition they can play an instrumental role in destinations' ability to improve their economic, socio-cultural and environmental impacts and to sustain their resources. They can achieve that by educating both consumers and service providers about the needs of consumers and suppliers, as well as by increasing their awareness of endangered environmental, economic and socio-cultural resources through the system. Therefore DICIRMSs are strategic tools for destination management and marketing. DMSs should be "*intelligent*" as they should simulate the human functions of memory, connections and creativity.

Business Process Re-engineering in the Tourism Industry

ITs have a great influence on the strategic management of contemporary organisations, as a paradigm-shift is experienced, transforming the "best" business practices. ITs can introduce great benefits to the efficiency, differentiation, cost reduction and response time of tourism organisations. Consequently, ITs stimulate radical changes in the operation, distribution and structure of the tourism industry. The proliferation of technology throughout the tourism distribution channels essentially means that both consumers and professionals use the newly available tools in order to retrieve information, identify suitable products and perform reservations. Thus, the visibility of tourism principals in the marketplace will be a function of the technologies and networks utilised to interact with their individual and institutional customers, as this will determine their ability to distribute their product efficiently and communicate interactively with their clientele. Should tourism principals neglect the significance of ITs in their distribution function, they will effectively jeopardise themselves and become marginalised from the mainstream of the tourism industry. As a result, tourism enterprises need to understand, incorporate and utilise ITs, in order to be able to serve their target markets, improve their efficiency, maximise profitability, enhance services and maintain long term prosperity for both themselves and destinations.

Perhaps the most apparent example in tourism is the re-engineering of the booking process which gradually becomes rationalised and enables both consumers and the industry to save considerable time in identifying, blending, reserving and purchasing tourism products enabling a closer match between tourism demand and supply. Ultimately, prospective tourists will be able to browse through the Internet and identify a rich variety of offers in order to make travel choices suited to their personal requirements. The focus is thus shifted towards individual travel and dynamic packages, targeting mini-segments. Using ITs empowers organisations to offer personalised services as they can research and recognise the needs of individual customers. Inclusive tourism is also facilitated as people can use technology to minimise the time spent on identifying the availability and price of suitable packages. Eventually it will be easy to access information and reserve products for the entire range of principals and destinations from the convenience of someone's armchair.

IT developments introduce a wide range of *opportunities and threats for the various players* in the tourism industry. *Airlines* have been pioneering the use of technology for their marketing and management. Increasingly they take advantage of ITs in order to achieve a better control of their distribution costs and processes as well as to establish innovative and interactive partnerships with consumers and intermediaries. *Hotels* enjoy an increase in their efficiency and take advantage of technology for promoting and distributing their products. International corporations also utilise ITs in order to co-ordinate remote properties and to expand their operations globally. Smaller properties on the other hand need to take advantage of the emerging ITs in order to reduce their marginalisation from the main stream tourism industry and make their products available to institutional and independent buyers. Co-operation at the local level will enable them to increase their presence in the international markets and also to reduce their handicaps emerging through their lack of expertise, resources and capital.

Traditional travel intermediation is to a certain degree endangered, as some of its conventional functions, such as information provision and communication with wholesalers and principals, become directly available to consumers through the Internet. *Travel agencies* (retailers) are more threatened as a certain degree of disintermediation is evident, partly due to the fact that the majority of travel agencies limit their role to that of booking agencies, jeopardising the quality of information they provide and the value that they add to travel arrangements. Travel agencies will not be eliminated from the distribution chain. However, unless they enhance their service to travel counsellors they will be severely threatened and they will lose market share. *Tour operators* seem to take advantage of ITs in order to increase their efficiency in the current distribution channel, although there is a reluctance to re-engineer their business processes in order to strengthen their position. Tour operators should perhaps use ITs in order to build individual packages. The provision of electronic brochures is expected not only to improve tour operators' flexibility by enabling them to amend the information provided without massive costs, but also to reduce their promotional and distribution cost. Tour operators can also utilise ITs in order to increase their value-added to the tourism package by differentiating elements of the tourism experience. Smaller and independent operators will probably benefit more from the ITs' developments, as larger ones are expected to continue their cost-advantage strategy which helps them deliver low cost packages.

Finally *destinations* emerge as major beneficiaries of the ITs developments as they can take advantage of new strategic tools for management, planning and marketing. This will enable them to offer a much more co-ordinated tourism product as well as to increase their intra-channel power in tourism. As a result, both locals and consumers will benefit in the long term, while the sustainability of local resources can be augmented. To a certain extent these developments will assist destinations to reverse the trend where they were becoming powerless to control their destiny, due to the pressures they receive from multinational intermediaries and other organisations to accept a cost-orientation strategy, rather than differentiate and attract niche markets. Hence ITs introduce a great opportunity for closer co-operation at the local level and bridge the gap between suppliers and consumers. Consequently, destinations are empowered to communicate directly with their prospective tourists and thus gain intra-channel distribution power. Destination Management Systems are expected to be instrumental in achieving a certain degree of disintermediation, which in turn will improve returns on investments for both the private and public sectors. Finally, tele-working is expected to allow holiday-makers to extent their stay, as they will be able to keep in contact with their working environment from remote holiday resorts via the Internet and tele-working centres.

However in order to achieve the above benefits a *closer partnership and co-operation* is required throughout the tourism industry as well as a certain degree of standardisation and interconnectivity. The need for co-operation emerges through the need to improve service and provide seamless travel experiences, as well as through the new realities imposed by contemporary economic developments, such as deregulation and globalisation. ITs provide an unprecedented opportunities for horizontal, vertical and diagonal integration which enable the industry to improve its provision to consumers as well as to strengthen its effectiveness. The degree of standardisation achieved in interfaces and processes will determine the compatibility and interactivity among technologies, partners and users. Consequently, few prototype interfaces and platforms are required to reinforce inter-active tourism product design, presentation and delivery, intermediation, payment systems, and telecommunication infrastructure. The development of the Internet is therefore instrumental as it establishes a robust and universally standard interface for communication. ITs penetration and

by marketing. Thus the industry should utilise ITs in order to delight individual and institutional consumers, rather than forcing product-driven technologies.

Conclusion

Technology presents both an opportunity and a challenge for the tourism industry. Although there is a fair degree of uncertainty in the developments of information technology in tourism there is a certainty that the "*only constant will be change*". In this environment, organisations which need to compete will need to compute. Unless the current tourism industry improves its competitiveness by utilising the revolutionary technology there is a danger for exogenous players to enter the marketplace jeopardising the position of the existing players. Only creative and innovative suppliers will be able to survive the competition in the new millennium. Therefore a continuous business process re-engineering in the tourism industry needs to ensure that a wide range of prerequisites such as rational organisation, training, and quality assurance methodologies are in place in order to enable destinations and suppliers to capitalise on the emergent capabilities of technology. Training and education of human resources in new technologies are therefore becoming even more critical in order to empower the tourism industry to strengthen its competitiveness.

The *key to future success* in the competitive tourism industry will most definitely be determined by a combination of ITs, intellect and management vision. The tourism industry lives in a rapidly changing world and needs to adapt constantly in order to be able to satisfy the demand needs and at the same time remain competitive. Vision is perhaps the most significant strategic consideration of an organisation as it is consisted by the corporate philosophy, the mission, policies and corporate values of an organisation. Intellect will also empower organisations to practice constant innovation and change towards reacting to the challenges of the business environment in order to satisfy the demand whilst maximising the returns on resources utilised for the production and delivery of tourism products.

Therefore, the tourism industry should regard ITs as a pivotal strategic issue and opportunity and identify ways which will enable them to achieve long term prosperity for both destinations and enterprises, as well as to add value to their products and enhance consumers' experience and satisfaction. Taking advantage of the emergent ITs will be instrumental for destinations and tourism organisations if they are to maintain their competitiveness and avoid competitive disadvantages in the new millennium. Suppliers who will be left behind will suffer major competitive disadvantages and may be forced out of the marketplace. Finally there is a need for inter-connectivity, compatibility and standardisation of information technology utilised in tourism in order to enable inter-and intra-organisational co-operation, avoid "technology islands", and facilitate access for consumers.

BIBLIOGRAPHY

Buhalis, D., 1993, Regional Integrated Computer Information Reservation Management Systems as a Strategic Tool for the Small and Medium Tourism Enterprises, Tourism Management, Vol. 14(5):366-378.

Buhalis, D., 1994, Information and Telecommunication Technologies as a Strategic Tool for Small and Medium Tourism Enterprises in the Contemporary Business Environment, in Seaton, A., Wood, R., Dieke, P., and Jenkins, C., (eds), Tourism—The state of the art: the Strathclyde symposium, J., Wiley and Sons, England:254-275.

Buhalis, D., 1997, Information Technologies as a Strategic Tool for Economic, Cultural and Environmental Benefits Enhancement of Tourism at Destination Regions, Progress in Tourism and Hospitality Research, vol.3(1):71-93.

Buhalis, D., 1998, Strategic use of Information Technologies in the Tourism Industry, Tourism Management, Vol.19(3):409-423.

Buhalis, D., 1999, Information Technology for Small and Medium-sized Tourism Enterprises: Adaptation and Benefits, Information Technology and Tourism, Vol.2(1).

Buhalis, D., 2003, eTourism: Information Technology for Strategic Tourism Management, Pearson, London.

Buhalis, D., and Main, H., 1998, Information Technology in Small and Medium Hospitality Enterprises: Strategic Analysis and Critical Factors, International Journal of Contemporary Hospitality Management, Vol.10(5):198-202.

Emmer, R., Tauck, C., Wilkinson, S., and Moore, R., 1993, Marketing Hotels Using Global Distribution Systems, The Cornell Hotel Restaurant Administration Quarterly, Vol.34(6):80-89.

Inkpen, G., 1998, Information Technology for Travel and Tourism, 2nd ed, Addison Wesley Longman, London.

Kärcher, K, 1997, Reinventing Package Holiday Business, DeutscherUniversitätsVerlag, Berlin.

O'Connor, P., Horan, P., 1999, An Analysis of Web Reservations Facilities in the Top 50 International Hotel Chains, International Journal of Hospitality Information Technology, Vol1(1), pp.77-87.

O'Connor, P. and Frew, A. (2000). Evaluating Electronic Channels of Distribution in the Hotel Sector: A Delphi Study, Information Technology and Tourism, 3(3/4), 177-193.

O'Connor, P., 1995, Using Computers in Hospitality, London: Cassell.

O'Connor, P., 1999, Tourism and Hospitality Electronic Distribution and Information Technology, Oxford: CAB.

Peacock, M., 1995, Information Technology in Hospitality, London: Cassell.

Pollock, A., 1998, Creating Intelligent Destinations for Wired Customers, in Buhalis, D., Tjoa, A.M., Jafari, J., (eds) Information and Communication Technologies in Tourism, ENTER 1998 Proceedings, Springer-Verlag, Wien:235-248.

Sheldon, P., 1993, Destination Information Systems, Annals of Tourism Research, Vol.20(4):633-649.

Sheldon, P., 1997, Information Technologies for Tourism, CAB, Oxford

Wanhill, S., 1998, Intermediaries, in Cooper, C., Fletcher, J., Gilbert, D., Shepherd, R., and Wanhill, S., (Eds), Tourism: Principles and Practice, 2nd Ed., Longman Publishing, London: 423-446.

Wardell, D., 1998, The Impact of Electronic Distribution on Travel Agents, Travel and Tourism Analyst, No.2:41-55.

WTO, 1988, Guidelines for the Transfer of New Technologies in the Field of Tourism, World Tourism Organisation, Madrid.

WTO, 1999, Marketing Tourism Destinations Online, Madrid: World Tourism Organisation.

WTO,2001, eBusiness for Tourism: Practical; Guidelines for Destinations and Businesses, Madrid: World Tourism Organisation.

8

Generation Y: Building a Future Through Volunteer Tourism?

**Tara Rowe, **C. Michael Hall*

Generation Y: Knowledgeable, skilled, and increasingly conscientious travellers. This chapter identifies Generation Y as a considerable market opportunity for volunteer tourism. This generation along with volunteer tourism is capable of enhancing a practical and positive vision for the tourism industry. The WTO (2001) estimates that youth travel is developing faster than the growth rate of the entire tourism industry. This hybrid culture of volunteers, youth and travellers is gaining momentum as a category of a completely new generation of travellers.

Many of the youth, aged 18-25, are preparing to leave school and enter a challenging workforce that is in an era of downsizing. Generation Y are seeking unique experiences that will enhance their skills and education; many are looking to

* Graduate Student, Department of Tourism, University of Otago, New Zealand.

** Professor and Head, Department of Tourism, School of Business, University of Otago, PO Box 56, Dunedin, New Zealand.

volunteer vacations to obtain this 'real life training'. This is a high spending group with flexible incomes, moreover, they are eager to spend money on 'active' vacations.

Drawing on a range of studies this article will provide a detailed account of research surrounding the youth market, commonly referred to as Echo Boomers, Millennials or Generation Y involved in volunteer tourism programs. Motivations will be identified as well as a more detailed discussion on how volunteer travel experiences are serving today's youth through the development aptitudes that will assist them with the choices they make in the future. This chapter concludes by identifying the value this sector holds for the tourism industry on a wider scale and the long-term implications of the youth volunteer market for destinations.

Introduction

This chapter focuses on two areas that have the potential to enhance and develop a positive trend and vision in the tourism industry: volunteer tourism and the current youth market, Generation Y. This newest generation, also known as 'Echo Boomers' (Neuborne and Kerwin 1999), or the 'Net Generation' (Tapscott 1996), are a population of knowledgeable, skilled and, increasingly, conscientious travellers (Wolburg and Pokrywczynski 2001). In an era of corporate downsizing and incredibly competitive workforce, evidence suggests that these individuals place great importance on education, flexibility and personal potential (Mitchell and Hall 2001, 2003; Pekala 2001). However, because of the changing nature of work in industrialised society the average Generation Y'er expects to be unemployed four to six times in their life (Pekala 2001) and will therefore likely turn to leisure activities, such as travel and volunteering to further educate themselves, and to gain skills that will help them realize their individual potential.

This chapter identifies Generation Y as a considerable market opportunity for volunteer tourism, and argues that they also have the ability to improve the overall reputation of western tourists in some locations (Woy-Hazelton 1999). This hybrid culture of volunteers, youth and travellers is gaining momentum as a category of a completely new generation of travellers, and, as a means of gaining experience to develop diverse capabilities and expand their resumes, Generation Y are looking to volunteer vacations to obtain this 'real life training'.

Because a growing number of employers are accepting volunteer experience as a valid part of work history (Volunteer Canada 2002), it is likely that Generation Y will offer major opportunities as a major target market for managed volunteer tourism programs. Generation Y are now entering the workforce, they began graduating from college in 1998 and continue to seek ways to enhance their skills and gain experience in different areas. This generation is believed to have unique characteristics that are different from preceding generations (Wolburg and Pokrywczynski 2001). Their numbers vary, depending upon how the groups are divided (see table in Appendix A for variations in age and characteristics of Generation X and Y). However, the United Nations report there are over 1,066 million youth (defined as ages 15-24) on the planet (UN 2001). Furthermore, Cheng (1999) estimates that Generation Y is three times the size of the recent group, Generation X.

Volunteer tourism has the capacity to offer a quality educational experience for volunteers that enhances personal development (Spaeth 2001). Generation Y is known to be a large spending group (Cheng 1999) and because they are likely to remain single throughout their 20s and early 30s (Wolburg and Pokrywczynski 2001) they will have increased leisure time and more disposable income, more so than their previous generations. There is an increasing trend towards more individualised travel packages (Lutz and Prosser 1994), and this trend might be inviting to many youth seeking a different type of experience. A survey conducted in 1999 by the largest travel company for 18-35 year olds, Contiki Vacations, reported that 43 per cent of students say active vacations are "in" (Inglesi 2000). Participants who are actively volunteering on vacation are gaining knowledge and acquiring skills that are helping them to develop aptitudes that will assist them with the choices they make in the future. Nevertheless, relatively little formal research has been carried out on the volunteer and tourism phenomenon (Uriely et al. 2002), and little is known about how many people are involved in volunteering, what they do, what motivates them (IYV, 2001). In particular, information and data is lacking about the overall area of volunteer tourism although its importance is becoming increasingly recognised (e.g. Wearing 2001). However, in order for this segment to be developed to its full potential, more research and reliable information is clearly needed in this area.

Volunteering or Tourism?

The more research that is conducted about volunteer tourism, the more we will be able to define how and where the concept of tourism fits into volunteer organisations. In addition to providing extensive benefits to youth who volunteer, properly managed volunteer tourism programs have the potential to shift some of the negative labels associated with traditional forms of tourism and tourists. Most volunteer programs are cautious to not market the international travel component of their programs, as to enable them to remain separate from mainstream tourism. Organisations who offer these programs usually focus on the volunteer and philanthropist components rather than promoting the travel and tourism side, which at times has been cast in a negative light. For example, Raleigh International's mission statement is:

> "To inspire people from all backgrounds and nationalities to discover their full potential by working together on challenging environmental and community projects around the world" (Raleigh International 2002).

Similarly, Cross Cultural Solutions mission is"

> "to empower communities, foster cultural sensitivity and understanding, and further social progress" (Cross Cultural Solutions 2002).

Many programs do not emphasise the international travel component, which is often a major draw for participants. Both of these organisations have volunteer programs around the world, and offer free leisure time to the volunteers for travel and sightseeing, yet they do not use this as a type of promotional pull to attract volunteers. Essentially these volunteer organisations are trying to attract the type of traveller whose main priority is to volunteer, and to work with a community, instead of seeing the sights and commodifying the experience of assisting a community or area in need.

Generation Y is resistant to being 'labeled'; they are not as susceptible to mass marketing and advertising schemes as previous generations (Wolburg and Pokrywczynski 2001), and will therefore tend to stay away from overdeveloped mass tourism destinations. It is not likely they will willingly conform to the title of "tourist" or the idea of mass tourism, and thus will be drawn more to volunteer organisations that offer a 'working vacation' to destinations that are off the beaten track, places they may not have the opportunity to visit on a traditional packaged holiday. Many of this generation are looking for a means to 'give back' in some form or another (Buck and Rembert 1997). Not everyone has the capability or the resources to dedicate two years service with the United States Peace Corps or the New Zealand Volunteers Abroad for example, yet the same altruistic sense of accomplishment can be achieved by way of volunteer travel. These volunteers are not only gaining an alternative travel experience but the programs are also providing valuable assistance to the communities they visit. This unusual form of vacationing is proving to be a powerful means of a quality educational experience, at the same time expanding the values and beliefs of those who participate in them.

Volunteer Tourism

What is it?

Volunteer tourism is a phenomenon that is changing the face of the traditional holiday market. People are paying large amounts of money to work as a volunteer—while on vacation —in number of different projects around the world, yet not all volunteers consider the vacations work. Many programs are designed for hobbyists, or for people who want to learn a new skill, to further educate themselves. These holidays are finding travellers helping scientists track koalas off the coast of Australia; weeding tropical islands in the Pacific; or learning about organic farming, among countless other projects around the world. The increase in demand for these holidays also appears to be expanding, Bill McMillon, author of "Volunteer Vacations" has seen the number of organisations in his annual guidebook grow from 83 to more than 280 in the past eleven years, 1990-2001 (Kuchment, Koh et al. 2002).

The International Volunteer Programs Association (2000) indicate there has been considerable interest from professionals who want short term, meaningful vacations. A large part of the volunteer tourism market is made up of individuals from more mature generations, people in ranging in age from their 30s to their 60s. The profile of this market is changing however, with the rapid increase in youth who are participating in volunteer activity we can expect to see Generation Y becoming very active in this growing area of volunteer tourism.

Wearing defines volunteer tourism as: "tourists who, for various reasons, volunteer in an organised way to undertake holidays that might involve aiding or alleviating the material poverty of some groups of society, the restoration of certain environments or research into aspects of society or environment" (2001 p1). Because of the diversity of tourists and the tourism industry, the definition of volunteer tourism is likely to continually evolve. As more research is conducted about this form of travel, more similarities with other tourism segments are also becoming apparent due to crossovers with other tourism forms such as ecotourism, educational tourism, cultural tourism, adventure tourism, amongst others.

Many sections make up the concept of volunteer tourism. Volunteer activity is a component of serious leisure (Stebbins 2000; 2001), however in relation to tourism it is equally found under the realm of alternative tourism (Weaver 1998). Figure 1 depicts a model of volunteer tourism outlining three main areas of tourism that overlap: ecotourism, educational tourism and volunteer tourism. All of these fall within the scope of alternative tourism. From this model a new definition for volunteer tourism evolves:

> "travellers who vacation to volunteer in an organised, responsible way to learn new skills or improve existing ones, while at the same time restoring or researching certain aspects of the environment; all the while aiding some groups of society".

As illustrated in Figure 1, the undertaking of volunteer activity while on vacation shares many similar features with educational tourism and ecotourism. Ecotourism is known as "responsible travel that conserves natural environments and sustains the well-being of local people" (Ecotourism Society 1992). Volunteer tourism is similar in that people also wish to travel in a responsible manner (because of the altruistic purpose of the holiday), the volunteer activity is normally of a sustainable or conservative approach involving the environment, additionally the results of the volunteer's actions and presence educates themselves as well as assisting the local community.

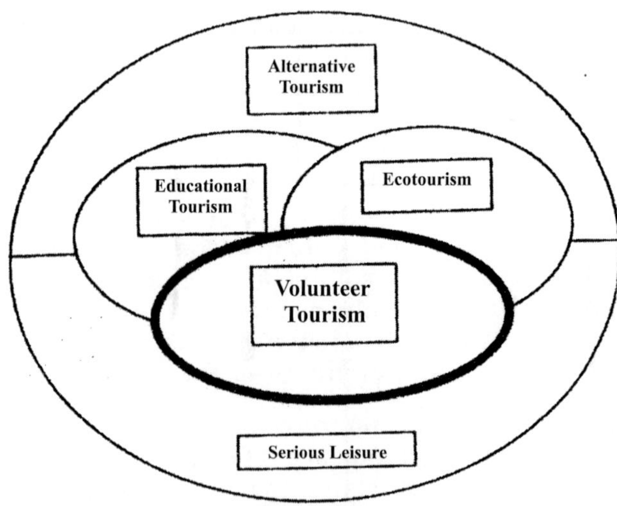

Fig. 8.1. Volunteer Tourism Model

Who is Doing It?

People who are choosing the option of volunteer vacations are a mix of different backgrounds and generations. The United Nations (2001) reports that most voluntary service agencies (VSA) are sending out people in their 30s and 40s, as well as a number of 'baby boomers'. Many of these individuals participating in international volunteer programs have Post-Graduate degrees and qualifications and several years of practical experience in their own field (United Nations 2001). Nonetheless, youth do make up a significant market for volunteer tourism programs. Furthermore, Generation Y may stand to learn a great amount from professionals who have experience in the labour force.

Trends are developing with respect to the increasing number of youth who are volunteering (Ellis 1985; Inglesi 2000; IVR 1998; Taemsamran 1999; USDED, 1999; Volunteer Canada 2002). Some authors offer differing opinions on the prediction that youth are becoming a significant market for volunteer tourism. Gibson (1998) states that although some men and women (18-22 age range) took educationally oriented vacations, this may not fulfil this group's need for adventure and excitement. This statement suggests that the label of educational tourism needs to expand beyond the ideas associated with a 'study tour', and recognise that hands-on learning, such as volunteering, can be an effective, exciting and adventurous means of education (Spaeth 2001).

In support of the argument against the significance of today's youth market, the Federation of International Youth Travel Organisations (FIYTO) and the International Student Travel Confederation (ISTC) reported in 1999 that "considering worldwide trends, youth and student travel is poised to become the largest and most highly specialised niche market in travel" (Taemsamran 1999). Furthermore, the World Tourism Organisation (WTO) states that youth travel accounts for 20 percent of the total travel market worldwide (1999). It is estimated that the youth travel industry is growing by six to seven per cent annually, higher than the average four to five per cent growth rate of the total tourism industry (WTO 2001). This leaves little uncertainty that youth are a key influential travel market of the near future, despite any negative labels that may be connected with them or the previous youth group, Generation X.

Some literature questions whether we should believe the stereotypes between one generation and the next. Generation X has been labelled with some contradictory descriptions over the past two decades. During the 1980s, Gen Xers were called "determined, career minded, ambitious, planners with priorities", but by the 1990s they became "slackers, cynics, whiners, drifters" (Wolburg and Pokrywczynski 2001). What is to say that this type of reverse labelling will not happen to Generation Y? Will the optimistic and skilled youth of Generation Y turn into the couch computer hacker of tomorrow? It was speculated that the recession of 1990 affected large numbers of the middle class and this is why the negative stereotype rolled over onto Generation X (Wolburg and Pokrywczynski 2001). Nonetheless, Generation X has been one of the most discussed and criticised generation to date (Pekala 2001), yet the next ten years may see Generation Y take over this title. In contrast, the patterns of altruistic behaviour that are being documented about Generation Y may make this an unlikely event.

At present there are few documents in relation to volunteer tourism and little information with regards to numbers of youth who volunteer. Even less is known about the range of people who are participating in volunteer tourism programs. It is therefore difficult to make authoritative accounts about this emerging tourism sector. The United Nations International Year of the Volunteer in 2001 was successful in raising awareness around the globe about the varying and key roles volunteers play. This event also prompted many governments, organisations and businesses to take an active role in future research in the area of volunteerism. Because of this international exposure, it is promising that all areas involving volunteerism will continue to develop further.

Volunteer Motivations and Benefits

The people who participate in volunteer tourism programs are seeking more than a typical holiday, they are looking for a meaningful type of journey and a responsible means of travel. Studies show that volunteering brings about a deep development of self, and this can be seen as a motivation to continue volunteer activity and travel (Wearing 2001). Volunteer travellers want a chance to become immersed in a community or assist with projects when they travel, rather than just passing through (PIRT 2000). A great deal of research is still needed to determine why people, especially youth, are participating as international volunteers. In a general sense, Murnighan et al. (1993) suggest that people volunteer for four key reasons:

1. To improve their skills and make themselves more employable;
2. To stimulate social interactions that may develop friendships;
3. To put themselves in position for employment when it becomes available;
4. To obtain other self-oriented benefits.

Wearing (2001) discusses seven motivation categories with respect to volunteer tourism:

1. Altruism
2. Travel / adventure
3. Personal growth
4. Cultural exchange/learning
5. Professional development
6. Right time/right place

The similarities between these sets of motivations lie in the realm of professional development, education and learning. The notion that volunteering will improve one's skills and put them in a positive status for gaining employment is supported in recent literature (Gibson 1998; Independent Sector and UN Volunteers 2001; Spaeth 2001; Wallis 2001; Hirst 2002; Hunt 2002) The fact that there are high rates of unemployment (aged 20-24 in US is at 9.6%—a six year high), many are choosing voluntarism as a way out (Mestheneos, Schumacher et al. 2001). Research conducted in 2000 indicated that over 54 per cent of volunteers believed that their volunteering experience would help them get a job, or had helped them get their current job (Hirst 2002). These facts offer support for youth who believe volunteering will be an asset in helping them secure employment in the future.

In 1997 a survey was conducted about volunteering by the Institute for Volunteering Research. The results suggested that one barrier to participation was that volunteering suffers from out-dated associations with 'worthy philanthropy', and conjures up images that do not appeal to the young. The question was posed 'are young people losing interest in volunteering?' The conclusion drawn was that the answer is a qualified no—youth are becoming more involved with volunteering, not the reverse. The report also demonstrated that experience is high on young people's 'wish list' for volunteering. Volunteering needs to offer opportunities to learn new skills, explore different careers, to get work experience. These motivations are not new, but are increasingly important among Generation Y (IVR 1998).

Volunteer travel can serve as an option for Generation Y to sample different career paths before making a long-term commitment to it. It allows youth to discover what they like, what they are good at (and not good at), and this experience allows them to make informed decisions without disrupting their resume, all the while offering a leisure experience. They can situate themselves in an environment they want to learn about, and because of the presence of older generations that have extensive life experience, they can learn from other people, in an unstructured setting (compared to a classroom for example). Volunteering and all that is connected to it, is a form of real life, hands on training.

Levinson (1996) suggests that "people in their early twenties are busy experimenting with new identities, establishing their independence, and generally searching for adventure". Volunteer tourism meets this criteria for young people, by offering a new identity (volunteer), establishes independence through travel, and adventure in the combined experience of travelling to a new place and living and working in another culture.

As previously noted, many people who participate in 'working holidays' are doing so to learn something. The concept of young people who gain education through travel has a long history. Travelling to enhance one's education dates back to the beginnings of tourism. The Grand Tour exposed young, noble gentlemen (evidence of some women travellers as well) to a romantic education of different cultures, arts, languages and politics (Gibson 1998). It was looked upon as a 'fashionable' way to complete a youth's education. This learning travel served as a 'rite of passage' from their youth into the working world. Although much has changed in the world since this type of 'Grand Tour' travel in the 18th century, the facts remain the same. Young people will choose travel to further their education, and the opportunity to volunteer is developing their skills and experience to enter today's workforce.

Benefits to Tourism

Many of the organisations and programs that make up volunteer tourism maintain an advantage when battling the negative images that have been cast over tourism. Although volunteer tourism is the term the tourism industry has attached to this type of travel, many volunteer programs may not want the term 'tourism' associated with what they promote. Wearing (2001) supports this, observing: "organisations that recruit volunteers for community aid projects overseas do not promote the fact that they offer a richer form of tourism". Their primary focus is usually on the volunteering feature of the experience and they may not want to be associated with the negative stigma connected to more popular forms of tourism. Today, tourism is often a mass activity often characterised by rudeness and disorderliness and lack of respect for local culture (Jamieson 2001). Therefore, many of the youth of Generation Y might not want to be associated with common, or mass tourism and are choosing this form of holiday to be recognised as a volunteer and to escape being labelled a 'tourist'.

The value of the youth and student market has been recognised as early as the 1920s and has been a popular target since that time (Burns 1926; Dumont 1929; George 1920 cited in Wolburg and Pokrywczynski 2001).The reasons are many, but include:

- — Their size makes students and youth an important market in the short-term and the potential for return travel make them a significant long-term market;
- — The small but significant disposable income of students may make them an attractive market for some destinations which provide budget accommodation (such as backpackers)
- — Students are often put in the role of trendsetters by setting examples to the remainder of the population;
- — Students influence parental choices for major purchases.

Considering these reasons from a tourism perspective, one can understand why youth should be considered a valuable asset to the volunteer tourism segment. Additionally, they can produce benefits for the entire tourism industry. For example, if a group of students were to participate in an international volunteer program, it is highly likely that their tales of adventure upon their return may entice other students to partake in a similar activity; they would set a 'trend' for a unique type of vacation. Furthermore, it is expected that the parents and families of students who learn how to volunteer and travel responsibly will follow in their footsteps and maintain similar, sensible travel patterns.

Overall, volunteer tourism has the ability to benefit the tourism industry in two ways. First, it has the potential to offer a positive image towards the tourism industry which has traditionally caused damage to some cultures and the environment. People who become familiar with volunteer tourism and it's associated outcomes may see it as a means of 'giving' instead of 'taking'. Second, properly designed volunteer programs have the ability to teach youth, and all those involved how to travel responsibly, have respect for the environment and the host community. These programs may have a positive influence on all participants in that they have an educational and leisure experience tied into one unique, adventurous working holiday. The following are some quotes from some international volunteer tourism programs:

"Our expeditions are designed as purposeful, challenging and rewarding experiences. We recognise the need for volunteers to balance skill development, community education and hard work with fun activities. Opportunities and social events are unique to each expedition, but always include barbecues, parties and day or weekend excursions. Through the combination of both hard work and play, past Volunteers have developed skills and friendships that will last a lifetime."

Global Vision International 2002

"VolunTours represents an opportunity to fulfill one's interest in community service in just a few hours, or, if preferred, a longer duration of service to the community, the environment, or the residents of a particular destination. This short time commitment allows VolunTourists to still experience the wealth of discovery via local attractions, arts and culture, and the finer amenities of shops and restaurants".

Voluntours 2002

"Volunteering on an expedition means that you will be living, working and travelling in some of the most beautiful and remote locations in the world. Taking part on one of our expeditions means existing skills are developed and many new ones are discovered and developed. The locations in which Frontier work means that you will not be short of beautiful and remote places to visit afterwards, or like-minded friends to travel on with! If you are looking to live and work in a challenging overseas destination, learn valuable skills, and help to conserve fragile areas but are short on time, then a Frontier expedition could be for you".

Frontier Projects 2002

Conclusion

The rapidly developing volunteer tourism market has the ability to adopt and communicate solid experiences and responsible travel behaviour. This wisdom will stay with youth throughout their lives, and subsequently benchmark sustainable practices for the next generation of travellers. Properly developed and managed volunteer programs have the ability to inspire such standards in their participants, and volunteers will walk away with more than memories of a two week holiday.

There is an obvious movement of more youth involved in volunteer activity, for various reasons. The most prominent motive for Generation Y is to gain valuable and real life experience, followed by an exciting and rare opportunity to volunteer and vacation in a remote, undeveloped area. They can use this experience to assist in making career decisions; developing skills and talents; and preparing themselves to enter the workforce. In this age of corporate downsizing and competitive job markets, the youth of Generation Y may find themselves changing jobs 4 - 6 times in their lifetime. To fill the gaps, gain new expertise, and as a means of leisure, volunteering will find it's way into many youth's lives. The increasing number of youth travellers (growing faster than the rate of the total tourism industry), combined with spending power in the billions (Inglesi 2000), are pointing to an innovative trend that can not be ignored. The tourism industry must recognise this pattern of the future and prepare for the next generation of volunteers, and travellers.

REFERENCES

(1998). What Young People Want from Volunteering, Institue for Volunteering Research.

Buck, W. R. and T. C. Rembert (1997). Just doing it: Generation X proves that actions speak louder than words. *E*. 8: 28-36.

Cheng, K. (1999). Setting Their Sites on Generation Y. *Adweek*. 40: 46-48.

Cross Cultural Solutions. www.crossculturalsolutions.org

Ellis, S. J. (1985). "Research on Volunteerism...What Needs to be Done." *Journal of Voluntary Action Research* 14(2-3): 11-114.

Frontier Projects. www.frontier.ac.uk

Gibson, H. (1998). "The Educational Tourist." *The Journal of Physical Education, Recreation and Dance* 69(4): 6-9.

Global Vision International. www.gvi.co.uk

Hirst, A. (2002). "Links Between Volunteering and Employability." *Labour Market Trends* 110(1): 45-50.

Hunt, J. W. (2002). Workers with attitude: Why Generation Y is turning out to be every employer's nightmare. *Financial Times*. London: 12.

Independent, S. and U. N. Volunteers (2001). Measuring Volunteering: A Practical Toolkit, International Year of Volunteers: 1-39.

Inglesi, E. M. (2000). "Youth Invasion." *Travel Agent* 302(5).

International Volunteer Programs Association. www.ivpr.org

Jamieson, Bill (2001). Word of the Week: Tourist. *The Scotsman*: 15.

Kuchment, A., B. Koh, et al. (2002). Lending a Helping Hand. *Newsweek International*: 66.

Levinson, D. (1996). *The Seasons of a Woman's Life*. New York, Knopf.

Lutz, J. and B. Prosser (1994). "The Changing World of Tourism." *Geographical Magazine* 66(12): 53-56.

Mestheneos, L., J. Schumacher, et al. (2001). Main Trends in Voluntarism, European Volunteer Information Pool.

Mitchell, R. , Hall, C.M. (2001) "The Winery Consumer: A New Zealand Perspective", *Tourism Recreation Research*, 26(2): 63-75.

Mitchell, R. & Hall, C.M.. (2003) "Consuming Tourists: Food Tourism Consumer Behaviour", *Food Tourism Around the World: Development, Management and Markets*, eds C.M. Hall, E. Sharples, R. Mitchell, B. Cambourne, & N. Macionis, Butterworth-Heinemann, Oxford, in press.

Murnighan, J. K., J. W. Kim, et al. (1993). "The Volunteer Dilemma." *Administrative Sciene Quarterly* 38(4): 515 - 539.

Neuborne, E. and K. Kerwin (1999). Generation Y. *Business Week*.

Pekala, N. (2001). "Conquering the Generational Divide." *Journal of Property Management* 66(6): 30-37.

Partners in Responsible Tourism. www.pirt.org

Raleigh International. www.raleigh.org.uk

Spaeth, M. (2001). "Volunteer Visibility." *Risk Management* 48(7): 10-14.

Stebbins, R. A. (2000). World Leisure International Position Statement on Educating for Serious Leisure, World Leisure Commission on Education.

Stebbins, R. A. (2001). "Serious Leisure." *Society* 38(4): 53-57.

Taemsamran, J. (1999). Youth and Student Travel. *Bangkok Post*. Bangkok.

Tapscott, D. (1996). The Rise of the Net-Generation. *Advertising Age*.

The International Ecotourism Society. www.ecotourism.org

United Nations, General Secretary (2001). Implementation of the World Programme of Action for Youth to the Year 2000 and Beyond, United Nations.

United Nations Volunteers International Year of Volunteers 2001. www.iyv2001.org

United States Department of Education. www.ed.gov

Uriely, N., Z. Schwartz, et al. (2002). "Rescuing Hikers in Israel's Deserts: Community Altruism or an Extension of Adventure Tourism?" *Journal of Leisure Research* 34(1): 25-37.

Volunteer Canada "The Potential of Volunteer Work for Developing Skills". www.volunteer.ca

Voluntours Travel. www.voluntour.com

Wallis, T. J. (2001). "Volunteering: Getting Work Experience by doing Good." *Career World* 30(1): 16-19.

Wearing, S. (2001), Volunteer Tourism: Experiences that make a difference. Oxon, CABI International

Weaver, D. B. (1998). *Ecotourism in the Less Developed World*. Oxon, CABI International.

Wolburg, J. M. and J. Pokrywczynski (2001). "A Psychographic Analysis of Generation Y College Students." *Journal of Advertising Research* 41(5): 33-53.

World Tourism Organisation. www.world-tourism.org

Woy-Hazelton, S. (1999). "Ecostudents: The New Wave of Students Abroad." *Social Education* 63(2): 89-90.

APPENDIX A

Table—8.1 Variations Among Age and Characteristics of Generation X and Y

Label	Age Range	Author	Characteristics
Generation X	15-30	Stepp, 1996	– alienated from traditional media – utilitarian
Generation X	16–29	Benezra, 1995	– complex mix of contrasts – introspective searching for sense of community
Generation X	18–30	Frengut, 1994	– honest, humorous, subtle – leaders, trendsetters – resistance to being labelled – media savvy
Generation X	18–34	Thau, 1996	– cautious with money – individualism and practicality – optimistic about their futures – want to be as responsible as they can in their lives

(Contd...)

Generation X	25–34	Janoff, 1999	– influence purchase adults – aggressive investors – less loyalty to traditional brands
Generation X	25–34	Stapinski, 1999	N/A
Generation X	25–34	Wellner, 1999	N/A
Generation X	20–39	Cheng, 1999	– 'slackers'
Generation Y	18–24	Janoff, 1999	– do not want to be targeted the same as Gen X – buying habits influenced by the Internet
Generation Y	18–24	Stapinski, 1999	– more savvy, tolerant than previous generations – more optimistic than Gen X
Generation Y	18–24	Wellner, 1999	– more willing to take a risk – shorter job tenure – heightened expectations for information
Generation Y	12–19	Cheng, 1999	– multimedia / multitasking people – sceptical

(Contd...)

Generation Y	Born 1977-1994 (ages 7 - 24)	Gill, 1999	– sophisticated generation – do not care to know brands
Generation Y	Born 1979-1994 (ages 7 - 22)	Duff, 1999	– technologically literate – more demanding, looking for overall quality – want to express themselves more individualistically
Generation Y	Born 1979-1994 (ages 6-21)	Kapner, 1999	– anti corporate – idealistic – socially conscious – individualistic
Generation Y	Born 1979-1994 (ages 6-21)	Neuborne and Kerwin, 1999	– radically diverse, ethnic and racially – distinctly practical worldview

Source: **Adapted from Wolburg and Pokrywczynski, 2001**

9

Yield Management: Issues for Tourism and Hospitality Strategic Decision Making

**Ray Leggo*

Introduction

Strategic decision making in relation to yield management needs to be a dominant focus of tourism and hospitality managers. Yield management is primarily concerned with maximising revenue through the manipulation of price in periods of low, medium and high demand (Bardi, 2002; Cross, 1997; Kimes, 1997; Luciani, 1999; Noone and Griffin, 1997). This chapter discusses contemporary issues that are important for the tourism and hospitality strategic decision makers to consider in order to achieve their revenue and profitability objectives. Issues such as market segmentation, competitive advantage, external intended and unintended forces, internal intended and unintended forces, organisational culture, forecasting, computerisation, teamwork, networking, ethics of

* Griffith University, School of Tourism and Hotel Management, Gold Coast Campus Griffith University, PMB 50 Gold Coast Mail Centre, Queensland 9726 Australia

overbooking, seasonality, empowerment, revenue generation and cost allocation are discussed. Examples are provided from a range of tourism and hospitality enterprises to reinforce the key points from the chapter. Because yield management for tourism and hospitality is both process and outcome oriented this chapter also examines strategic decision-making that deals with the implementation, monitoring, feedback and adaptation of yield management techniques. These decisions are made in a complex, dynamic environment and as a consequence tourism and hospitality decision makers need to be responsive and flexible in order to accommodate changing circumstances and maintain a competitive advantage.

Market Segmentation

Effective yield management requires tourism and hospitality enterprises to define their market into clearly distinguishable segments (Donaghy, McMahon-Beatie and McDowell, 1997). Hence these enterprises need to look inwards and determine where their strengths are in relation to their competitors. Yield management strategic decision-making is required to maximise the strengths and minimise the enterprise's weaknesses when marketing within its complex, dynamic environment. A mix of target market segments must be selected that will provide the tourism and hospitality enterprise with the highest possible revenue and profit throughout the year. For example, a number of tourism and hospitality enterprises operating at the Cold Coast, Australia used to specifically target the Japanese segment before the Asian financial crisis in the late 1990's and now the decision-makers at these enterprises target a much broader mix of market segments. Tourism and hospitality enterprises need to develop separate pricing structures for each segment based on their characteristics and willingness and ability to pay different rates (Jauncey, Mitchell and Slamet, 1995). By setting clear market segmentation goals that are realistic and attainable it gives both the staff and management a 'reason' to work hard at yield management. Once the target markets have been selected it is then imperative to forecast demand from these segments accurately.

Forecasting

The ability to forecast effectively and accurately future patterns of demand is a key issue in yield management (Jauncey et. al., 1995; Yeoman and Watson, 1997).

Internal Intended and Unintended Forces

An important basis of accurate forecasting is the establishment of internal policies and procedures regarding how yield management is to be used within tourism and hospitality enterprises. This systematic foundation accommodates the internal intended forces where yield management meets the normal day-to-day decision making requirements. However unintended internal forces, such as a double booking or an unexpected extended stay, have a tendency to occur and therefore tourism and hospitality yield management systems must incorporate responsiveness and flexibility in order to assist staff and management with decision-making should disputes, problems or queries arise. One such problem facing tourism and hospitality enterprises that adopt yield management is possible alienation of customers (Bardi, 1996). Making tactical yield management decisions is therefore crucial. These tactics will vary during periods of low, mid, and high demand. Such decisions make involve 'block outs' for periods of high demand and special promotions and holiday packages for periods of low demand. This illustrates how yield management decision-making is dynamic in nature, constantly adjusting to changing conditions.

External Intended and Unintended Forces

To be effective forecasting must be done on a daily basis and must encompass more than 30 or 60 day projections (Huyton and Peters, 1997). External intended and unintended forces such as the weather, economic conditions and natural disasters influence the decision-maker's ability to forecast yield (Yeoman and Watson, 1997). Choi and Cho (2000) state that tourism demand is influenced by affects from the global economy, events occurring, seasonality, and the booking level of competitors. Therefore it is important that management and staff have a satisfactory understanding of what is happening in the world around them. Yield management does not replace employee decision-making and control; rather it is used to guide the manager and staff to implement well-structured, well-researched decisions (Liberman, 1993). Hence having vast quantities of timely, accurate and relevant information at their disposal is crucial for decision-makers. Processing this information is being made easier via computerisation.

Computerisation

A fundamental decision that a tourism and hospitality establishment must make is whether or not to accept or reject a booking. Given the complex nature of enhancing revenue and profitability using yield management techniques a large amount of information has to be gathered and analysed. Hence the analysis and adjustment by computerised systems is a fundamental element of yield management within tourism and hospitality enterprises (Baker, Bradley and Huyton, 1994). Computerised systems use large amounts of data from past history and current trends, and are capable of producing forecasts and predictions on the best configuration for revenue maximisation (MacVicar and Rodger, 1996).

However, yield management is not simply a computer system. Lee-Ross and Johns (1997) suggest that computer yield management systems that apply algebraic or statistical techniques to the analysis of information should be used as a tool for aiding staff and management in their decision-making. Kasavana and Brooks (1995) state that yield management software does not make decisions for managers, it provides a lot of helpful information regarding such things as booking patterns that can be used to help support managerial decision-making.

Seasonality

It is essential that tourism and hospitality enterprises know the pattern in which customers book reservations, recognise the customers needs, desires and especially seasonal demand patterns by customer market segment (Czinkota, 2000). Decision makers therefore need well-kept customer records and profiles to match market segments to low, mid and high seasons. Reed, McKibben and Associates (1998) identify that a successful yield management program means that different marketing plans are required for different market segments at different times of the year.

Networking

One way that tourism and hospitality enterprises keep abreast of occupancy levels in their region is to set up a network where information regarding occupancy and average rates for each hotel is shared. This assists decision-making because strategies can be framed in terms of what the competition is achieving from a revenue perspective. Something that is not readily apparent from these shared figures is the profitability that each enterprise is achieving. However such a network does indicate those tourism and hospitality enterprises that are utilising an overbooking strategy.

Ethics of Overbooking

According to Lee-Ross and Johns (1997) tourism and hospitality enterprises find it acceptable to overbook to a certain degree. However this can lead to an ethical dilemma of guests (who may well have a guaranteed booking) arriving and being told that there is nothing available. In order to assist with overbooking strategic decision making, tourism and hospitality enterprises must keep accurate and up-to-date data concerning 'no show' rates, especially information concerning the segments most likely not to show up (Yeoman and Ingold, 1997).

Boella (2000) argues that overbooking is an essential part of normal business practices and few people in the tourism industry question its ethical basis. However there is the danger that overbooking will result in a loss of good will for the enterprise and often a transfer of costs incurred by having to rebook the customer with a rival, or by offering some other compensation for 'bumping'. Norman and Mayer (1997) state that the tourism industry's concerns over the fairness of yield management has retarded the embrace of yield management techniques. Johns (1999) warns tourism and hospitality enterprises to be careful when it comes to deciding whether or not to take a booking from a regular customer when a one-off customer is willing to pay a higher price. In order to make ethical decisions that are consistent across the entire enterprise, teamwork is an important consideration.

Teamwork

A team approach is essential for the success of yield management (Burgess and Bryant, 2001).

Yield Management Team

The yield management team usually consists of the General Manager, the Marketing Manager, and the Reservations Manager. Yeoman and Watson (1997) argue that it is important for the yield management team to take risks and have an understanding of realistic timescales. After each meeting the members of the team need to disseminate the information amongst the rest of the members in their departments because tourism and hospitality staff should be empowered to make strategic yield management decisions.

Empowerment and Training

Tourism and hospitality enterprises must be responsive and flexible in order to gain the maximum benefit from using yield management techniques. Many situations such as a regular guest wanting to stay during a 'blockout' period require staff to make yield management decisions on a case-by-case basis. It is therefore imperative that staff are empowered to make the best possible yield management decision in any given context. Regular training for everyone involved in yield management is vital so that everyone understands the principles involved and their role in the process. Seminars need to be organised where the staff and management learn how to make informed decisions and the benefits that these decisions will have for themselves and the customers they serve. Donaghy et al. (1997) believe that managers and staff require training in both the operational techniques of yield management and also the development of its conceptual understanding.

Revenue Generation and Cost Allocation

Profitability will differ between market segments because of the varying levels of service and support needed to meet the needs of each customer or group (Jauncey et al., 1995). Customer profitability analysis is a decision making tool that has been developed to assist tourism and hospitality enterprises by identifying the revenues, costs and profits by individual customers or customer groups. It thus identifies which segments generate greatest profit contribution thus providing management with vital information regarding their customer base (Noone and Griffin, 1997). Hence customer profitability analysis is an important issue for yield management decision-makers.

Costs need to be identified to support the yield management decisions being made associated with delivering the service (Burgess and Bryant, 2001). Yield management is concerned with offering different prices to different market segments in response to demand and ability to pay. This is identified by Kimes (1994) as a form of discrimination. But it has been long recognized by economists that price discriminators sometimes make more money than single-price sellers (Weigand, 1999). What this means is that the focus of tourism and hospitality enterprises needs to shift from high-volume to high-profit bookings and the yield management decision-makers need to find ways to attract those high-profit clientele and keep them coming back.

Organisational Culture and Implementation

The first stage of implementing successful yield management is the development of a 'yield culture' within the organisation where the concept becomes an integral part of everyone's daily routine (Jones and Hamilton, 1992). Huyton and Peters (1997) state that it is the people who are the driving forces behind the successful implementation of yield management. Yeoman and Ingold (1997) recognize the importance of top management showing a strong commitment to yield management. Cooperation and communication within the tourism and hospitality enterprise is also identified as an important element of yield management success (Kasavana and Brooks, 1995).

Feedback, Monitoring and Adaptation

Feedback, monitoring and adaptation are the final issues for discussion presented in this paper. Jauncey et al (1995) proposes that yield management is a continuous approach to maximising revenue, and this paper argues that the same is true for strategic decision-making to enhance revenue and profitability. Customer satisfaction is one of the key operational goals of tourism and hospitality enterprises. Yield management helps facilitate this objective when it focuses on the issues of feedback, monitoring and adaptation because the hotel is ensuring the delivery of quality service to their most profitable segments. Staff and management know that the customers they serve are the ones who should be staying at the hotel and who should be encouraged to return to the hotel. The recording and review of favourable or negative feedback from these customers will help shape future yield management strategic decision-making.

Conclusion

This chapter has identified a number of important issues regarding tourism and hospitality yield management decision-making such as market segmentation, forecasting, revenue generation and cost allocation, teamwork, ethics, organisational culture and implementation. Because tourism and hospitality yield management operates in a dynamic environment and is process oriented, issues that dealt with monitoring, feedback and adaptation were also examined.

REFERENCES

Baker, S., Bradley, P., and Huyton, J. (1994), *Principles of Hotel Front Office Operations: A Study Guide*, London: Cassel.

Bardi, J. (1996), *Hotel Front Office Management (2nd Ed.)*, New York: John Wiley and Sons.

Boella, M. (2000), *Human Resource Management in the Hospitality Industry (7th Ed.)*, Cheltenham: HCIMA.

Burgess, C., and Bryant, K. (2001), "Revenue Management: the Contribution of the Finance Function to Profitability", *International Journal of Contemporary Hospitality Management*, Vol. 13. No.3, pp. 144-150.

Choi, T. and Cho, V. (2000), "Towards a Knowledge Discovery Framework for Yield Management in the Hong Kong Hotel Industry", *Hospitality Management*. Vol. 19, pp. 17-31.

Cross, R. (1997), "Launching the Revenue Rocket: how Revenue Management Can Work for Your Business", *Cornell Hotel and Restaurant Administration Quarterly*, April, pp.32-43.

Czinkoa, M. (2000), *Marketing Best Practices*, New York: Drayden Press.

Donaghy, K., McMahon-Beattie, U. and McDowell, D. (1997), "Implementing Yield Management: Lessons from the Hotel Sector", *International Journal of Contemporary Hospitality Management*, Vol. 9 No. 2, pp. 50-54.

Huyton, J., and Peters, S. (1997), *Yield Management: Strategies for the Service Industries*, London: Cassell.

Jauncey, S., Mitchell, I. and Slamet, P. (1995), "The Meaning and Management of Yield in Hotels", *International Journal of Contemporary Hospitality Management*, Vol. 7 No. 4, pp. 23-26.

Jones, P. and Hamilton, D. (1992), "Yield Management: Putting People in the Big Picture", *Cornell Hotel and Restaurant Administration Quarterly*, Vol. 35 No. 1, pp. 89-95.

Jones, P. (1999), "Yield Management in UK Hotels: a Systems Analysis", *Journal of the Operational Research Society*, Oxford, Nov 1999, Vol. 50 Iss. 11, pp. 11-21.

Kasavana, M., and Brooks, R. (1995), *Managing Front Office Operations*, East Lansing, Mich: Institute of the American Hotel and Motel Association.

Kimes, S. (1989), "Yield Management: a Tool for Capacity Constrained Service Firms" *Journal of Operations Management*, Vol. 8, No. 4, pp. 348-363.

Kimes, S. (1994), "Perceived Fairness of Yield Management", *Cornell Hotel and Restaurant Administration Quarterly*, Vol. 35 No. 1, pp. 22-29.

Lee-Ross, D. and Johns, N. (1997), "Yield Management in Hospitality SMEs", *International Journal of Contemporary Hospitality Management*, Vol. 9 No. 2, pp. 66-69.

Lieberman, W. (1993), "Debunking the Myths of Yield Management", *Cornell Hotel and Restaurant Administration Quarterly*, Vol. 35 No. 1, pp. 34-41.

Luciani, S. (1999), "Implementing Yield Management in Small and Medium Sized Hotels: an Investigation of Obstacles and Success Factors in Florence Hotels", *International Journal of Hospitality Management*, Vol. 18, Iss. 2, pp. 129-142.

MacVicar, A. and Rodger, J. (1996), "Computerized Yield Management Systems: a Comparative Analysis of the Human Resource Management Implications", *International Journal of Hospitality Management*, Vol. 15 No. 4, pp. 325-332.

McEvoy, B. (1997), "Integrating Operational and Financial Perspectives using Yield Management Techniques: an add-on Matrix Model", *International Journal of Contemporary Hospitality Management*, Vol. 9 No. 2, pp. 60-65.

Norman, E., and Mayer, K. (1997), "Yield Management in Las Vegas Casino Hotels", *Cornell Hotel and Restaurant Administration Quarterly*, October, pp.28-33.

Noone, B. and Griffin, P. (1997), "Enhancing Yield Management with Customer Profitability Analysis", *International Journal of Contemporary Hospitality Management*, Vol. 9 No. 2, pp. 75-79.

Reed, McKibben and Associates (1998) "How to Make Money From Your Accommodation Business [on-line], *Interim Report: June 1998 Tasmania Tourism Council*. Available: http://www.tourism.tas.gov.au/ym [2002, February 12].

Weigand, R. (1999), "Yield Management: Filling Buckets, Papering the House", *Business Horizons*, Sept/Oct, pp. 55-64.

Yeoman, I. and Ingold, A. (1997), *Yield Management: Strategies for the Service Industries*, London: Cassell.

Yeoman, I. and Watson, S. (1997), "Yield Management: a Human Activity System", *International Journal of Contemporary Hospitality* Management. Vol. 9 No. 2, pp. 80-83.

10

Hotel Management and Tourism Policy in Greece: A Critical Assessment

**Paris Tsartas, **Dimitris Lagos*

Executive Summary

The scope of the present paper is to identify the main characteristic of hotel management of Greek hotel businesses in relation to tourism policies. To this end, we will examine the broader framework of the tourism industry, the current tourism policy in force as well as the tourism market sector, which will help us define those factors which shape hotel business management. Further on we will examine the characteristics of those business's management and will then draw critical conclusions which will in turn let us formulate

* Associate Professor of Tourism Development, Director of the Interdepartmental Program of Graduate Studies in Tourism Planning, Management and Policy, University of the Aegean, Greece. e.mail:ptsar@aegean.gr

** Assistant Professor of Tourism Economics and Tourist Business Administration Department of Business Administration, University of the Aegean, Greece. e.mail:D.lagos@aegean.gr

proposals and suggestions with a view to improving yield hotel management as well as enhancing Greek tourism competitiveness.

Our analysis has led us to realize that the Greek tourism industry consists of a particularly large number of small-sized enterprises with specific development characteristics, which sets the tone of a monopolistic market and which suffer from a series of weaknesses and malfunctions (i.e. seasonal operation, lack of economies of scale, low quality in services, narrow profit margins, concentration of such businesses on islands). We have also discovered that the majority of tourist businesses manage their affairs in an empirical manner and that a variety of obstacles hinder the introduction of more effective managerial approaches.

Development of Greek Tourism

Greece is a Mediterranean country located at the southern tip of the Balkan peninsula with a population of 19.9 million people and her political system is that of a presidential democracy. Greece became a full member of the European Union in 1982 and ever since her adhesion, she has been the recipient of significant financial aid to a number of sectors of production. More recently, the country's economy has witnessed significant improvements and today it's been stabilized.

The country's evolution of tourism indices (arrivals, overnight stays, tourist exchange) has been generally deemed satisfactory. If the different scenarios on world tourism trends are proved more or less accurate and considering that fact that Greece has been visited by growing numbers of tourists from Europe (who, by the way, are the majority of tourists in Greece) then it is estimated that in 2006 the country will witness the arrival of more than 14 million tourists (WTO 2000).

It is a truism to say that tourism is one of the most important factors of development of the Greek economy. In light of this, the contribution of the hotel sector in the Gross Domestic Product (GDP), employment and regional development is obviously particularly crucial. In-depth knowledge of the development potentialities of the sector and the character and orientations of hotel management are elements deemed sine qua non for the accurate assessment of their yield and performance.

According to the World Tourism Organization, Greece ranked 15th on the list of tourist destinations in 1999 and 23rd as per tourist revenues. Additionally, the country was 10th on the list of the most preferred destinations in the world in 2000.

Tourism is a particularly significant economic activity, contributing to GDP by approximately 18.3 per cent, and creating 16.3 per cent of jobs. In addition to these, tourism accounts for almost 35 per cent of invisible exchange resources, 6.5 per cent of investments on fixed assets and half the trade balance deficit.

In terms of demand, we can see a relatively steadily growing number of arrivals of foreign tourists for the period 1990-2000 (see Diagram 1). More particularly, in 2000, 12,500,000 foreign tourists visited the country, made 46,636,293 overnight stays and spent US$ 10,061,200 mn. Of the arrivals mentioned hereabove, 90 per cent came from Greater Europe, of which 76.2 per cent from member states of the European Union.

Foreign tourist arrivals in Greece account for almost 3.1 per cent of the European tourist traffic and 1.8 per cent of the international tourist traffic.

Table—10.1 shows (see on page 206) the number of tourist arrivals in Greece, Europe and worldwide, during the period 1950 - 2000. More specifically, we can easily see therefrom that throughout the decade of 2000, foreign tourist arrivals showed a total increase of 40.88 per cent, while in the decade of 1990, total increase rose to 76.63 per cent.

DIAGRAM 10.1

Arrivals of Foreign Tourists in Greece (1990-1999)

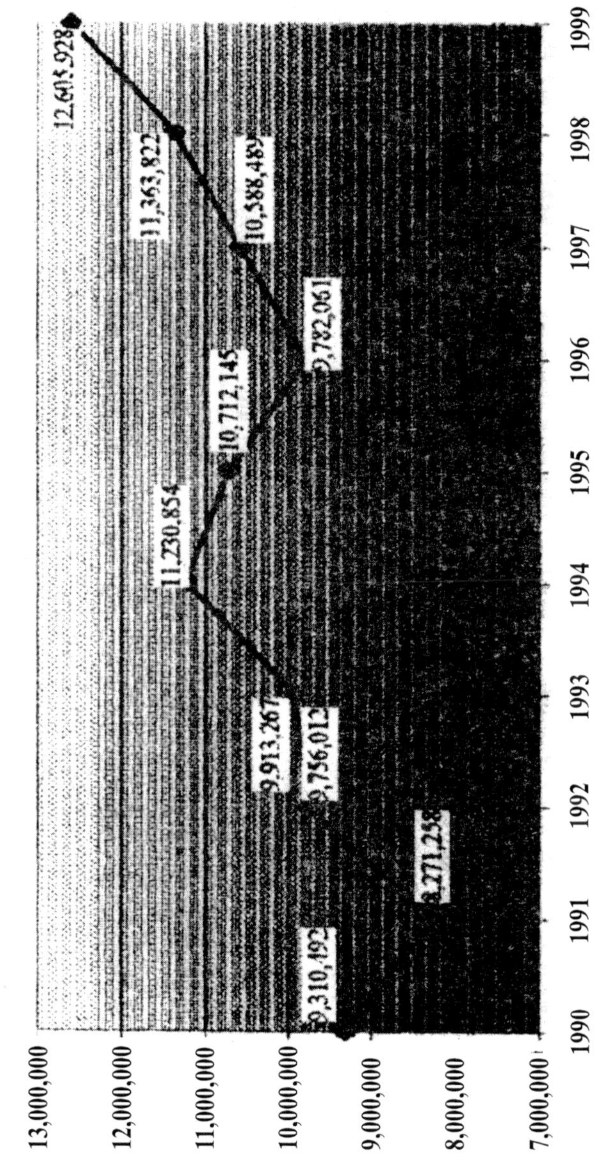

***Source*: Greek National Tourism Organization. National Statistical Department of Greece.**

Table—10.1 Arrivals of foreign tourists in Greece, Europe and worldwide, per decade (1950 - 2000)

Decade	*Greece (thou.)*	*Modification (%) per decade*	*Europe (mn)*	*Modification (%) per decade*	*Worldwide (MN)*	*Modification (%) Per decade*
1950	33.3	-	16.8	-	25.3	-
1960	399.4	1,098.33	50.4	199.70	69.3	174.11
1970	1,609.2	302.87	117.3	133.01	165.8	139.25
1980	5,271.1	227.56	188.3	60.50	286.0	72.50
1990	9,310.0	76.63	282.7	50.13	457.2	59.86
2000	12,5000.0	40.88	402.7	42.44	696.7	52.38

Sources: WTO, Compendium of Tourism Statistics.

DIAGRAM 10.2

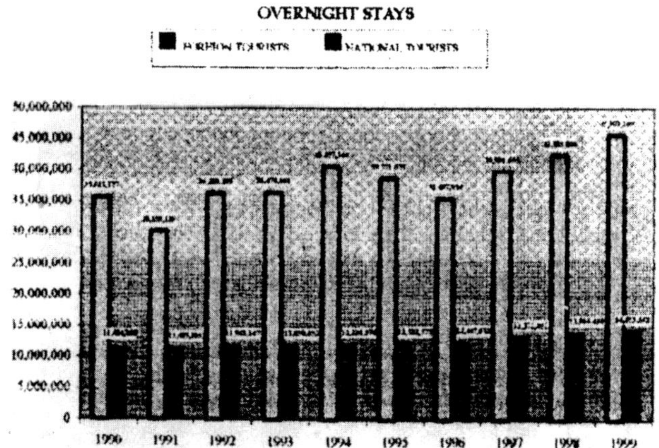

***Source*:** **Greek National Tourism Organisation**

The costs of outgoing tourism account for 25 per cent of official incoming tourism revenues. In 1999, outgoing costs amounted to US$ 2.3bn.

Diagram 10.2 shows the total number of overnight stays in the period 1990-2000; the number is on the rise. Foreign tourists overnight stays have increased by 30 per cent and those of domestic tourists have been steadily increasing.

Diagram 10.3 shows the evolution of hotel infrastructure (hotel units and beds).

In Diagram 3 we can see that during the period 1990 - 2000 the slight increase of hotel units corresponds to an average increase, by 4 per cent, of the number of beds.

Based on the geographic distribution of hotels, it is evident that tourist activity is mainly concentrated in a limited number of regions (Tsartas - Lagos, 2002). More specifically, the islands of South Aegean and the island of Creta have half of all overnight stays. The Ionian islands, Central Macedonia and Attica follow with smaller tourist shares. The concentration of both the tourist traffic and the

DIAGRAM 10.3

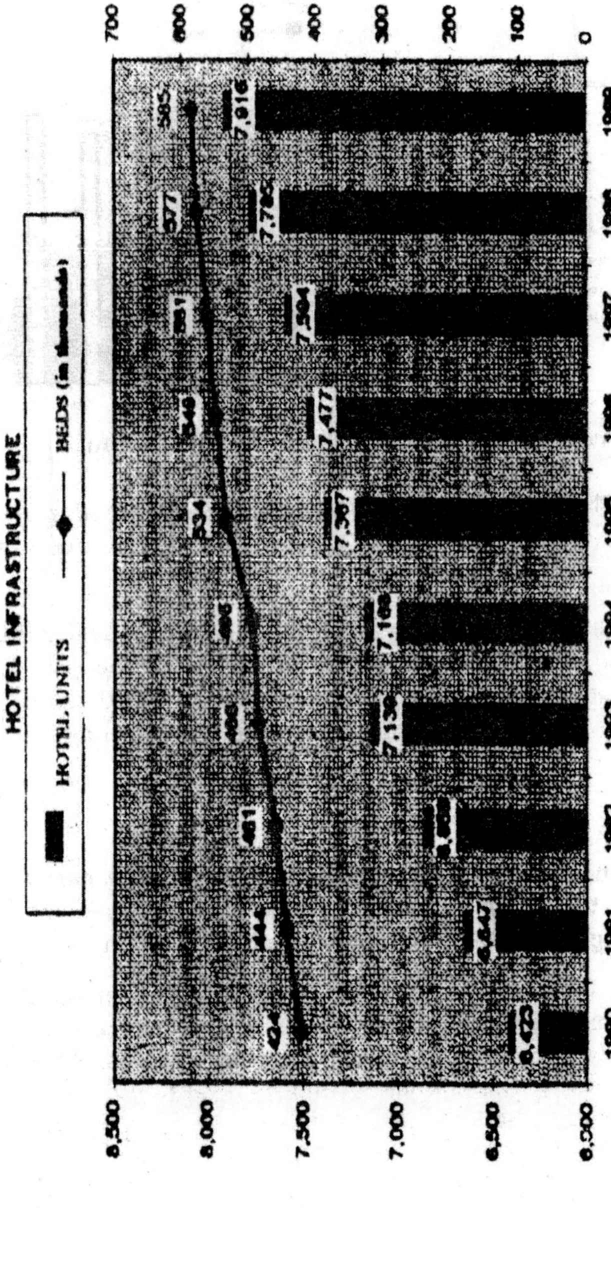

Sources: Greek National Tourism Organization. Hellenic Chamber of Hotels

hotel infrastructure in specific geographic areas can be easily understood since the said areas enjoy numerous advantages (i.e. tourist, commercial, generic as well as special infrastructures) which transform them in turn, in poles of attraction for tourists.

In terms of what is being offered in Greece, the specialized infrastructures/facilities indicated herebelow are also providing support to tourist activity:

- 5 Conference Centers with a capacity of 2,400 have received GNTO's special badge. 9 new Congress Centers have been placed under the new law for development, another 12 have received approval by GNTO for their architectural plans and finally, 9 more have received approval for their feasibility study to be placed under the said law or not.
- 453 congress halls and rooms with a capacity ranging between 10 and 1000+ attendants in 150 hotels operating under NGTO's special badge.
- 5 gold fields (of which 4 with 18 holes and one of 9 holes), with one more golf field being placed under the law for development.
- 2 centers of thalassotherapy operating under NGTO's badge and one more under construction and 5 more such centers with their feasibility studies already approved by NGTO.
- 1 modern thalassotherapy center and another one with its feasibility study already approved by NGTO.
- 4 private marinas and hotel-owned harbors (under construction).
- 5 international airports and 31 other airports wherefrom domestic and charter flights are made. Of the total number of 68 islands enjoying full tourist infrastructure, 26 have an airport.
- 70 ports.

The above data indicate the degree of development of Greek tourism, a development which positively affects various aspects of the socio-economic activity in a mostly crucial way. Such influence bears on the economic sector (i.e. increase of national income, increase of employment, higher living costs), the social sphere (i.e. higher living standards, better lifestyles), the cultural sphere (development of folk art), and last but not least, the environment (Lagos 1995, Coccosis and Tsartas 2001).

The strengths and weaknesses of Greek tourism are outlined in the table herebelow (Table—10.2).

Table—10.2 Strengths and Weaknesses of Greek Tourism

Strengths (S)	Weaknesses (W)
Abundance and variety of natural resources (island complexes, natural ecosystems, forests, rich and rare flora and fauna, different regions of particular natural beauty) which allow for tourism on a 12 month basis.	Strong seasonal character (during the summer season)
	Aggravation of the natural environment mainly due to the development of tourist activities without observing any measures for the protection of the environment.
Important destination of tourists, worldwide (high ranking both in terms of arrivals and revenues).	Reduction of the competitiveness of the tourist product - high dependence on organized holiday tourism which is first and foremost based on travel costs (low package price and low exchange yield)
Paramount historical as well as cultural heritage combined with modern cultural output.	Change of the cultural character of local societies in particular

(Contd...)

	The Greek tourist product is not diversified
Tourism plays very important role in regional development (i.e. keeps local population from immigrating, contributes to new jobs, helps economic revival)	Imbalanced development of the different regions of the country.
Hosting of the Olympic Games of 2004; hosting of the Cultural Olympics	Significant lack of infrastructures and superstructures (transports, congress halls, installations for special forms of tourism etc)
Positive contribution of the Law for Development in the upgrading of hotel units and the establishment of facilities for special forms of tourism	High rate of medium- and low- class beds as well as high dependency on low prices to ensure full capacity
During the last decade there has been a growth of significant businesses, in all sectors, which offer diversified products for the attraction of demanding tourists or tourists of specialized interests.	The majority of tourist units (>95%) are medium and small enterprises with low marketing capabilities, insufficient exploitation of new technologies and inefficient financial management
Rich output of traditional products on both primary and secondary levels	Insufficient and non specialized human resources

***Source*: 3rd Community Support Framework 2000**

From the table hereabove it becomes evident that Greece enjoys comparative advantages in natural and cultural sources, in infrastructures and superstructures which shape the country's tourist image and support entrepreneurship in the tourism sector. These elements have traditionally attracted tourists and created revenues, brought in exchange and established job openings. However, in more recent years there has been a gradual decrease of the competitive character of the Greek tourist product, a growing dependence on mass tourism, loss of high end tourist exchange, problems in hotel business viability and a difficulty to adjust in and exploit new technological possibilities.

Tourist Policies with Consequences on the Operation of the Hotel Sector

The tourist strategy for the period 2000-2006 provides for both broader and narrower goals, which have been incorporated in the 3rd Community Support Framework of the European Union: (3rd Community Support Framework 2000: 61):

The broader goals are the following:

Upgrading demand by means of achieving visibility in new markets and market segments on the one hand, by means of offering new forms of tourism in order to attract different types of tourists on the other hand. Diversifying the Greek tourist product through the provision of better services and the availability of enhanced tourist offers.

The narrower, *i.e.* more specific, goals are as follows:

- modernization of quality of the existing tourism businesses and facilities as well as differentiation and enrichment of their product
- establishment of a diversified tourism offer of high quality
- development of specialized and alternative types of tourism
- enhancement of the competitiveness of all the medium and small companies of the sector
- enhancement of the tourism sector's contribution to the creation and increase of employment
- better connection between the tourism sector, the sectors of traditional products and modern Greek cultural output.

The broader and narrower goals are further specialized and aim at the following:

- Exploitation of the projects financed under the 2nd Community Support Framework and completion of their operational characteristics, under the broader efforts to upgrade and enrich the Greek tourism offer.
- Exploitation of the comparative advantages of the regions in view of diversifying the tourism product through alternative form of tourism which are finely tuned to the physical and cultural resources of mountainous, border and island regions.
- Upgrade and diversification of demand for developed areas, so that the latter are less and less exposed to demand fluctuations and the seasonal character of tourism.

The goals described hereabove will be implemented on the basis on protection of the environmental and cultural landscape as well as on the principles of sustainable development, according to the relevant European Community directives and the national commitments of Greece (EE1993, WTO 1993).

More specifically, the Ministry for Development, which is responsible for drawing up the tourism policy, has elaborated the general framework for the tourism development policy and the mechanisms for the implementation thereof:

- A reassessment of the tourism investment map of Greece, with first priorities given on rational tourism development and elimination of weaknesses born from the current regulatory landscape (modification of certain aspects of the Law for development, establishment of new hotel units of higher category—luxury—and redress of the status of saturation wherever it applies)
- Development of the program for the public owned tourism property in order to achieve the broader goals

in general and support the organization of the Olympic Games to be held in 2004

- Conclusion of a memorandum between the Ministry for Development and the Organization "Athens 2004" for the prompter implementation of the Olympic Projects, relating to the modernization of tourism infrastructure on the shores of Attica (marinas, beaches, theme parks), the establishment of integrated tourism facilities at the periphery (Creta, Rhodes, Peloponnese, Phthiotida, Chalkidiki) as well as the development of spa related products at such resorts as Edipsos, Ypati, Kam. Vourla, Caiafa, Nigrita, Methana etc.
- Introduction of licensing processes similar to those for the Olympic projects for GNTO's property development
- Establishment of a General Tourism Secretariat at the Ministry for Development and transfer of responsibilities thereto from GNTO
- Establishment of Tourism Departments at the periphery
- GNTO will focus more on commercial ads and visibility, training, certification and monitoring
- Establishment of a state of the art Conference Hall with a capacity of 10,000 attendants at the installations of the Eastern Terminal
- Adoption of the star-based classification system for hotels
- Submission of Athens's candidacy for the organization of the World Tourism Congress to be held in 2003
- GNTO's call for papers for the drafting of a special marketing plan for the broader area of Attica
- Provision of support to the tourism entrepreneurship by means of the various projects funded by the European Union

- Upgrade of tourism education by making better use of Community funds. To this end a number of initiatives have been undertaken for the construction of a Balkan Centre for Tourism Education in Thrace and a call for interest has been submitted for the acquisition of 4,500 sq. m. in Athens in view of this modern educational center.

The above general framework establishes the short term policy for the Greek tourism and more particularly the hotel sector. This framework includes a number of structural suggestions which will contribute to the new image of the Greek tourism product in view of the Olympic Games of 2004.

In order to implement the goals of its policy, tourism, along with certain other activities, has ensured funding amounting to approximately US$ 2 bn for the period 2001-2006.

The Hotel Market Sector in Greece

Tourism businesses in Greece can be distinguished in the following three categories (Tsartas - Lagos, 2002):

Main hotel businesses, which include all kinds of hotel units distributed under a classification systems. In the first category, in 2001, there were 8,284 hotel businesses with 390,484 rooms and a total capacity of 608,140 beds (73 beds per hotel unit).

Secondary hotel businesses which include all kinds of complementary accommodation (rooms and apartments to let, camping). In this category, in 2001, there were 28,000 units of rooms and apartments; these units are small businesses with 15 - 20 rooms. Additionally there have been 320 camping facilities with 28,504 sites, accommodating 43,288 campers.

Other tourism businesses in the tourism industry (travel offices, transportation offices, rent-a-car offices, restaurants, charter offices). In this category in 2001 there were 8,893 businesses, broken down into 4,500 travel offices, 738 tourism transportation offices, 1,455 rent-a-car companies,

200 charter companies, approximately 2,000 licensed tour operators, working as free lancers. More than 98 per cent of this category's businesses are small, employing less than 10 persons each.

Table—10.3 Greek Demand Indices (2001)

		Greece				
		Units		**Beds**		**Av. Capacity (beds)**
Category						
AA (5*)		90		37,936		422
A (4*)		816		155,719		191
A (3*)		1,543		146,214		95
C (2*)		4,189		215,146		51
D (1*)		1,083		36,973		34
E (1*)		536		16,152		29
	Total	8,284	22,6%	608,140	55,9%	73
	Other accommod.	28,000	76,5%	450,000	41.4%	16
Camping	320	0,9%	43,228	2,7%		89
Total Accommodation and Camping		28,320		493,228		16
Grand Total		36,604	100%	1,101,368	100%	30

***Source*: Greek National Tourism Organization**

Table—10.3 presents the total number of legal tourism accommodations under each category, along with the number of beds. The number of tourists that can be simultaneously accommodated amounts to 1,101,368. In addition to that there are 27,435 businesses with 414,916 beds, which have received GNTO's badge and illegal accommodation with 100,000 to 150,000 beds, which serves tourism.

Unlike in most other countries, in Greece hotels classified in 6 categories are (Lux, (5*) A (4*), B (3*), C (2*), D and E class (1*)) according to criteria which relate to the hotels' construction and not to the quality of their services.

Hotel unit distribution per the above system for 2001 was as follows: 6.3 per cent of beds are luxury hotels (AA) or 5*, 25.6 per cent in Class A' or 4*, 24 per cent in Class B' or 3* and 44.3 per cent in lower classes (C,D,E) or 2* and 1* (Diagram 10.4).

DIAGRAM 10.4

Distribution of the Hotel Force Per Category (2001)

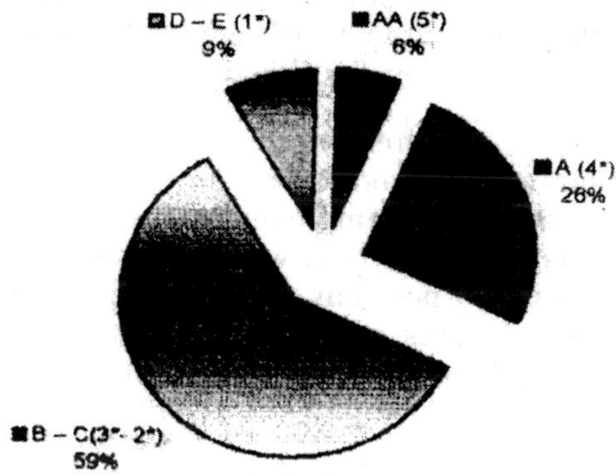

70 per cent of Greece's hotel force is located in areas identified as "saturated" or "areas of tourism development control"; this generates additional problems at local and regional levels since a lot of tourism areas have exceeded their tourism caring capacity, something that necessitates structural modifications in the tourism policies followed.

The hotel market sector is characterized by small capacity, since 58.9 per cent of units have 50 or less beds and 24.9 per cent have between 51 - 100 beds. With more than 300 beds we find 290 units or 3.5 per cent of the total.

Table—10.4 Distribution of Hotel Units Per Number of Beds (2001)

Number of beds	Number of Hotels Units	Rate (%)
Up to 50 beds	4,879	58.9
51-100 beds	2,063	24.9
101- 300 beds	1,052	12.7
300+ beds	290	3.5
Total	**8,284**	**100**

Source: Hellenic Chamber of Hotels, 04/2002

The average fullness per year of hotel accommodation in Greece for 2001 amounted to 65 per cent, while it ranged between 55 - 63.5 per cent for the period 1990 - 2000.

Lastly, based on the time of operation of different accommodations as well as other conditions, it is estimated that 35 per cent of people employed in the hotel sector works on a full year basis, 40 per cent works between 5 to 8 months and the remaining 25 per cent works for only 3 months. The above mentioned figures are relating to employment in the tourist sector, which represents 7.25 per cent of the country's workforce.

The hotel sector is comprised of a lot of small, family run companies which offer limited scope of services, have unsophisticated organization and management while at the same time suffering from fierce competition amongst them as well as narrow margins of profit.

Lastly, one of the most important problems of the hotel sector is the lack of quality in the provision of services, a factor which results in irregular customer satisfaction indices and low levels of competitiveness.

Structural Problems of the Hotel Sector and Characteristics of the Hotel Business Management in Greece

Despite the forecasts of the World Tourism and Traveling Council (WTTC:1995) for a steady increase in international tourism (arrivals and exchange revenues), Greece's image is not similarly promising. Greece must resolve paramount structural problems which hinder the country's efforts to upgrade on the one hand the management of hotel businesses and achieve on the other hand a well balanced tourist development.

Competition that has existed between Mediterranean countries has become fiercer because their tourism product is not diversified enough. Therefore, it is only in terms of lower prices that tourists can be attracted. In this tourism market compete, in addition to the European countries (i.e. Italy, Spain), new countries from Northern Africa (Morocco, Tunisia). The Mediterranean Sea is trying to maintain her leading position in tourist preferences, ahead of other micro-peripheries such as Indonesia and the Caribbean. In the competitive environment described hereabove, Greece cannot be very efficient because of the inelasticity of her adhesion to the Euro zone (Papatheodorou 1999).

Foreign tourists overnight stays are not regularly on the rise. This is due to a number of occasionally political situations (i.e. war in Yugoslavia) which have put off tourists from visiting the country, kept hotel fullness to low levels and translated in limited increase of tourist exchange.

Illegal hotel accommodation has grown and resulted in serious dysfunctions in the whole hotel sector (unfair competition, low quality in services).

The average capacity of hotel accommodation is 73 beds per hotel. This capacity is deemed small to explore economies of scale and ensure adequate service quality levels. The majority of hotels fall under category B (or 4*), followed by hotels in category C (3*) and D (1*). The small capacity of hotels on the one hand and the concentration of hotels in category B does not follow the trends identified in competitive countries.

The problems hotel business face (financing, professional specialization, high operation costs, narrow margins of profit etc.) are basically due to their small capacity which poses threats to their very viability.

The seasonal character is also another factor hindering improvements in quality, and keeping production costs of the Greek tourism product high. This character has a negative influence on the product's competitiveness and extends on all peripheral tourist businesses, which operate where and when there is significant hotel capacity.

The existing competition has become fiercer and led a lot of businesses in acquisitions mergers and different co-operations, such as franchising. However this trend of increasing hotel capacity is considered weak. A verticalization with other segments of tourism chain is witnessed in limited cases (i.e. cruising ships, tour-operating, sight-seeing etc).

The different regional characteristics of Greek hotels are related to their location (islands, sea shores, mountainous regions) and the development patterns identified in each region.

From a relevant study it has been found that hotels in the Mediterranean region (Greece, Spain, Italy, Portugal) do not have high level management, the local branches of international chains being an exception to the rule (E.C. 1997). This means that hotel conditions are similar in all these countries and their problems are due both to their inherent characteristics and more generally to the policy followed in the tourism sector.

The structural problems of hotels mentioned hereabove impede the introduction of yield management. These problems fall in two specific categories: in the first, problems relate to the internal characteristics of the hotels and they are a direct result of their operating mentality; in the second category we identify problems relating to infrastructure, competition, competition in relation to regulatory frameworks (Patsouratis 2002 : 165).

Tourism Policy Measures for the Development of the Hotel Sector

In order to face the structural problems of the sector, a number of strategic initiatives must be undertaken within the broader 3rd Community Support Framework, which will enhance Greek tourism internationally. These initiatives must include specific measures which will help hotels adopt yield management approaches. Amongst the said measures, the following are necessary:

- Technological upgrade of hotels. Introduction of IT systems which will familiarize small and medium businesses with modern technology and help them adopt digital technology. Use of advanced, environment friendly technologies (i.e. energy saving).
- Upgrade of hotel service quality and maintenance at high levels, through integrated modernization of the business. Quality throughout the tourism chain. Emphasis on programs and motivations which will improve service quality through the appropriate types of management (ISO etc). Promotion of tourism excellence in businesses.
- Reduction of the seasonal character of tourism activities and financing of domestic tourism schemes in order to create tourism demand during winter months.
- Promotion of Greece as tourism destination by means of modern marketing methods, appropriate commercialization and promotion of tourism products or packages.
- Revision of tourism education and training. Planning and development of a program of environmental education which will aim at both tourism entrepreneurs and the inhabitants of tourist regions.
- Better stuffing, organization and operation of tourism entities, emphasizing on small and medium

businesses which are the majority of such types of businesses in Greece.

- Increase of the medium capacity of the Greek tourism business, through mergers and acquisitions, with a view to achieving economies of scale and better efficiency in performance rates. Introduction of strategic alliances between tourism companies in order to improve their financial indices.
- Differentiation of tourism incentives and development framework as per the competitive advantage of each region and according to the needs, potentialities and identify of each tourism destination.
- Involvement of the local authorities in undertaking initiatives which will have devolve monitoring and control from the center to the periphery.

All the above measures, integrated in the current tourism policy will enhance efficiency and competitiveness, either directly or indirectly and will encourage hotel managements to adopt new, efficient management tools.

Conclusions—Findings

Greece, in her capacity as a tourist destination, has endless potentialities to diversify and strengthen her position in the international market, making the most of her unique comparative advantages in relation to other Mediterranean tourist destinations.

In order to be efficient, Greek tourist policies must be conformant with the goals set by the European Union and connected operationally to the domestic processes of development of each region of the country (Konsolas, Papadaskalopoulos, Plaskovitis, 2002: 8-10).

The strategic goals of the current Greek tourist policy are in line with and part of the broader strategic framework set by the European Union and relate to the improvement of the production basis of each and every tourist destination, the balanced and sustainable tourist development, the enhancement of competitiveness and the quality upgrade of tourist related services on offer.

Greece is described as "low cost destination" or "mass tourism destination" since in comparison to her competitors —the country has low levels of incoming exchange per overnight stay, small domestic tourism market, deficiency in overnight stays and the average size of hotel units, deficiency in making the most of her accommodation force, deficiency in providing tourist related training to her work force active in the sector as well as deficiency in adequate professionalism and mentality. All these weaknesses are due to the structural problems of the hotel sector and hinder badly the introduction and application of efficient hotel management. Despite these problems, Greece enjoys a good number of comparative advantages which place her ahead of all her competitor destinations in terms of tourist exchange per capita, and this, against the odds of the seasonal character of the Greek tourist activities and the insufficient visibility and commercial campaigning of the country's tourist product. (Konsolas 2002: 129-130).

It is proposed to complement the tourism policy framework currently under implementation with a series of measures which will aim at enhancing hotel management and create competitive advantages for the sector. Offering high quality hotel services requires the introduction of changes in the ways of organizing and managing hotels; this will be achieved through yield management strategies, prioritizing on pricing policies, asset and sales management; additionally, new strategic orientations (i.e. alliances, mergers and acquisitions) will have to be taken into account in parallel with all the other priorities, in order to help the hotel industry integrate into the international tourist reality.

REFERENCES

Coccosis Har. and P. Tsartas (2001) "*Viable Tourist Development and the Environment*". EXANTAS, Athens.

European Commission, (1997), *"Yield Management in Small and Medium—Sized Enterprises in the Tourism Industry"*.

European Union, (1993), "Europe - Environment : Goal: Sustainability" Number C 138/1-2-93.

Konsolas I. (2002),"The Cmpetitive *Advantage of Greece"*. Ashgate.

Konsolas N., A. Papadaskalopulos and I. Plaskovitis (2002) *"Regional Development in Greece"*. Springer.

Lagos D. (1995), "Growth of Tourism in Greece and Environmental Protection" in *EAST-WEST European Environmental Research*. V. 1 pp 105-101.

Ministry for Development : 3rd Community Support Framework 2000-2006

Patsouratis B. (2002), *"Competitiveness of the Greek Tourism Sector"*, Research Institute for Tourism.

Papatheodorou, A., (1999), The Demand for International Tourism in the Mediterranean Region, *Applied Economics*.

Tsartas P. and D. Lagos, (2002), "Small Hotel Firm in the Tourism and Hospitality Sector of Greece", Conference Proceedings of International Conference *"Small Firms in the Tourism and Hospitality Sectors"* 12-13/09/2002, Leeds Metropolitan University

WTO, (1993), *"Sustainable Tourism Development: A Guide for Local Planners"* Madrid, Spain.

WTO, (2000), *"Tourism Vision 2020"* , Vol. 1-6. Madrid, Spain.

WTO , (2001), "Compendium of Tourism Statistics", Madrid , Spain.

WTTC (World Travel and Tourism Council), (1995),.*"Travel and Tourism's Economic Perspective"*. Brussels, Belgium.

11

Using Revised Business Process Reengineering Methodology as an Improvement Tool for Tourism

Ian Bickerstaff and Peter Bolan***

Introduction

The tourism product is an important ingredient to the overall economic performance of many nations and different countries have struggled to capitalise on the potential that could be realised if tourism was fully exploited. These problems have become even more pronounced in recent years in light of the threat of terrorism and policy makers across the globe have attempted to put in place measures that seek to eradicate the difficulties associated with achieving a country's full tourism potential. This paper seeks to outline how nations could use a business improvement tool, namely Business Process Reengineering, as a way of systematically improving the provision of the tourism product.

* Lecturer in Economics, Accounting Strategic Development and Small Business Enterprise in School of Hotel Leisure and Tourism, University of Ulster, Northern Ireland.

** Lecturer and Course Director in Travel and Tourism Management, University of Ulster, Northern Ireland.

Business Process Reengineering achieved widespread acclaim throughout the early 1990's and was embraced by many organisations who used its ideas as a way to improve on business performance. After the initial citing of many success stories critics however began to focus on the shortcomings of the approach. This lead to its widespread abandonment. Recent studies however have suggested that the BPR methodology was not flawed but that any shortcomings were attributed to the way that it was implemented. Managers adopting the approach did not fully embrace all the requirements needed for a successful outcome but left out strands that they felt could be ignored. This attitude was diametrically opposed to the fundamentals of BPR methodology which advocated a clean slate approach to organisational change.

In light of these recent studies this paper proposes that the traditional BPR methodology be revisited and a tailor made methodology for tourism be developed. This methodology could then be applied to countries that have experienced difficulties in achieving the full GDP contribution that tourism could potentially achieve.

What is Business Process Reengineering ?

Business Process Reengineering has attracted considerable attention over the last decade since its introduction (Hammer 1990, Hammer and Champy 1993).The approach was widely embraced by senior management in many organisations as the "Holy Grail" that would save them from the onslaught of globalisation, increased competition and rapidly changing technology. In recent years however there has been a raging debate on how useful the phenomena has actually been with many examples cited in which the adoption of the approach has actually made things worse for organisations. There exists a plethora of views in relation to BPR ranging from its supporters, through to those who believe it can work, but only if conditions are met, to those who have described it as an expensive fad.

BPR involves radically redesigning key processes in an attempt to improve organisational performance in areas such as quality speed and cost. The concept seeks to provide managers with a business model that will reinvent their organisations, creating one that has the potential to be

> "...flexible enough to adjust quickly to changing market conditions, lean enough to beat any competitors price, innovative enough to keep its products and services technologically fresh, and dedicated enough to deliver maximum quality and customer service." (Hammer and Champy 1995 pp7)

BPR questions the usefulness of fundamental business concepts such as specialisation, whose roots can be traced back to Adam Smith's seminal book, The Wealth of Nations (1776). This approach advocated the division of labour whereby efficiency was created as a result of individuals specialising in individual tasks rather than attempting to act as "Jack of all Trades". This thinking was further developed by Henry Ford and has formed the basis for the traditional divisional structure of the firm, with the organisation being set up along functional lines. Although this type of structure had the advantage of making jobs themselves simpler, it had the drawback of complicating the overall process. This resulted in inefficiency as a direct result of the problems associated with co-ordinating people and attempting to combine their work tasks. Such difficulties lead to the need for bureaucracy resulting in diseconomies of scale. This was diametrically opposed to what benefits the system had intended to provide.

Coupled with this was the fact that these traditional work methods were developed in order to meet needs for a completely different environment as is evident today. Tasks which individuals carried out were not performed with the aim of meeting customer needs, but were completed in order to meet the organisations own demands. A perfect example of this was the assembly line production techniques carried out by Henry Ford where the customer could chose any colour of car they liked, as long as it was black. Such an attitude towards customers cannot exist in today's turbulent environment where the customers needs and desires must be at the forefront of all organisations if they are to survive.

Business Process Re-engineering recognises these limitations of the traditional organisational model and promotes the view that organisations need to look beyond and across the traditional functional arrangements, concentrating instead on the organisations' core processes.

Hammer and Champy (1995) define reengineering as

"The fundamental rethinking and radical redesign of business processes to achieve dramatic improvements in critical, contemporary measures of performance such as cost, quality, service and speed."

This definition identifies four key areas in that organisations need to examine if successful reengineering is to take place.

1. ***Fundamental:*** This requires organisations to ask the most basic questions about themselves and how they operate in an attempt to force them to question their underlying rules and assumptions.
2. ***Radical:*** If the organisation is to truly reengineer all existing structures and procedures must be disregarded and replaced with completely new ones. This is perhaps one of the most difficult concepts for organisations to carry out, as an attempt to implement superficial change will not be conducive to a successful reengineering exercise.
3. ***Dramatic:*** The reengineering process must seek to make dramatic improvements in organisational performance. True reengineering does not simply make small or marginal improvements, but rather aims to achieve substantial results.
4. ***Processes:*** This is the fundamental concept of reengineering according to Hammer and Champy whereby processes should form the heart of the organisation and businesses should be managed around these processes. A process according to these

authors is a collection of activities that turn inputs into an output that is of value to the customer.

Processes are vital to the organisation because it is these that create the value-added product. Traditional functional organisation structures and the division of labour result in individuals, and indeed individual departments, losing sight of the fundamental objective of the organisation. Although individual tasks within the process are vital, they are of limited use if they are not performing in a manner that leads to customer satisfaction.

Peppard and Rowland (1995), define BPR as

"... an improvement philosophy. It aims to achieve step improvements in performance by redesigning the processes through which an organisation operates, maximising their value-added content and minimising everything else. This approach can be applied at an individual process level or to the whole organisation."

This definition also reiterates the importance of redesigning processes as a method of improving performance. In addition to this it also highlights the importance of value as perceived by the customer whereby it is essential that the redesigned processes strive to magnify the value added as seen by the customer. Therefore the customers' needs and expectations need to be known in order to ensure that the outcomes of these redesigned processes are in tandem with their requirements.

Macdonald (1995) emphasises the need to adopt an approach that creates major improvements in the organisation, as it is believed that continuous incremental improvement is not enough to meet the challenge of the global market place. In order to achieve these improvements, organisations need to uncover the key processes that drive an organisation's performance and customer satisfaction and completely redesign these processes using a "clean slate approach"

Talwar (1993) provides a simple definition of BPR as

"rethink, restructure and streamline the business structure processes, methods of working, management systems and external relationships"

It is evident from the literature that there is not one single concise definition of what business process reengineering actually is, although all definitions exhibit the common factor of the need to identify the core processes used by the organisation. Once these processes have been identified and understood they may be reengineered. This will require the organisation to examine its' organisation structure from a different angle. Traditional organisations are structured vertically in functional departments whereas a process-based approach will run horizontally through departments.

BPR and Information Technology

Today, many organisations now see the value and benefit of using information communication technology (ICT) to improve their business and its competitiveness. However, keeping existing business processes intact and just using ICT to speed them up is no longer seen as being enough.

Developments in information technology and the role it has to play in the operation of the organisation have had an impact on business process reengineering. Alavi and Yoo (1995) take account of this in their definition

> *"Business reengineering induced by information technology is being offered as a paradigm to redesign processes and to achieve dramatic gains in productivity and quality"*

Towers (1995) reiterates the role which technology can play in aiding the possibility of a successful BPR initiative. Information technology not only removes unnecessary tasks allowing people to get on with what they are supposed to but it also provides a means by which new ways of working can emerge.

Hammer and Champy (1996) however stress that care must be taken when implementing information technology as a means of assisting a BPR initiative as there is the danger that the adoption of such measures may simply reinforce old methods and work practices. Therefore those involved in the project need to examine ways in which information technology can allow the organisation to do things which they are not already doing rather than looking for ways of improving what is already being done. Thus the real power of information technology is the fact that it can act as an enabler allowing organisations to break old rules and create new ways of working. In order for this to be truly effective, it is imperative that the organisation is not only aware of current developments in technology but that it is looking to what future developments may take place. This allows the organisation to be prepared in advance for new emerging technological developments, ensuring that processes can be developed which will be able to cope with future innovations.

These points are clarified by Zairi (1995) who stresses that BPR initiatives are not necessarily dependant on information technology but that they can be used as a

> "powerful enabler in the redesign of organisational processes."

Developments in information technology (like eCommerce) and the role they have to play in the operations of organisations has had an impact on BPR. This was recognised as far back as 1995 by Alavi and Yoo when they offered this definition

> *"Business reengineering induced by information technology is being offered as a paradigm to redesign processes and to achieve gains in productivity and quality"*.

This view is supported by authors such as Certo (1997) who believes that one important reason for reengineering is the need to integrate computerised production and information systems. Not only can such technology-change be expensive, but it is very difficult to accomplish successfully in a piecemeal incremental approach. It should be an integral part of BPR.

This view is reiterated by Louvieris, (2002),

> *"Simply automating ineffective processes cannot remove their inherent deficiencies. Most companies are waking up to the fact that business as usual, in all likelihood, can be a recipe for corporate death"*

It is further postulated that new reengineering opportunities emerge from immediate access to customers and suppliers via the internet (Finklestein,2002).The development of eBusiness has radically modified how transactions are made, how customers are managed and how a competitive edge is achieved. Those who advocate eBusiness argue that the 'old' approaches and methods of adding value to customers are no longer sufficient. Obliteration of wasteful activities, non-added value functions, unprofitable practices etc is a logical way to proceed with IT-based innovation (Zairi, 2001).

Thus an organisation wishing to redefine their business scope by embracing eCommerce will need to undertake BPR.

How Does Business Process Reengineering Work?

Towers (1995) suggests that four main approaches to BPR have emerged. These range from the big bang approach whereby an organisation attempts to reengineer all aspects of the organisation to the pilot method where the project is tested within a controlled environment. Other approaches include a low risk technique where an existing project is examined and opportunities identified where BPR may be feasible. This may result in a pilot approach being undertaken. The final approach identified which in many respects may be the easiest is that described as the Greenfield site where new businesses are created, discarding the old problems that existed in the past.

The Criticisms of BPR Initiatives

Despite the wide number of efforts that have been made by organisations globally, many end up in failure. Hammer and Champy(1995) estimate that as many as 50 per cent-70 per cent of organisations that attempt reengineering do not achieve the dramatic results intended.

Hall, Rosenthal and Wade (1993) also highlight similar scenarios where companies are successful in their attempts to reengineer individual business processes and are in fact successful in achieving improvements only to see overall results decline. Some suggestions offered for these phenomena are due to increased business unit costs and declining profits. Manganelli (1993) would support this suggesting that the success rate is very low with only four out of five reengineering programmes being successful.

However, we have to view such an approach with some caution. BPR is no business panacea and certainly no guarantee of success. In January 1995, a survey by Arthur D Little found that only a rather low 16 per cent of business executives were fully satisfied with BPR programmes. In addition figures quoted in the mid 1990's showed that at least 70 per cent of these projects were failing (Peltu, 1996). Even more startlingly, Hayward (1995) mentions estimates of successful BPR initiatives as being as low as 1%. This of course does not mean that BPR is bad, or the wrong approach to take for an organisation.

Byrne (1997) is even more critical in his discussion, outlining the high rates of dissatisfaction obtained by many firms pursuing popular management theories. Quoting from the 1997 annual Bain Survey[1], he describes Business Process Reengineering as being the least successful in terms of the numbers of respondents being dissatisfied with the results of the strategy.

Although there are many authors who are critical of the merits of reengineering, many have outlined reasons for their lack of success. Manganelli (1993) believes that despite the poor track record associated with BPR, if the concept is adopted correctly, it can help organisations to improve upon their performance. If this is to be achieved however, certain guidelines need to be followed. Projects need to be fully backed up by senior executives providing visible leadership and they must also include entire processes rather than functions. It is also important that organisations are careful in their selection of the processes that they are intending to reengineer and adopt a carefully selected methodology to help with its implementation. Hammer and Stanton (1995) have identified ten reasons why there has been a relatively low success rate in reengineering programmes.

1. High-level managerial misunderstanding;
2. Reengineering where it cannot fit
3. Spending too much time analysing existing processes
4. Lack of leadership
5. Timidity in redesign
6. From new process design to implementation
7. Reengineering slowly
8. Placing some aspects of business off limits
9. Adopting a conventional implementation style
10. Ignoring the concerns of employees

Mumford and Hendricks (1996) are more critical in their attack of the "disastrous experiment" blaming the tendency of firms to copy others, the absence of theory, and the use of consultants. They further suggest that many of the followers of BPR simply did not understand people and change management techniques and used the concept as an excuse for staff cuts. Tonnessen (2000) is also aware of the people element, suggesting that many projects have seen the human factor as a cost that may be reduced rather than as a resource that may be developed. In order to ensure success, it is believed that the human element needs to be given full consideration and that an environment is encouraged in which employee involvement is nurtured.

The Future of BPR

Despite the failures that are evident among many reengineering projects, many believe that the success stories make the approach a risk worth taking. (Sincoe(1998) Gunasekaran and Adebayo (2000). Verespej (1995) who claims that 80 per cent of companies that had engaged in significant reengineering efforts had met or exceeded their expectations reiterates these points. In addition to these supporters of BPR it is evident that even in cases were criticisms have been made, causes of the poor results have been identified, with the suggestion being made that the concept of BPR should not be discarded. At face value it is evident that there have been conflicting reports in relation to its usefulness, but in many cases, it is not the concept which is at fault, but the methodology used to implement it. One recurring criticism of BPR methodology that has been cited time and time again is the impact of the human element and how important a role that it has to play in determining the success or failure of an initiative.(Steininger, 1994, Bolman and Deal, 1997, Knights and McCabe, 1998, Evans et al., 1999). It is imperative therefore that this element is given full consideration during the implementation of any BPR initiative.

It has also been argued that one of the main downfalls of BPR initiatives has been related to the inability to understand a firms goals, not paying enough attention to personnel retraining, and not fully comprehending business processes. (Fernandes, Raja and Antony, 2001). Raja (1998) reiterates these points by outlining the importance of goal consideration in a BPR exercise. It is therefore postulated that far from being an outdated and unworkable idea, BPR has a role to play in performance improvement but the key factors outlined above must be given adequate consideration. These points become even more salient if we consider the widely held view that BPR can act as a suitable vehicle to embrace developments in information technology and in particular to enable e-business.

BPR/eCommerce/Tourism

There are many and varied examples around the globe of tourist destinations that are not fulfilling their full potential. In recent times especially we have seen the damage external events can cause to such tourist locations. Countries such as Eygpt, the former Yugoslavia, parts of the Middle East (Israel and Jordan), Northern Ireland and even the United States of America have seen their tourism industries suffer in the face of terrorism and negative media coverage. Other destinations have suffered due to increasing competition from new emerging destinations and changes in tourist preferences.

Bearing this in mind, the question of how such destinations could regain their tourism standing and strive towards their true tourism potential must be answered.

A possible avenue to explore is increased and more efficient use of ICT (information and communications technology) to improve tourism within the destination and market it effectively to those who provide ready potential tourist markets. The Internet and especially eCommerce has had an enormous impact on the way we do business and the tourism industry has been at the forefront of this. Indeed it has been this industry and the travel sector in particular that has led the way in effective, efficient utilisation of just what eCommerce can do. The 'no-frills' airline Easyjet are a prime example carrying out close to 90 per cent of their business online in 2001 and making extensive profits at a time when many other airlines were finding things difficult (www.eyefortravel.com, May 2002). Easyjet research on the effectiveness of their website through log file analysis also shows that almost everyone who visits their site buys a ticket compared to telephone enquiries where only about 1 in 6 callers actually make a purchase (Chaffey, 2002).

Organisations in the travel sector are therefore in a position to show the way forward for effective use of eBusiness. It is time now for NTO's (National Tourist Organisations) and other policy makers at a destination and regional level to catch up and focus on how such new measures can turn around and improve tourism as an industry within their geographical location. Organisations at this level are not by and large making the most of what eBusiness and other ICT aspects can do for their destinations. Individual organisations such as the airlines have shown much more progressive and effective vision and utilisation in this regard. This needs to be scaled up to destination level by those responsible for marketing and managing tourism.

Keeping existing business processes intact and just using ICT to 'speed' things up is not enough nor is making small changes here and there in a gradual way with a piece-meal approach. Simply automating practices which have already grown ineffective cannot turn things around nor remove inherent deficiencies. Business as usual for many suffering tourism destinations is no longer an option. Taking a more radical approach through the use of Business Process Reengineering (BPR) could be what is now called for.

New reengineering opportunities are now emerging from immediate access to customers and suppliers via the Internet (Finklestein, 2002). The whole premise of eBusiness is essentially to radically modify how transactions are made, how customers are managed and how a competitive edge is achieved. As far as many tourism destinations are now concerned obliteration of wasteful activities, non-added value functions, unprofitable practices etc is a logical way to proceed with ICT-based innovation (Zairi, 2001).

For an ailing tourism destination or indeed one which is simply not achieving its potential for whatever reason developing a more effective web presence and embracing eCommerce may well be the answer to remaining competitive in the ever changing world of global tourism. Rather than develop such aspects gradually and bring them in small stages into the way things are normally done such destinations should consider BPR, a key component of which these days is ICT.

There are already signs that again the Travel sector and the airlines in particular are at the forefront of utilising the latest innovations. mCommerce (mobile commerce) is now with us and will radically grow in importance in the coming years. This essentially means business using mobile technologies. In a sense any transaction enabled by 'wireless technology'. British Airways have already been exploring this new aspect. Through BA research they identified that 74 per cent of business travellers take a laptop computer with them, 36 per cent use a PDA (Personal Digital Assistant), with some 92 per cent using a mobile phone - a third of whom use SMS text messaging and 14 per cent making regular use of WAP services (Matthewson, 2002).

British Airways have launched a new eBusiness process designed to operate across other channels, expanding their already successful website which attracts over 3.5 million visits per month and generates around £1million in sales revenue per week (Matthewson, 2002, 12). BA are now targeting integrated digital television, WAP enabled mobile phones, SMS text messaging and PDA's (personal digital assistants). The development and integration of these newer channels are seen as critical to the success of BA's eBusiness strategy. For other tourism sectors and destinations introducing such crucial issues needs to be handled through the effective use of BPR to make the most of what can be achieved.

Tourists and travellers are constantly changing and have different information needs. Business travellers especially want to be able to change travel plans at a moments notice and have the latest tourism and travel information at their fingertips.

The tourism industry needs to cater to this much more. Not just the airlines but all sectors of the industry. eCommerce is here to stay and mCommerce is further developing these issues. NTO's and policy makers at destination level must give serious attention to current and evolving technology and its benefits and not just simply give such issues what might be described as 'token notice' without really exploring the full potential of what it can help achieve.

Tourism can be a vital tool for spurring economic growth and even development projects in a country but many destinations need to radically rethink the way things are done, make use of techniques such as BPR to turn themselves around and make the most of what they can really achieve.

Post September 11th many people worry about the effects of negative external events like terrorism much more so than ever before eg, in the USA the airline industry lost an estimated $1 billion to $2 billion in the first week after the tragedy alone (Goodrich, 2002), the airlines laid off thousands of staff, the hotel industry suffered the knock-on effects, major sporting events in the country suffered badly or were cancelled. All this brought about serious managerial implications for those involved in tourism.

While there is undoubtedly some cause for concern in relation to the future of the tourism industry the belief of these authors is that these hiccups can be overcome. Such events will affect certain destinations in a temporary way but people will always want to take a holiday, it's in our nature to do so. After such events travel patterns alter, some destinations suffer but others gain, tourists still travel, still take a holiday and globally the effects are not great. Some sectors such as the 'no-frills' airlines and the budget hotel sector have actually done better in the aftermath of September 11th due to changing travel habits. Destinations do have to figure all of this much more into their planning and through BPR they can do this, refocus how to improve their potential, look to alternative markets perhaps closer to home to avoid or at least reduce the impact of such external effects on the industry.

It is time for tourism destinations to make more of the opportunities from ICT based innovation and especially so the continually evolving open architecture environment of the internet coupled with developments in emerging areas such as mCommerce (mobile commerce) using BPR techniques to do so effectively and efficiently.

Using BPR Methodology as an Improvement Tool For Tourism

Based on the successes of properly implemented BPR initiatives and the opportunities that exist from ICT innovation, the authors believe that Business Process Reengineering has an important role to play in the development of tourism for nations experiencing difficulties in achieving their full potential. One realistic approach that could be used to achieve such goals would be to adapt the model outlined by Towers (1994), specifically relating it to the tourism industry. This ten step methodology would provide tourism policy makers with a framework that could be followed when seeking to develop the tourism product.

The First step that policy makers should consider is a definition of the goals to be achieved. These goals will be different for individual nations but there will exist a common

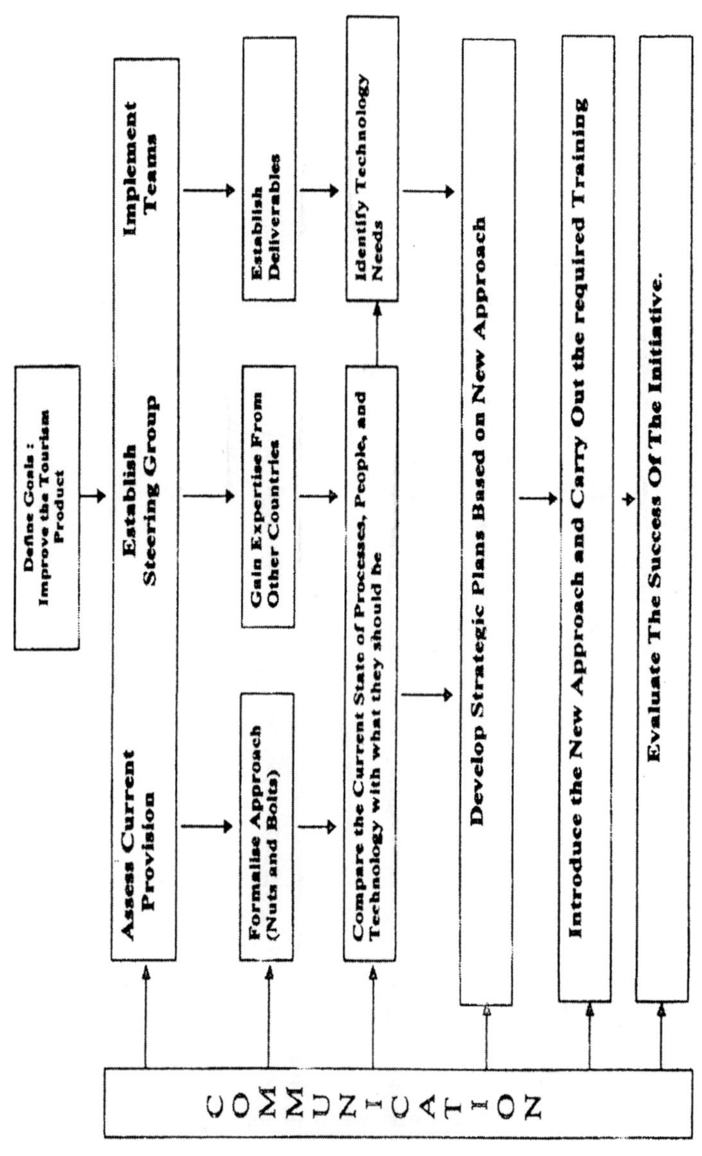
Define Goals :
Improve the Tourism
Product
Assess Current
Provision
Establish
Steering Group
Implement
Teams
Formalise Approach
(Nuts and Bolts)
Gain Expertise From
Other Countries
Establish
Deliverables
Compare the Current State of Processes, People, and
Technology with what they should be
Identify Technology
Needs
Develop Strategic Plans Based on New Approach
Introduce the New Approach and Carry Out the required Training
Evaluate The Success Of The Initiative.
COMMUNICATION

underlying thread of trying to improve on the potential of the tourism product. Each nation will have its own unique problems but these will be assessed at a later stage of the process. This stage has particular importance if we consider the fact that many BPR initiatives fail as a result of a lack of understanding of the goals to be achieved.

Policy makers should establish a steering group to oversee the entire initiative. This group should be made up of representatives from both the tourist industry and the education sector. It is envisaged that membership might include representation from bodies such as the National Tourist Organisations, Tourist Trade Bodies, various Tourist related industries and educational establishments involved in the delivery and development of tourism courses.

Once policy makers are clear about the goals to be achieved and have clearly defined them for the steering group, the second stage will involve an assessment of what the country already has to offer. This stage will examine the current provision that exists and may involve conducting a SWOT analysis. Thus, the nations strengths, weaknesses, opportunities and threats will be examined in order to gain an insight into what is already occurring in relation to the tourism product. This stage will be conducted by teams selected by the steering group.

It is important that the teams selected at this stage also have a good representation from the various bodies outlined above as they need to be fully committed to the philosophy of Business Process Reengineering. Without this commitment there is the danger that interested parties will view the initiative as just another expensive management fad.

These three stages are interlinked, and should be viewed as such, and this will allow the Steering group to make an assessment of the overall tourism product on offer. It will also allow the group to examine the strengths and weaknesses of the nations' tourism provision and perhaps for the first time, really gain an insight into the overall state of affairs of tourism.

The next stage of the process will involve formalising how the initiative will actually operate. This will be achieved through the steering group aided by the teams selected during the initial stages of the project. The timeframe and the mechanics of how the methodology will be implemented will also be decided at this time. An essential element of this part of the implementation process will require the reinforcement of the necessity to adopt a clean slate approach and investigate the adoption of creative solutions to the problem. This will undoubtedly prove to be a difficult phase and may require substantial training and development for all parties involved. The appointment of a BPR specialist will be required at this stage to ensure that the aims of the program are realised and that the teams focus on processes.

Consideration should also be given to developments taking place in other countries and this will involve an examination of not only nations with a successful tourism product but also nations that are experiencing difficulties. This will allow the implementing nation to identify critical success factors as well as measures that are not working successfully.

Based on the research carried out the steering group should be in a position to ascertain what the existing provision is, what the possibilities are and how these may be realised. It will therefore now be possible to draw up a list of what realistically can be achieved from the nations' tourism product. If the research has been conducted properly these deliverables will be both realistic and achievable.

The next stage is one of the most important as far as the BPR methodology is concerned. As already noted, some of the factors that have detracted from the overall success of previous initiatives have been identified as a lack of knowledge of processes and not enough attention paid to the people element. Given these experiences, it is imperative that these two areas are examined in detail and comparisons made with what they are at present and what they should be. Lessons should be learnt from both successful and unsuccessful initiatives and remedial action taken to ensure that shortcomings are not repeated. A final aspect of this stage, and perhaps one that has particular importance to the tourism industry is the state of technology. It has already been noted that the speed of development in this area is phenomenal and that any organisations hoping to take advantage of ICT need to embrace BPR if their actions are to be successful. The implementing nation should therefore examine their current actions and compare these with what they should be doing if they want to fully capitalise on the benefits that can be achieved. Such actions are fundamental to the overall success of tourism development.

Additionally, it has been noted, that not only is it important to assess current technological capabilities but it is also important to ensure that the nation has the technological capability of capitalising on the full potential of the implementation of BPR. This will require an assessment of possible future developments in technology and putting in place measures that ensure that any initiatives have the capability of meeting future needs.

Once it is clear as to what needs to be done to achieve the initial goals the next step involves policy makers developing a strategic plan based on the new approach that has been developed. This can then be put in place alongside any identified training and suitable evaluation instrumentation tools that have been developed in order to assess and monitor the effectiveness of the approach.

It should also be noted that effective communications need to be evident throughout the entire process to ensure that each phase is fully aware of other developments. This is particularly true if we consider the fact that some of the phases will be developed alongside others.

Conclusion

It is evident that many nations have a tourism product that is failing to meet its full potential. Despite many varied and innovative efforts to capitalise on the possibilities of the tourism product, the full potential for many countries has not been realised. The increased threat from terrorism has further detracted from these efforts and many nations are now struggling to keep a vital industry alive.

From a positive perspective, there has been a rapid development in technology and the potential benefits that can be achieved from its use. It is believed however that if such technology is to be fully embraced, then old methods are unsuitable to deal with its demands. It is argued that one way of introducing and capitalising on the potential of technology is to introduce it using Business Process Reengineering techniques. It is the belief of these authors that such an approach could be used to help nations to develop their tourism product but only if it is adopted using a systematic approach. The ten step methodology that has been described is one such way that these aims could be realised. This methodology will not only aid policy makers in the examination of their current provision, but will also encourage them to assess the processes that will ensure that their product is customer focused whilst embracing the technology that is available to them.

NOTE

1. A survey of management techniques created by Darrell Rigby on the success rate of management ideas.

REFERENCES

Alavi, M and Yoo, Y, (1995), *Productivity Gains of BPR—Achieving Success Where Others Have Failed*, Information Systems Management, Fall pp 43-47

Bolman, L, G, and Deal, T, E, (1997), *Reframing Organisations* 2nd Edition, Jossey-Bass, San Francisco, CA.

Byrne, J, (1997), *Management Theory or Fad of the Month?*, Business Week, June 23

Certo, SC (1997) *Modern Management - International Edition*, 7th Edition, New Jersey, Prentice Hall

Chaffey, D (2002) *E-Business and E-Commerce Management*, Prentice Hall, Essex

Evans, G.N., Mason-Jones, R. and Towill, D.R., (1999), *The Scope Paradigm of Business Process Reengineering*, Business Process Management Journal, Vol 5, No. 2.

Fernandes, K and Raja, V, and Antony, J, (2001), *Optimum Level of Goal Mapping in a Reengineering Environmemt*, Business Process Management Journal, Vol 7, No 1.

Finklestein, C (2002) *Business Re-engineering and the Internet: Transforming Business for a Connected World*, http://members.ozemail.com.au/~visible/papers/bripaper.htm

Goodrich, JN (2002) *September 11th, 2001 Attack on America : A Record of the Immediate Impacts and Reactions in the USA Travel & Tourism Industry*, Tourism Management, 23, pp 573-580

Gunasekaran, A, and Adebayo, J, (2000), *GEC Alsthom Learns Many Lessons From BPR*, Production and Inventory Management Journal, Second Quarter

Hall, G, Rosenthal. J, Wade, J (1993), *How to Make Reengineering Really Work*, Harvard Business Review, November-December pp119-131

Hammer, M, (1990), *Reengineering Work: don't Automate, Obliterate*, Harvard Business Review, July-August pp 104-112

Hammer, M and Champy, J, (1993/5) *Reengineering the Corporation: A Manifesto for Business Revolution* Nicholas Brealey Publishing Limited

Hammer, M, and Stanton, S, (1995), *The Reengineering Revolution*, Harper Collins

Hayward, D (1995) *Facing the Firing Squad*, Computing, 2Nov, pp 36-7

Knights, D, and McCabe, D, (1998), *When Life is But a Dream, Obliterating Politics Through Business Process Reengineering*, Human Relations, Vol 51, No 6

Louvieris, P (2002) *Unit 6—Business Process Reengineering*, eBusiness Management, University of Surrey

Macdonald, J, (1995) *Understanding Business Process Reengineering* Hodder and Stoughton

MacIntosh, R, and Carrie, A, (1995) *The Use of the GRAI Method in Reengineering*, Proceedings of IFIP Conference on Reengineering the Enterprise, Galway, pp 411 - 421

Manganelli,R, (1993), *Its not a Silver Bullet*, The Journal of Business Strategy, Nov/Dec

Martilla, J, and James, J, (1997), *Improvement—Performance Analysis*, Journal of Marketing, January 1997

Matthewson, JA (2002) *e-Business - A Jargon-free Practical Guide*, Butterworth Heninemann, Oxford

Mumford, E, and Hendricks, R, (1996), *Business Process Reengineering RIP*, People Management, May 2, 1996

Nwabueze, U, and Gopal, K, (1997) *A Systems Management Approach for Business Process Reengineering*, Total Quality Management, October

Peltu, M (1996) *Death to Cuts*, Computing, 9th May, p 34

Peppard, J, and Rowland, P, (1995) *The Essence of Business Process Reengineering*, Prentice Hall

Raja, V, (1998), *Business Process Reengineering at Marconi Marine*, Company Report.

Sincoe, M, (1998), *A CFO Defends Reengineering*, Manufacturing Engineering, Feb

Steininger, D, (1994), *Why Quality Initiatives are Failing: The Need to Address the Foundation of Human Motivation*, Human Resource Management, Vol 33, No4.

Talwar, J, (1993) *Business Reengineering—A Strategy Driven Approach*, Long Range Planning, Vol. 26, No. 6 pp 22-40

Travel Trade Gazette, April 2002

Tonnessen, T, (2000), *Process Improvement and the Human Factor*, Total Quality Management, July

Towers, S, (1994), *Business Process Reengineering: A Handbook for Executives.* Stanley Thornes

Verespej, M, (1995), *Reengineering isn't Going Away*, Industry Week, 1995 *www.eyefortravel.com*

Zairi, M, (1995), *BPR and Process Management*, Management Decision, Volume 33, Issue 3.

Zairi, M (2001) *Editorial—Bring Back BPR - All is Forgiven, Business Process Management Journal*, Vol 7, No1, pp 6-7

12

Research and Indigenous Tourism—Cultural Collision or Collaboration

*Alicia Boyle**

Abstract

A recent scoping study was undertaken with the principal aim of developing broad proposals for the cultural, social, economic and environmental sustainability of Indigenous tourism. This scoping study identified that in both academic and government literature as recent as 2001, that there was little real research underlying the nature of Indigenous tourism in Australia. However, on a national level, those involved at both operational and government levels appeared to think that Indigenous tourism was 'over-researched' and that insufficient attention may have been given to implementation. This paper highlights the issues raised by both academics and practitioners and identifies some common ground on which the two may meet to facilitate the participation of Indigenous people in the Australian tourism industry.

* Northern Territory University, Faculty of Law, Business and Arts, School of Tourism and Hospitality, Casuarina Campus B22.65, Darwin Northern Territory 0909, Tel: 08 8946 6084 / Fax: 08 8946 6777 / e-mail: alicia.boyle@ntu.edu.au

Introduction

The scoping study reviewed in this paper was undertaken to develop a report that would identify, prioritise and develop broad research proposals that have the potential to enhance the cultural, social, economic and environmental sustainability of indigenous tourism. It was aimed at involving all major stakeholders across Australia in the development of a blueprint for the short to medium direction of indigenous tourism research. This extensive scoping study was the first of its type in terms of its aims and methodology to be undertaken. Its results have not been published yet but should be of interest to some in the tourism industry, both at government and non-government levels.

Australia's tourism industry and more importantly, Australia's indigenous people have an unparalleled but to date relatively unrealized opportunity to capitalize on their unique past and contemporary cultures. There is burning need to identify how academic researchers and those more experienced in the ways of working in the tourism industry can facilitate the participation of indigenous people in Australia's fourth largest export industry. The publishing of the outcomes of this scoping study may assist to increase the representation of Indigenous Australians in the tourism industry and to ultimately enhance their social and economic well-being.

The principal aim of the scoping study was to build on the national frameworks provided by the National Aboriginal and Torres Strait Islander Tourism Industry Strategy (ATSIC (Aboriginal and Torres Strait Islander Commission) and ONT (Office of National Tourism) National Aboriginal and Torres Strait Islander Tourism Industry Strategy 1997) and the National Aboriginal and Torres Strait Islander Cultural Industry Strategy(ATSIC (Aboriginal and Torres Strait Islander Commission) and ONT(Office of National Tourism) National Aboriginal and Torres Strait Islander, Cultural Industry Strategy 1997). These frameworks, although clearly setting the directions and actions required to turn the potential of Indigenous tourism into reality, recognised that much work needed to be done to:

1. assist Aboriginal and Torres Strait Islander peoples to understand the demands of the tourism industry
2. remove obstacles to their participation
3. build Indigenous Tourism business development capabilities within the Indigenous community
4. raise the awareness of non-Indigenous tourism business people of the potential of Indigenous Tourism.

Initially, a review of the available literature was undertaken to identify the apparent gaps in indigenous tourism research and/or lack of research implementation. The review began with Heather Zeppel's. 'Aboriginal Tourism in Australia: A Research Bibliography' (Zeppel 1999a) and was extended to encompass texts, journal articles, national and State/Territory publications and electronic resources related to indigenous tourism published since May 1999.

A draft report was sent Australia-wide to all State Tourism Authorities, Offices of Aboriginal Affairs/Development, ATSIC, Aboriginal Tourism Australia, Department of Industry, Science and Resources, Cooperative Research Centre (CRC) for Sustainable Tourism researchers (and others) for distribution throughout their networks and for comment. The report did not present any new material related to indigenous tourism, nor did it to 'speak' on behalf of indigenous peoples, but merely identified the apparent gaps in indigenous tourism research and/or lack of research implementation. It was made clear that I was Balanda, not indigenous, and my interpretation of the literature was given with full respect to my cultural limitations.

A workshop was held with representatives from the above organizations to identify, given the knowledge that already existed and, given the identified gaps in research and its implementation, and given the knowledge of existing strategies, what research needed to be undertaken to increase the participation of indigenous people in the Australian tourism industry. This workshop, and additional comments received from those who were invited but could not attend, provided the basis on which the scoping study report was written.

Heather Zeppel's 'Aboriginal Tourism in Australia: A Research Bibliography (Zeppel 1999a) comprehensively identified the range of research undertaken on a national and State/Territory basis with respect to indigenous tourism. A review of additional comparable literature to May 2001 highlighted similar gaps in research and strategy implementation. However, when presented with what academics considered fundamental research needs, indigenous people currently involved in the tourism industry, their representatives from the State/Territory tourism authorities and their State/Territory Aboriginal Development/Aboriginal Affairs departments, generally considered indigenous tourism to be 'over-researched'. It was their opinion that it was the implementation of past research findings and the implementation of the various State/Territory/National Indigenous/Aboriginal tourism strategies that was now needed.

The question is now, how to identify and more specifically, in what directions do we move forward to meet the needs of both groups.

Existing National and State/Territory Strategies Issues

A principal aim of the scoping study was to build on the national and State/Territory frameworks that had been developed for developing Indigenous Tourism in Australia. The overarching strategies are the National Aboriginal and Torres Strait Islander Tourism Strategy (ATSIC (Aboriginal and Torres Strait Islander Commission) and ONT (Office of National Tourism) National Aboriginal and Torres Strait Islander Tourism Industry Strategy 1997) and the National Aboriginal and Torres Strait Islander Cultural Industry Strategy ([ATSIC (Aboriginal and Torres Strait Islander Commission), 1997 #178]. The 1991 Royal Commission into Aboriginal Deaths in Custody initiated the development of these strategies.

Strategies that currently exist include:

Year	Strategy	Agency
1994	National Ecotourism Strategy	Commonwealth Department of Tourism
1995	Aboriginal Tourism Strategy	South Australian Tourism Commission
1995	Cultural Tourism Three Year Development Strategy	Geelong Otway Tourism
1996	Aboriginal Tourism Strategy	Northern Territory Tourist Commission
1996	Kimberley Aboriginal Cultural Tourism Strategy	Kimberley Aboriginal Tourism Association
1996	Queensland Cultural Tourism	The Arts Office and Queensland Tourist and Travel Corporation
1996	The Cultural Landscape: A Cultural Action Plan for Western Australia	
1996-1998	Western Australian Tourism Commission and Arts Western Australia	
1996	Cultural Tourism Opportunities for South Australia	South Australian Tourism Commission
1997	Indigenous Tourism Product Development Principles	Tourism New South Wales
1997	National Aboriginal and Torres Strait Islander Tourism Industry Strategy	ATSIC and the Office of National Tourism
1997	National Aboriginal and Torres Strait Islander Cultural Industry Strategy	ATSIC and the Office of National Tourism
1997	Queensland Ecotourism Plan	Queensland Department of Tourism, Small Business and Industry

(Contd…)

1997	Nature-based Tourism Strategy for Western Australia	Western Australian Tourism Commission
1997	Aboriginal Economic Development in Western Australia	Department of Commerce and Trade
1998	Aboriginal Tourism Industry Plan	Tourism Victoria
1998	Tourism A Ticket to the 21st Century	Office of National Tourism
1998	Aboriginal Cultural Tourism Plan 1998/1999 - 2000/2001	Tourism New South Wales
1999	Koori Business Network	Aboriginal Affairs Victoria
1999	Aboriginal Business Network	NSW State and Regional Development

It is apparent that although these strategies have been developed and released by governments very little has been done toward implementation. All State and Territory representatives believed that the strategies are still relevant, the problems and issues identified still the same and the needs still unmet. Some of the reasons given for the lack of implementation included: insufficient resources to provide the drivers of existing strategies and initiatives; lack of Key Performance Indicators (KPIs) that identify current benchmarks and set new targets, allocated timeframes and responsibilities for action; the lack of commercial reality for partnerships to eventuate and changes in government that resulted in programs being abolished or changed, leaving programs inconsistent with the existing strategies.

Some States/Territories are attempting to implement their own strategies. The Northern Territory has possibly been the most proactive in this endeavour. Foundations for the Future, released in June, 1999, was a series of documents identifying where the Northern Territory wanted to be and how it was going to get there. Foundation Four was about developing partnerships with Aboriginal people, its implementation underpinned by a focus group that includes representatives from a broad range of departments, organizations and agencies. This focus group is supported by a series of task forces, one of which is the Aboriginal Tourism Task Force, whose primarily role is to revisit the 1996 Aboriginal Tourism Strategy and implement its identified priorities. The Northern Territory could provide us with a useful model on which to base strategy implementation.

What is now required is a macro evaluation of what has happened, what has not happened, what is working and what is not working and an identification of the key drivers that will realise the identified outcomes of the strategies. Such an evaluation is required before, or at least concurrently with a micro level evaluation of small business. We need to know what has occurred on a policy program basis to identify how these were operationalised in the marketplace and the effects they have had on small business. We need to identify the criteria that will allow us to evaluate the strategies.

Following the National Indigenous Tourism Forum in Sydney 2000 the Department of Industry Science and Resources (DISR) established an Indigenous Tourism Leadership Group to look at the gaps in the national strategies, what has happened, what has not happened and why. To date this group has primarily looked at accreditation, product development and access to finance although even this group admits it does not have all the information it needs to undertake such an evaluation.

Definition Issues

Indigenous tourism as a field of study is relatively new and is considered to have begun with Smith's anthropological study (Smith 1977) concerned with the impacts of tourism on Indigenous peoples. Many authors since have provided alternative definitions for indigenous tourism and its associated activities (Hinch and Butler 1996), (Clark and

Larrieu 1998), (Moscardo and Pearce 1999), (Pitcher, van Oosterzee et al. 1999) and (Zeppel 2001). ATSIC and the ONT (ATSIC (Aboriginal and Torres Strait Islander Commission) and ONT (Office of National Tourism) National Aboriginal and Torres Strait Islander Tourism Industry Strategy 1997) defined indigenous tourism as all forms of participation by Aboriginal and Torres Strait Islander people in tourism as: employers; employees; investors; joint venture partners; providing indigenous tourism products and providing mainstream tourism products.

An impediment to the involvement of indigenous people in the tourism industry has perhaps been its frequent association with cultural tourism, exacerbated by the fact that the majority of operators promote their indigenous tourism product as offering an 'indigenous cultural experience'. There is general consensus in the literature about indigenous tourism that the Northern Territory holds an advantage in attracting tourists (Clark and Larrieu 1998) although results from a 1996 study (AGBMcNair 1996) highlighted that the majority of travellers were drawn to the Northern Territory because of the natural environment and well known icons and while Aboriginal art and culture was a contributing factor to these people's decision to come to the Northern Territory, it did not appear to be the primary motivation for the majority of visitors.

However, the Northern Territory's competitive advantage is largely the result of tourists believing that authentic indigenous culture only exists in its pre-European state. This stereotyping does not reflect the strength and adaptability of indigenous culture to exist in contemporary form and for the ability of indigenous people to participate in the tourism industry at any other level. The scoping study identified that it may in fact be the participation of indigenous people at other levels that offers the greatest benefits. It recognized that the very fact that individuals in business provided a cultural 'flavour' allowed the cultural experience to 'value-add' to the product rather that it being the primary promotional message.

Demand Issues

Although inbound tourism has more than doubled in the past ten years, domestic tourism continues to remain the most important sector of Australia's tourism industry. Interesting to note however, is that this statement applies least to the Northern Territory. A report prepared by the South Australian Tourism Commission (South Australian Tourism Commission 1998) suggested that the dominant market for indigenous tourism continued to be international visitors, a suggestion also supported by figures provided in the 1999/2000 Territory Tourism Selected Statistics (Northern Territory Tourist Commission 1999/2000). Jackie Kelly, Minister for Sport and Tourism in the proceedings of the National Indigenous Tourism Forum (DISR (Department of Industry Science and Resources), ATSIC (Aboriginal and Torres Strait Islander Commission) et al. 2000) stated that about 80 per cent of our overseas visitors wanted authentic Indigenous experiences. However Don Freeman, Managing Director, Tjapukai Aboriginal Cultural Park, expressed concern with such figures. Other authors, (Ryan and Huyton 2000b) also commented on the dubious success of a range of indigenous tourism products presented in ' A Talent for Tourism', (Commonwealth of Australia 1994) as did Pitterle when she told tourist operators in Darwin that only a small minority of international visitors had a strong interest in indigenous cultural tourism product (Pitterle 1999).

The scoping study similarly questioned the validity of these figures, given the limited number of commercially sustainable existing businesses. It considered that the thinking of the Australian tourism industry continued to be dominated by the needs of the seller rather than those of the consumer, a situation inhibiting appropriate product development and product marketing. There is a need to know much more about the marketplace, both international and domestic. There has to date been little quantitative work undertaken to ascertain the motivations, perceptions and demand for indigenous tourism product (Ryan and Huyton 2000b). This is more acutely apparent when searching for such information relating to our largest market, our domestic visitors.

Research Issues

The scoping study literature search adopted a similar view to many authors that there is little real research underlying the nature of indigenous tourism in Australia. Ryan and Huyton (2000b) commented that without such data there cannot exist economic reality as to the level of demand nor its subsequent socio-cultural or environmental effects (Ryan and Huyton 2000b). Zeppel (1998b) stated that most research was very recent (post 1989) and much of it descriptive, existing principally in the form of reports and conference papers but little appearing in peer reviewed journals (Zeppel 1998b). Others, including the author, take the view that although there appears to have been a substantial amount of research undertaken regarding Indigenous tourism, to date there has been limited application of this research to aid indigenous involvement in tourism (Schuler, Aberdeen et al. 1999). It is worth commenting however, on the obvious lack of indigenous academic tourism industry researchers at either quantitative or qualitative levels.

Various academic authors have attempted to categorise the research undertaken to date. Ryan and Huyton (2000b) presented the research as being descriptive, conceptual, empirical or strategic or planning (Ryan and Huyton 2000b). The Australian Institute of Aboriginal and Torres Strait Islander Studies reported more broadly on current research gaps of relevance to indigenous people and subdivided their findings into the areas of anthropology, education, economics and other (Australian Institute of Aboriginal and Torres Strait Islander Studies 1999). Other academic authors such as, (Burchett 1992), (Altman 1993a), (Pitcher, van Oosterzee et al. 1999) and (Zeppel 1999a) and (Zeppel 2001) have identified gaps in the knowledge base on which to develop policy and/or practices. Other authors in governmental roles such as (ATSIC (Aboriginal and Torres Strait Islander Commission), Northern Territory Tourist Commission et al. 1993), (Altman 1993b), (South Australian Tourism Commission 1998) and (DISR (Department of Industry Science and Resources), ATSIC (Aboriginal and Torres Strait Islander Commission) et al. 2000) have identified similar gaps.

	Area of Research	Authors
1.	Aboriginal involvement in cultural tourism enterprise	(Finlayson 1991), (Finlayson & Madeen 1994), (Zeppel 1998d), Zeppel 1999b), (Pitcher 1999), (Pitcher van Oosterzee et al. 1999)
2.	Sustainable development of Aboriginal tourism	
3.	Small scale Aboriginal tourism	
4.	Detailed case studies of a range of Indigenous tourism businesses to identify factors contributing to economic success and failure	
5.	Aboriginal entrepreneurs	(Burchett 1992), (Finlayson 1992), (Altman and Finlayson 1993c), (Palmer 1999), (Pitcher, van Oosterzee et al 1999), (Schaper 1999), (Zeppel 1999a), Muloin, Zeppel et al., 2001)
1.	Social, cultural, environmental or economic impacts of tourism on Aboriginal commnities	(Kesteven 1987), (Altman 1988b), (Altman 1989), (Ross 1991), (Altman 1992), (Altman 1996), (Boyd and Ward 1996), (Pitcher, van Oosterzee et al., 1999) (Schuler, Aberdeen et al. 1999)
1.	Aboriginal involvement in National Parks	(Altman and Allen 1991), (Birckhead, De Lacy et al. 1992), (Mercer 1994), (Press, Lea et al., 1995) (Gillespie 1998), (Hall 2000)

(Contd...)

	Area of Research	Authors
2.	Industry perspectives on developing and marketing tourism	(Fourmile 1993), (ATSIC (Aboriginal and Torres Strait Islander Commission), Northern Territory Tourist Commission et al. 1993) (Northern Territory Tourist Commission 1995)
1.	Representation of indigenous peoples and indigenous tourism	(Wells 1996), (Zeppel 1998b), (Zeppel 1998c), (Waitt 1999), (Wells & Kauffman 1999)
2.	Indigenous intellectual property rights	(Janke 1998), (Australian Institute of Aboriginal and Torres Strait Islander Studies 1999)
3.	Visitor perceptions, needs, expectations and demands–domestic and international	
4.	Indigenous peoples' expectations of visitors	
5.	Ability to meet the needs and expectations of visitors	
6.	Segment the demand for Indigenous tourism	(Burchett 1992), (Altman & Finlayson 1992) (Altman 1993a) (ATSIC (Aboriginal and Torres Strait Islander Commission), Northern Territory Tourist Commission et. al. 1993)

(Contd...)

Area of Research	Authors
	(Langton 1994), (AGBMcNair 1996), (Clark & Larrieu 1998) (Pearce 1998) (South Australian Tourism Commission 1998), (Pitcher, van Oosterzee et al. 1999) (Zeppel 1999a) (DISR (Department of Industry Science and Resources), ATSIC (Aboriginal and Torres Strait Islander Commission) et al. 2000), (Ryan & Huyton 2000a), (Ryan & Huyton 2000b), (Ryan & Huyton 2001)
1. Indigeneous tourism in urban areas	
2. Development of more positive urban Indigenous tourism experience.	
3. Aborginal tourism in southern Australia	(Finlayson 1991), (Clerk & Larrieu 1998), (Zeppel 1999c)
1. Innovative induction and training programs that ensure service delivery	
2. Review of existing training programs and establishment of a realistic training needs	
3. Education of community members not directly involved in tourism.	

(Contd...)

Area of Research	Authors
4. Identification and implementation of the most effective training and support mechanisms that minimise obstacles to employment	
5. Development of Business and tourism management skills	
6. Linking of funding for business development and training	(Burchett 1992) (Altman & Finlayson 1992), (ATSIC (Aboriginal and Torres Strait Islander Commission), Northern Territory Tourist Commission et al. 1993) (Weiler 1997), (DISR (Department of Industry Science and Resources), ATSIC (Aboriginal and Torres Strait Islander Commission) et al. 2000) (Muloin, Zeppel et al., 2001)
1. Indigenous involvement in mainstream tourism	
2. Creating partnerships with mainstream tourism	(Zeppel 1999a) (DISR (Department of Industry Science and Resources), ATSIC (Aboriginal and Torres Strait Islander Commission) et al. 2000), (Zeppel 2001)
1. Analysis of government policies and programs for Indigenous tourism	(Pitcher, van Oosterzee et al. 1999) (Zeppel 1999a)

(Contd...)

	Area of Research	Authors
2.	Authenticity–its identification, role use and marketability	(Altman & Finlayson 1992), (ATSIC (Aboriginal and Torres Strait Islander Commission), Northern Territory Tourist Commission et al.. 1993) (Pitcher, van Oosterzee et al. 1999)
3.	Database of tour operators	(Altman 1993a), (Altman 1993b) (ATSIC (Aboriginal and Torres Strait Islander Commission), Northern Territory Tourist Commission et al. 1993) (Pitcher, van Oosterzee et al. 1999)

The scoping study identified that over the years 1992 to 2001 the following areas were commonly cited in both the academic literature and in government publications as still needing further research or knowledge bases. The majority, if not all these research gaps, remain unfilled.

- Why then, did those participants in the scoping study representing operational and/or government interests insist that Indigenous tourism was 'over-researched'? They identified a real need for workplace-applied, commercial research and an equally strong antipathy toward academic research. Yet when asked what it was that was needed to advance Indigenous tourism the following were presented as common areas of need:
- development of a national database of Indigenous tourism product
- development, analysis and evaluation of a nationally-applied diagnostic tool profiling indigenous tourism product
- customer perceptions, needs, expectations and demands, both of our international and more importantly, domestic visitors
- identification of business success and failure factors to enable development of best practice models
- development and implementation of effective business mentoring programs
- higher levels of business management skills and knowledge
- identification of and minimisation of barriers to employment in mainstream tourism
- increased involvement in mainstream tourism
- simplified and more timely availability of and access to appropriate funding
- the knowledge and resources to facilitate the implementation of existing commonwealth and State/ Territory Indigenous tourism strategies

Are these not the same needs expressed as research, knowledge or information gaps identified by academic researchers? It may well be that these groups classify or identify 'research' as something quite different to those with academic interests. So how should we classify Indigenous tourism research? Should it in fact be by type (descriptive, conceptual, empirical or strategic), source (academic or government) or issue (education and training, supply and demand, anthropological, economic, product development, management and sustainability, employment)?

Directions

So how can academic research contribute to indigenous tourism? It is first worth considering that the methodology employed in this scoping study may have unintentionally resulted in the formation of a pseudo consensus. A fundamental reason for the lack of implementation of strategy and research may well be the fact that key drivers are localised, not generalised and thus a national approach may not be appropriate. It is doubtful that the processes and drivers are the same for all Indigenous people, products and situations. No gains will be made if strategies are implemented the wrong way or for no purpose. Commonly applied universal, 'one size fits all' approaches could be contributing to the lack of implementation. Facilitating a merger of the differentiated knowledge of Indigenous cultures (and their associated relationships) at the local level, with the data-dependent knowledge of research could prove to be the way forward.

Indigenous people should be empowered with appropriate tools to implement appropriate actions. They need to be empowered to accumulate their own information in their own homelands. Academic researchers can act as mentors and intermediaries in this process. Perhaps in this way, Indigenous knowledge can be appropriately integrated with the business and management knowledge required to sustain success in the tourism industry.

It is equally important to recognise that those actively involved in indigenous tourism and its management may also have set unrealistic expectations on what research can deliver. Academic researchers are not about setting policy but are about providing knowledge on which to base sound policy development and implementation. From an academic perspective, there remains an apparent lack of information on which to base decisions, further compounding the problems associated with policy and strategy implementation.

We need to make choices about the priorities we now set for indigenous tourism research. The scoping study identified a need to evaluate the products and associated experiences currently available, to collect and analyse information regarding their stage of development, funding and finance issues, their marketing strategies, technology use, their success and failure factors and the skill base that resides within these businesses. The development of a diagnostic tool, applied nationally, has been proposed to assist in providing answers to these questions and to enable existing and potential operators to learn from the experiences of others. The implementation of this tool however, is inhibited by the fact that no centralized, accessible national database of indigenous tourism products currently exists, a situation that urgently needs to be addressed by those given the task of managing the development of indigenous tourism. Without it, we have no true idea of the size of this sector of the tourism industry, its start and finish or its worth.

Conclusions

Collision or collaboration, the choice needs to be made by all those who identify as stakeholders in indigenous tourism. The scoping study reported in this paper facilitated the identification of some mutually agreeable priorities that should promote the future participation of indigenous people in the Australian tourism industry. It is important that indigenous people are appropriately mentored and empowered to identify local processes and drivers in any research undertaken. It is only hoped that by working collaboratively and with a better understanding of both how research is perceived and of what it can deliver, by those who best stand to benefit from its outputs, we can in fact provide some much needed answers to the questions posed by indigenous tourism.

BIBLIOGRAPHY

AGBMcNair (1996). *Aboriginal Culture: Qualitative Research Report: Reference No. Qg4831, Confidential Report Prepared for the Northern Territory Tourist Commission*, Darwin.

Altman, J. (1988b). *Aborigines, Tourism and Development: The Northern Territory Experience*. Australian National University, Northern Australian Research Institute, Darwin.

Altman, J. (1989). "Tourism Dilemmas for Aboriginal Australians." *Annals of Tourism Research* 16: 456-476.

Altman, J. (1992). Tourism and Aboriginal Communities. *Australian Tourism Outlook Forum 1992*. B. Faulkner and M. Kennedy (Ed). Bureau of Tourism Research, Canberra.

Altman, J. (1993a). Indigenous Australians in the National Tourism Strategy: Impact, Sustainability and Policy Issues. Discussion Paper No. 37/1993 Centre for Aboriginal Policy Research, Canberra.

Altman, J. (1993b). *Where to Now*? Some Strategic Indigenous Tourism Policy Issues. Indigenous Australians and Tourism: A focus on Northern Australia, Canberra, Goanna Print.

Altman, J. & Allen, L. M. (1991). *Living Off the Land in National Parks: Issues for Aboriginal Australians. Discussion Paper No. 37*. Centre for Aboriginal Economic Policy Research, Canberra.

Altman, J. & Finlayson, J. (1992). Aborigines, Tourism and Sustainable Development. Centre for Aboriginal Economic Policy Research, Canberra.

Altman, J. & Finlayson, J. (1993c). "Aborigines, Tourism and Sustainable Development." *Journal of Tourism Studies* 4(1): 38-50.

Altman, J. A. (1996). "Coping with Locational Advantage: Tourism and Economic Development at Seisia Community, Cape York Peninsula." *Journal of Tourism Studies* 7(1): 58-71.

ATSIC (Aboriginal and Torres Strait Islander Commission), Northern Territory Tourist Commission, et al. (1993). *Indigenous Australians and Tourism: A Focus on Northern Australia.* Indigenous Australians and Tourism: A focus on Northern Australia, Darwin, Commonwealth of Australia.

ATSIC (Aboriginal and Torres Strait Islander Commission) & ONT (Office of National Tourism) (1997). National Aboriginal and Torres Strait Islander Cultural Industry Strategy Commonwealth of Australia, Canberra.

ATSIC (Aboriginal and Torres Strait Islander Commission) & ONT (Office of National Tourism) (1997). National Aboriginal and Torres Strait Islander Tourism Industry Strategy ATSIC and the Office of National Tourism, Canberra.

Australian Institute of Aboriginal and Torres Strait Islander Studies (1999). *Research of Interest to Aboriginal and Torres Strait Islander Peoples. Commissioned Report No.59.* Australian Research Council, Canberra. www.arc.gov.au/publications/arc/99_05.pdf

Birckhead, J., De Lacy, T., et al. (Ed). (1992). *Aboriginal Involvement in Parks and Protected Areas. Australian Institute of Aboriginal and Torres Strait Islander Studies Report Series.* Panther Publishing and Printing, Canberra.

Boyd, B. & Ward, G. (1996). Aboriginal Heritage and Visitor Management. *Heritage Management in Australia and New Zealand: The Human Dimension.* C.M. Hall and S. McArthur (Ed). Oxford University Press, Melbourne.

Burchett, C. (1992). Ecologically Sustainable Development and Its Relationship to Aboriginal Tourism in the Northern Territory. *Ecotourism Incorporating the Global Classroom.* B.Weiler (Ed). Bureau of Tourism Research, Canberra.

Clark, I. D. & Larrieu, L. (1998). Indigenous Tourism in Victoria: Products, Markets and Futures Faculty of Business and Economics, Monash University, Caulfield East.

Commonwealth of Australia (1994). *A Talent for Tourism—Stories About Indigenous People in Tourism.* Commonwealth of Australia, Canberra. www.dist.gov.au/tourism/publications/talent/tjapukai.html

DISR (Department of Industry Science and Resources), ATSIC (Aboriginal and Torres Strait Islander Commission), et al. (2000). *National Indigenous Tourism Forum Proceedings* Report, Sydney.

Finlayson, J. (1991). Attitudinal Survey of International Visitors' Expectations of Cultural Tourism. in Australian Aborigines and Cultural Tourism: Case studies of Aboriginal involvement in the Tourist Industry, Working Papers on Multiculturalism No.15, Centre for Multicultural Studies, University of Woollongong: 79-98.

Finlayson, J. (1992). Issues in Aboriginal Cultural Tourism: Possibilities for a Sustainable Industry. *Ecotourism Incorporating the Global Classroom.* Weiler, B. (Ed). Bureau of Tourism Research, Canberra.

Finlayson, J. & Madden, R. (1994). *Regional Tourism Case Studies: Indigenous Participation in Tourism in Victoria.* Tourism Education and Research in Australia, Canberra, Bureau of Tourism Research.

Fourmile, H. (1993). *Cultural Survival Vs Cultural Prostitution.* Cultural Tourism Awareness Workshop, Cairns, James Cook University.

Gillespie, D. (1998). Tourism in Kakadu National Park. *Contemporary Issues in Development.* D.Wade-Marshall and P.Loveday (Ed). Australian National University, Darwin.

Hall, C. M. (2000). Tourism, National Parks and Aboriginal Peoples. *Tourism and National Parks: Issues and Implications*". R.W.Butler and S.W.Boyd (Ed). John Wiley and Sons, Queensland.

Hinch, T. & Butler, R. (1996). A Common Ground for Discussion. *Tourism and Indigenous Peoples*. T.Hinch and R.Butler (Ed). International Thomson Business Press, London: 3-19.

Janke, T. (1998). Our Culture: *Our Future; Report on Australian Indigenous Cultural and Intellectual Property Rights*. Cultural Industries Section, ATSIC, Canberra. www.icip.lawnet.com.au

Kesteven, S. (1987). *Aborigines in the Tourist Industry. East Kimberley Working Paper No.14*. Centre for resource and environmental studies, Australian National University, Canberra.

Mercer, D. (1994). Native Peoples and Tourism: Conflict and Compromise. *Global Tourism the Next Decade*. W. F.Theobald (Ed). Butterworth Heinemann, Boston.

Moscardo, G. & Pearce, P. L. (1999). "Understanding Ethnic Tourists." *Annals of Tourism Research* 26(2): 416-434.

Muloin, S., Zeppel, H., et al. (2001). *Indigenous Wildlife Tourism in Australia: Wildlife Attractions, Cultural Interpretation and Indigenous Involvement. Wildlife Tourism Report Series. (Unpublished) Status Assessment of Wildlife Tourism Series*. CRC for Sustainable Tourism, Griffith University, Gold Coast, Queensland.

Northern Territory Tourist Commission (1995). National Aboriginal Tour Operators Forum, Alice Springs.

Northern Territory Tourist Commission *(1999/2000). 1999/ 2000 Territory Tourism Selected Statistics*. www.nttc.com.au/statistics/

Palmer, L. (1999). Safari Hunting and Indigenous Peoples, paper presented at the 14th Australasian Wildlife Management Conference, Northern Territory University.

Pearce, P. L. (1998). *Proud to Be Aborigine: Visitor Responses to Tjapukai Cultural Park*. Eighth Australian Tourism and Hospitality Research Conference, Canberra, Bureau of Tourism Research.

Pitcher, M. J. (1999). *Tourists, Tour Guides and True Stories: Aboriginal Cultural Tourism in the Top End*. School of Social Sciences. Northern Territory University, Darwin.

Pitcher, M. J., van Oosterzee, P., et al. (1999). *Choice and Control: The Development of Indigenous Tourism in Australia*. Centre for Indigenous Cultural and Natural Resource Management, Darwin.

Pitterle, S. (1999). International Visitor's Interest and Experience with Indigenous Tourism Products, workshop for Northern Territory Tourist Operators, Northern Territory Tourist Commission, Darwin.

Press, T., Lea, D., et al. (Ed). (1995). *Kakadu: Natural and Cultural Heritage and Management*. Australian National University, Darwin.

Ross, H. (1991). "Controlling Access to Environment and Self: Aboriginal Perspectives on Tourism." *Australian Psychologist* 26(3): 176-182.

Ryan, C. & Huyton, J. (2000a). "Who Is Interested in Aboriginal Tourism in the Northern Territory, Australia? A Cluster Analysis." *Journal of Sustainable Tourism* 8(1): 53-88.

Ryan, C. & Huyton, J. (2000b). "Aboriginal Tourism - a Linear Structural Relations Analysis of Domestic and International Tourist Demand." *International Journal of Tourism Research* 2: 15-29.

Ryan, C. & Huyton, J. (2001). *Balanda Visitors to Australia: Their Perceptions*. Capitalising on Research. Eleventh Australian Tourism and Hospitality Research Conference, Canberra, University of Canberra.

Schaper, M. (1999). "Australia's Aboriginal Small Business Owners: Challenges for the Future." *Journal of Small Business Management* 37(3): 88-94.

Schuler, S., Aberdeen, L., et al. (1999). "Sensitivity to Cultural Difference in Tourism Research: Contingency in Research Design." *Tourism Management* 20(1): 59-70.

Smith, V. L. (Ed). (1977). *Hosts and Guests - the Anthropology of Tourism*. University of Pennsylvania Press, USA.

South Australian Tourism Commission (1998). *Indigenous Tourism: Background Research on the Demand for Indigenous Tourism Product in South Australia*. South Australian Tourism Commission, Adelaide.

Waitt, G. (1999). "Naturalizing the 'Primitive': A Critique of Marketing Australia's Indigenous Peoples as 'Hunter-Gathers." *Tourism Geographies* 1(2): 142-163.

Weiler, B. (1997). Meeting the Ecotourism Education and Training Need of Australia's Indigenous Community. *Tourism and Heritage Management*. W.Nuryanti (Ed). Gadjah Mada University Press, Yogyakarta.

Wells, J. (1996). Marketing Indigenous Heritage: A Case Study of Uluru National Park. *Heritage Management in Australia and New Zealand: The Human Dimension*. C.M.Hall and S.McArthur (Ed). Oxford University Press, Melbourne.

Wells, J. & Kauffman, P. (1999). *Saving the Dreamtime: Representations of Indigenous Tourism in Marketing*. Ninth Australian Tourism and Hospitality Research Conference, Canberra, Bureau of Tourism Research.

Zeppel, H. (1998b). "Come Share Our Culture: Marketing Aboriginal Tourism in Australia." *Pacific Tourism Review* 2(1): 67-82.

Zeppel, H. (1998c). Selling the Dreamtime: Aboriginal Culture in Australian Tourism. *Tourism, Leisure, Sport: Critical Perspectives*. D.Rowe and G.Lawrence (Ed). Hodder education, Rydalmere, NSW.

Zeppel, H. (1998d). Land and Cultural Sustainable Tourism and Indigenous Peoples. *Sustainable Tourism a Geographical Approach*. M.Hall and A.A.Lew (Ed). Addison Wesley Longman, UK.

Zeppel, H. (1999a). *Aboriginal Tourism in Australia: A Research Bibliography*. CRC for Sustainable Tourism, Australia. C:\My Documents\NITRSS\Indigenous Tourism Copy.enl

Zeppel, H. (1999b). Dreamtime in the City: The National Aboriginal Cultural Centre Sydney. *Ninth Australian Tourism and Hospitality Research Conference*. J.Molley and J.Davies (Ed). Bureau of Tourism Research, Canberra.

Zeppel, H. (1999c). *Hidden Histories: Aboriginal Cultures in Nsw Regional Tourism Brochures*. Ninth Australian Tourism and Hospitality Research Conference, Canberra, Bureau of Tourism Research.

Zeppel, H. (2001). Aboriginal Cultures and Indigenous Tourism. *Special Interest Tourism*. N.Douglas, N.Douglas and R.Derrett (Ed). John Wiley & Sons Australia Ltd, Brisbane.

13

Issues in Intellectual Property Rights: The Role of Tourism in Safeguarding the Integrity of Cultural Icons

*Malcolm Cooper**
*Maggie Asplet***

It has often been noted that a community's heritage and cultural life is an undervalued and under-utilised tourism resource. On the other hand tourism has also often been criticised as having a very high potential for adverse impacts on local and indigenous cultural values (Picard, 1995; Cohen, 1992; Mathieson and Wall, 1982; Pizam, 1978; Graburn, 1976). Within the context of this debate, this chapter discusses the increasing pressure in both Australia and New Zealand for local control of the use of indigenous cultural icons. The current legal background to intellectual property rights in those

* Professor Malcolm Cooper PhD LLM FPIA is Dean, Wide Bay Campus, University of Southern Queensland PO Box 910, Hervey Bay, Queensland, Australia.

** Ms Maggie Asplet was Dean, Waiariki Polytechnic, Rotorua, New Zealand and currently runs her own fashion design business.

Countries is referred to and used as a framework for determining the likely success of attempts to control the use of indigenous cultural imagery for tourism purposes.

Issues in the Use of Tourist Merchandise as a form of Cultural Expression

The concept of culture has been debated in anthropological literature for over two centuries (Mathieson & Wall, 1982). Modern thinking on culture is that 'Culture can be broadly defined as a way of life—the way we think, believe and behave as well as the way we make, do and use things. Culture is the way a people express themselves—not only verbally, but also in dress, lifestyle, beliefs and practices (Crocombe, 1983, 46). Ritchie and Zins (1978, 257), on the other hand have defined cultural tourism as: 'the consumption by tourists of features resembling the culture of a society'. They identified elements of culture that attract tourists to particular destinations. These are:

1. Handicrafts;
2. Language;
3. Traditions;
4. Gastronomy;
5. History of a region, including visual reminders;
6. The types of work engaged in by residents and the technology used;
7. Architecture giving the area a distinctive appearance;
8. Religion, including visible manifestations;
9. Educational systems;
10. Dress;
11. Leisure activities.

For the physical manifestations of cultural values on this list (1, 4, 5, 7, 8, 9, and 11), it has been often observed that a belief in their authenticity lends tremendous weight and value to cultural objects (Healy, 1994). The knowledge that a cultural souvenir is locally handmade is also an important ingredient in establishing its authenticity—things made by local hands are 'genuine'. Mass-produced commodities made elsewhere are in the realm of the 'plastic', a word connoting flimsiness, superficiality, flashiness, or artificiality, whether in concept or material. Cohen (1992) on the other hand observed that cultural products such as mass-produced handicrafts that might at first seem contrived or unauthentic could over time become recognised as authentic. He referred to this process as 'emergent authenticity', and noted that even experts may eventually accept such products as authentic.

Independent of this debate is the undeniable difficulty for many indigenous peoples is that, when offered for sale in retail outlets, their handicrafts, art and music are marketed not primarily as representations of their culture, or even as mementos of encounters between themselves and tourists. Instead they are offered as keepsakes of the *Country*, often as 'authentic' souvenirs of that country (Blundell, 1993), even when the originating group may make up only a small fraction of the total population. As Blundell noted, particular problems arise as a result from the practice of labelling souvenirs with claims as to their origin, their originality, and the materials/ manufacturing processes employed to produce them, without the involvement of local indigenous groups. These claims often mislead tourists, and may even be designed to mislead tourists as to that involvement.

Additionally, while it is important to control what tourists might like to buy and authenticate its cultural origins (if any), it is also necessary to educate the tourist about local products, culture and design traditions. This is not only because the tourist product may be said to be a composite of everything purchased, seen, experienced and felt from the time the tourist leaves home until his or her return, but is also because a tourist holiday package also includes the culture of the destination as part of that package. One of the adverse consequences of this truism is that cultures, however complex or ancient they might be, can and will be reduced to a few instantly recognisable characteristics. Culture thus becomes a commodity (Aotearoa Maori Tourism Federation, 1996) to be bought and sold.

Cultural Values and Intellectual Property

The World Intellectual Property Organisation (WIPO) is responsible for the promotion of the protection of intellectual property throughout the world. Article 2(viii) of the Convention Establishing the World Intellectual Property Organisation (1967) refers to intellectual property as rights relating to:

(i) literary, artistic and scientific works;

(ii) performances of performing artists, phonogram and broadcasts;

(iii) inventions in all fields of human endeavour;

(iv) scientific discoveries;

(v) industrial designs;

(vi) trademarks, service marks, and commercial names and designations;

(vii) protection against unfair competition; and

(viii) all other rights resulting from intellectual activity in the industrial, scientific, literary or artistic fields.

The principal international instruments for the protection of intellectual property are the Paris Convention for the Protection of Industrial Property (1883), the Universal Copyright Convention, and the Berne Convention for the Protection of Literary and Artistic Works (1886). They do not however have the binding force of a *treaty*. These conventions have been revised several times, and as at April 1992, 128 states were members of the World Intellectual Property Organisation and, as of January 1992, there were 103 State members of the Paris Union and 90 State members of the Berne Union. Both New Zealand and Australia are signatories to the Paris and Berne conventions, and are members of the

World Intellectual Property Organisation. Interestingly, neither the United States nor China are signatories to the Berne Convention.

In practice therefore, intellectual property rights are only given legally binding protection at National level, if at all (although see the Uruguay Round of the General Agreement on Tariffs and Trade). The New Zealand *Trade Marks Act 1953*, for example, gives a proprietor who registers a trademark the right to prevent other traders from using the same or similar mark. It confers a monopoly right to the use or licence of a trademark in relation to the goods or services in which registration is obtained. The *Patents Act 1953* allows a person to apply for a patent to protect their invention. This is also essentially a monopoly property right, and the protection is primarily intended to promote innovation and secondly to promote research and development by the inventor. Under this Act the patent holder has exclusive right for a limited period of 16 years to make use and sell an invention. This period can be extended by up to 10 years in certain limited circumstances (Note the recent GATT agreement on intellectual property rights resulting from the Uruguay Round (TRIPS) provides for a 20 year term with no extensions).

The New Zealand *Designs Act 1953* ensures that persons who develop a new design can profit from their work without others being able to exploit that work. The Act provides a registered proprietor of a design with a statutory monopoly throughout the Country and the objects of the Act aim to protect the external features of the product. This Act provides up to 15 years protection for any original design, whereas the *Copyright Act 1962* protects original artistic (literary, dramatic or musical) works, ensuring that they cannot be copied without consent of the copyright owner, for the lifetime of the author plus 50 years. Note that once an artistic work has been industrially applied (50 reproductions made) protection under the Copyright Act is reduced to 16 years.

While aspects of the above legal frameworks, and of commercial law such as the Fair Trading Act and the Commerce Act may be useful in protecting cultural values in

New Zealand, in general, current legislation in both Australia and New Zealand deals only with individual property and new knowledge. It does not protect collective property or traditional knowledge (Anderson, 1990). Protection of cultural values will only be provided by new legislation specifically designed to collectivise cultural expression and render these in law.

Cultural Tourism and Intellectual Property Rights in New Zealand

The intellectual property relating to the culture of New Zealand as portrayed to the tourist is that of the Maori indigenous people. It covers all taonga inherited and conceived by Maori. The Treaty of Waitangi (1840 - Article Two) between the British colonisers and the Maori indigenous population refers to 'taonga' as being:

"...te tino Rangatiratanga o o ratou whenua o ratou kainga me o ratou taonga katoa...

The translation of which reads:

"...the full, exclusive and undisturbed possession of their lands and estates, forests, fisheries, and other properties which they may collectively or individually possess..."

To understand this concept it is useful to refer to a United Nations paper (E/CN. 4/Sub.2/1992/30 - 6 July 1992), which classified the intellectual property of indigenous peoples into three broad groups:

- Folklore and Crafts—which includes various forms of oral literature, music, dance, artistic motifs and designs, crafts such as basketry, beading, quillwork, carving, weaving and painting;
- Biodiversity—plant varieties which have been developed through experiment and cultivation for use as food, medicine or materials for houses or boats (or crafts), and other kinds of construction or use;
- Indigenous Knowledge—the knowledge held, evolved and passed on by the indigenous peoples about their environment, plants and animals, and the interaction of the two.

In other words, all materials, knowledge and folklore/crafts are encompassed. Nevertheless, only Maori can define specifically what is taonga Maori, and this is where the potential problem lies. While the Tourism Industry in New Zealand does in many instances provide support for Maori cultural aspirations, the industry infrastructure can at times exclude appropriate Maori *participation* in decisions that have national and international implications.

Threats Posed To Taonga Maori from Tourism

The first issue in the protection of intellectual property rights in indigenous cultures is identifying what the threats and concerns are. The primary concern as noted above is that ethnic authenticity is put at risk by tourism commercial activities. This means more specifically:

Dilution of Tikanga (Culture)

The modern world requires Maori to make allowances to cater for the commercial demands of tourism. However this can have the effect of altering some aspects of the operation of culture in an everyday context—such as imposing culturally inappropriate restrictions on action time frames, inappropriate use of meeting grounds (marae) for tourist attractions, or requiring the waiving of marae formalities to accommodate tour groups.

Misuse of Taonga and Information Regarding Taonga

The misuse of names and language, mispronunciation, inappropriate use of images on souvenir and photographs, incorrect and inappropriate versions of and communication of tribal lore and history, threats to the biodiversity central to cultural practices—plant varieties, craft materials, methods of exploitation and sources of supply).

Exploitation of Taonga through Fake Reproduction

The mass production of machine carved souvenirs, and the non-recognition of indigenous quality controls are the major problem here. Reproduction by outsiders of cultural manifestations and objects of religious importance, or false representations of cultural icons is the result.

Threat to Ownership and Control of Taonga

A lack of respect or acknowledgement of ownership rights over Maori cultural and intellectual property often occurs. In this regard no enforcement of rights by Maori is possible unless copyright and other forms of registration of ownership are contravened, but the law in these areas does not take into account communal rights or the difficulties inherent in ascribing copyright to cultural concepts. Indeed, Australasian law has failed signally to protect 'moral rights' in a work even for individuals, and continues to do so.

Depreciation of Taonga Maori

Export of Taonga Maori—there are currently no controls to ensure that an indigenous product source is acknowledged and not disguised. Commercial viability does not support the protection and care of the intrinsic Maori value of taonga, but instead relies on a trade off between dollar value and cultural value. A famous example of this was the manufacture of plastic souvenirs depicting Maori cultural icons in Hong Kong.

Appropriate Protection Mechanisms

Legislation

There is a need to review existing legislation to see what opportunities already exist to protect indigenous cultural and intellectual property rights. There is also a need to investigate what new legislation is required to cover the question of community ownership of resources, including intellectual property, as distinct from private ownership and the structures of common law. In 1989 UNESCO adopted a Report entitled 'Recommendations on the Safeguarding of Traditional Culture and Folklore', which contained a set of Model Provisions (UNESCO, 1989). These provisions were in four categories covering:

- expressions (of culture) by words;
- expressions by musical sounds;
- expressions by action (movement);
- expressions incorporated in a material object.

These provisions prohibit creation of the impression that expressions of culture are derived from a particular community when, in fact, such is not the case, and recommends that Countries place restrictions on imports of foreign-made material objects purporting to be from their own culture. The creation of an international treaty governing these matters has not proceeded to date however, so very little actual advance in the worldwide protection of intellectual property rights has been achieved.

Industry Standards

As a result, national standards authenticating indigenous tourism products need to be developed and enforced. A trademark of authenticity could then be designed and marketed, an accreditation process established, and an enforcement body put in place. Education of indigenous tribal groupings in New Zealand and Australia in regard to the process, standards and any subsequent trademarks involved in protecting indigenous property rights would be required under this approach. Coupled with this is the need to ensure greater awareness and support from any enforcement body and the wider tourism industry.

The United States Legislation—A Model?

In 1935 the United States Congress approved an act 'to promote the development of Indian arts and crafts and to create a board to assist therein'. This Act created the Indian Arts and Crafts Board of five elected commissioners whose function it was to promote the economic welfare of the Indian tribes through the development and marketing of Indian Arts and Crafts. The Board was given the power 'to create Government trade marks of genuineness and quality for Indian products and the products of particular Indian tribes or groups;

to establish standards and regulations for the use of such trade marks; to license corporations or individuals to use them; and to charge a fee for their use; and to register them in the United States Patent Office without charge' (S 2(g)). The Board had recognition as a Government Agency and was resourced initially by Treasury. The Act also provided for penalties for misuse of the trademark and for offering 'for sale any goods ... as Indian products or Indian products of a particular Indian tribe or group (when) such goods are not Indian products or are not Indian products of the particular Indian tribe'.

The practical implementation of this legislation means, for example, that when dealing with the production of American Indian jewellery the finished product will be recognised as an authentic artefact provided:

(a) that the producer is an American Indian;

(b) that he or she is recognised as a qualified artist;

(c) that traditional materials are used;

(d) that the designs are traditionally Indian; and

(e) that the artefact is hand-made.

These provisions effectively assign ownership and control over intellectual property created within the American First Nations cultures. Unless all these conditions are met the artefact does not qualify for the term 'authentic Indian artefact'.

Conclusion

The United States model appears to provide the controls necessary for the proper protection of cultural forms and expression at the level of rights in intellectual property, if that is what is desired. This does not of course mean that cultural imitations cannot be found in that country, nor does it mean that tourists will not forsake the genuine for the often-cheaper imitation. It does mean however that the decision to do so will be informed one, and that tourists themselves cannot claim that they have purchased 'the real thing'.

It will not be possible to go further under existing intellectual property rights protection regimes until rights of cultural autonomy for indigenous peoples are recognised in international law. While agreeing with Picard that the cultural icons presented to tourists in most countries are often the inventive product of what is by now a long-standing dialogue between indigenous groups and tourism, the increasing ownership of tourism enterprise by indigenous peoples requires not only rights in land and infrastructure but also intellectual property rights in the expression of their cultural heritage. Only in this way will the full economic benefits of cultural tourism accrue to the originators of the cultures being visited.

REFERENCES

Anderson, P. (1990) *Aboriginal Imagery: Influence, Appropriation, Theft? Eyeline 12*: 8-11.

Aotearoa Maori Tourism Federation. (1996). *The Protection of Cultural and Intellectual Property Rights of Maori within the Tourism Industry*, Presented to the Aotearoa Maori Tourism Federation National Hui, Paparoa Marae, September.

Blundell, V. (1993) *Aboriginal Empowerment and Souvenir Trade in Canada. Annals of Tourism Research 20*: 64 - 87.

Cohen, E. (1992), *The Study of Touristic Images of Native People: Mitigating the Stereotype of a Stereotype*. In Pearce, D. and Butler, R., Eds. *Tourism Research: Critiques and Challenges*. London, Routledge.

Crocombe, Ron (1983) *The South Pacific: an Introduction. Auckland*, Longman Paul.

Graburn, N.H.H., Ed (1976) *Ethnic and Tourist Arts: Cultural Expressions from the Fourth World*. Berkeley, University of California Press.

Healy, R. G. (1994) *Tourist Merchandise as a means of generating local benefits from Ecotourism. Journal of sustainable Tourism 2*: (3), 137-151.

Mathieson, A & Wall, G. (1982) *Tourism Economic, Physical and Social Impacts*. London, Longman Group.

Picard, M. (1995) *Balinese Culture: Cultural Heritage and Tourist Capital*. In M-F. Lanfant, J. B. Allcock and E. M. Bruner, Eds, *International Tourism: Identity and Change*. London, Sage Studies in International Sociology 47.

Pizam, A. (1978) Tourism's *Impacts: the Social Costs to the Destination as Perceived by its Residents. Journal of Travel Research 16*: (4), 8-12.

Ritchie, J.R. and Zins, M. (1978) *Culture as a Determinant of the Attractiveness of a Tourist Region. Annals of Tourism Research 5*: 252-267.

14

Study on the Tourist Sustainability of the Eco-tourism Destination

*Zhang Mu**

Abstract

According to the eco-tourism development tendency around the world, this paper mainly researches some problems of the tourist sustainability and takes the case study about the Longsheng County, GuangXi province. At first, the tourists resources consist of multifarious natural landscape in this county are stated. Then the author analyzes the close correlation between the economical structure and its natural environment and then considers that the Longsheng County should be an eco-tourism destination. The eco-tourism exploitation would benefit to relieve the poor through the operating the tourism supported by the government. Therefore, some relevant advice of the eco-tourism development, especially about the tourist guideline and strategy, environment protection and sustainable development are put forward.

* (Zhang mu, Doctor of physical geography, worked as an associate professor in Tourism and environment department of Guangxi Institute of Education. Address: 37 Jianzheng road, Nanning, Tourism & Environment Department of GuangXi Institute of Education, Guangxi province, P.R.China, 530023. E-mail: zhangmu@163.com

Key words: Eco-tourism, tourist destination, sustainability, Longsheng County

Background

Eco-tourism, a kind of new tourist form, has been a mainstream of the tourist development in the world, especially in those new tourist destination. From the 80's, the eco-tourism have been popularized in the western countries and the production value increased in 10 per cent~30 per cent rate per year (higher than the 4 per cent of the average growth level of the world tourist industry). The main reason about that due to the revival consciousness of the environment protection and then the eco-tourism has been thought as the substitute of the mass tourism. So many people think of that the eco-tourism could be described as a special tourist form and given the different description such as the soft tourism, green tourism, low-impact tourism, alternative tourism, nature tourism, responsible tourism, appropriate tourism, sustainable tourism etc.(Zou Tong-Qian 1999). The core feature of them is that the tourist activities should be carried out on the basic of the efficient protection of the environment. In the new century, the conception of the eco-tourism has been profound defined. The whole content about it including the followings: the eco-tourism, no longer being thought of a kind of tourist product relied on the particular environment or tourist resources, should be regarded as a required morality of the tourist. The key problem around it is to establish a sustainable tourist mode which means we should do the protection of the physical surroundings and provid assistance for poor areas of the country through the tourist exploitation. Each people should make sure that the natural environment could not be thought as a conquered object and people's influence should be diminished at lower level. The harmony between the people and circumstances is the ultimate target of the eco-tourism.

This paper mainly researches the corresponding topic in relation to the eco-tourism in developing countries. Because the eco-tourism has obvious impact on the aid-the-poor program for the local government. In the south of China, there are more regions where are suitable for the tourist development and Guangxi province is an important tourist destination over there. The selection zone of this paper is Longshen County, located in the north of Guangxi and near to the famous tourist city - Guilin. It is one of the twelve-poverty counties in Guangxi province and has more minorities living there. Because the local government take the tourist development into account and the eco-tourism program just been in the beginning, so the author hope to summarize some useful countermeasure to building up a sustainable tourist mode in the similar area of China.

The Physically Basis of the Sustainable Eco-tourism

According to the above description to the eco-tourism, we can reach the agreement that the eco-tourism should be activated in the region where are free from the human's disturbance relatively. So, there are more aboriginal of the environment, there are better of the tourism development. Generally, the physical basis of the sustainable eco-tourism belongs to the nature environment system. The value of the natural feature is more than that of the economic feature.

Longshen County is situated on the juncture of three provinces, Hunan, Guizhou and Guangxi and the south border of the Yuechen mountains. The area of the county is about 2442 square kilometers and the mountainous region takes up 87 per cent to the total area. The whole area at an elevation of 700 meters and is a typical mountainous county. Within the boundaries of this county, it is rich in natural resources in particular there are four support industries, including the forest reserves, minerals, waterpower and tourist resources. The area of forest is about 132000 hectare and the percentage of the forest cover goes up 74.5 per cent, so the ecological environment has better quality and means that the exploitation of the tourist resources has a superior basis. For instance, there are number of the different tourist scenic spot: 1)Huapin National Nature Preservation, built up at 1978, mainly protected the rare and precious flora such as the typical broad-leaved forest ecosystem and the China fir. It is bounded on the northeast by Lingui County and near the Guilin just from 60 kilometers. Total area is about 15133.3 hectare and at an elevation between 1200~1600 meters. In this nature reserve, the average air temperature is about 2~14ºC. The developed tourist spot comprised Hongmao River, Chujiang River, Red waterfront and Guangfu Forest Spot where have beautiful scenery about the China fir and broaden virgin forest and there are more travellers come here every year. 2) Hot Spring National Forest Park is another valuable destination. Here the hot spring and forest landscape has a strong appeal to the visitor. 3) The Terrace Field on the Dragon Back is world-famous for its marvellous spectacle and long history, so as to become a most important spot in the Longshen County. 4) Because of the multiple minority living together, such as the Miao, Yao, Dong and Zhuang nationalities, there are multifarious tradition and custom to attract the tourist. All of these means that the foundation of the tourist development has been established. Now the five scenic spot of the total area of the county have been formatted and become one of the key support counties which financial come from the funds provided by the Guangxi province government. The theme of the local tourism is "the unique hot spring, the excellent nature landscape, the strong flavor of rural life, the majestic terrace field on the dragon back and the mysterious virgin forest". By comparison with the "the fascinating mountains, the beautiful waters, the monstrous cave and the grotesque rock " of the Guilin scenery, the landscape of the Longshen County is an apropos supplement. Some people hold that the nature reserve, forest park, scenic spot, zoological and botanical garden, multiple ecotope and artificial ecological zone are classified into the eco-tourism destination (WAN HUA-Bin, ZHOU Ling, 2001). In this region the characteristic of the tourist resources have been shown by the particular species of plant and animal, the special eco-system and landscape etc. They make up the main contend of the sightseeing to the tourist. In short, the destination of Longshen County is a typical eco-tourism attraction where all travel programs are suited for the eco-tourism.

In the light of the tourist development current, the purpose of the industry structure readjustment is to avoid the aggravation of the ecological environment in tourist destination. In the past decade, the ill effect of the "the eco-tourism exploitation damaged the ecological environment" take place generally in more new tourist destination in China. Because following with the tourist program opened to the popular, the urbanization proceeding would speed up and the pure agricultural field would irreversible change into town or urban land. The predictable result is the order of the primary environment would be disturbed and the sustainable development of the local tourist industry is effected also. So more and more people realized that the relationship between the mankind and environment is more important than the tourist exploitation itself. The tourist development stage of the Longshen County is still in the preliminary state and the local people with correct awareness about the eco-tourism exploitation are absolutely necessary.

Table—14.1 The Tourist Development Level in Longshen County during the Ninth Five-year Plan

Year	Reception number of tourist (Ten thousand people)	Business earnings (Ten thousand Yuan)	Financial Income (Ten Thousand Yuan)
1995	20.2	1150	–
1996	24.1	1810	–
1997	26.0	2061	–
1998	28.6	2320	110
1999	33.2	3200	135

In the ninth five-year plan, the tourism of the Longshen County come through from a high speed tourist industry development to a stable development period and acquired a good achievement (look at the Table—14.1):

From the table, the tourist industry development of Longshen County has a forward effect to the ecological environment and get profit from the core tourist resources such as the primitive ecotope and ancient habitat. In the past time, the single city usually is looked as a unity of "cell economy" which means that the different industry gather in a city. So much as we can say that the traditional tourist cities such as Beijing, Xi'an, Suzhou, and Guilin have been transformed to the industrial city in China now. The original nature and human environment has been damaged in the different level respectively. So the new city plan commonly considers the relations between the economic development and environment protection. The tourist vantage of Longshen County is eco-tourism and the "operating tourism to relieve the poor" has been making sure as the local government's economic development strategy. It means that the economy would ground on the good ecological environment and without it the economic basis would be loosed. When the local government starts to operate the new city plan and the tenth five-year plan, the specialization and the comparative advantages of the region economy should be forehand considered. Meanwhile, when taking the reconstitution of the urban economic structure into account, the decision-maker should be fully articulated realize the location of Longshen County in the big tourist cycle of Guilin and the advantage of the division of labour in this special space. In the other words, the target of the eco-tourism is to create an enjoyment nature landscape and traditional customs, restrict the blind activity hold by the tourist business company and the false behaviour of the tourist. Every organization or person should share the cost of the eco-tourism resources protection and make sure that the benefit from the eco-tourism could go down to the descendants and finally establish a sustainable eco-tourism development environment in Longshen County.

Building up the Proper Approach of the Eco-tourism Promotion the Principle of "Government Guiding Policy"

The affect factors of the tourist sustainable mainly shown up in the contradiction among of the nature environment and tourist activity. Because the target of the eco-tourism and the sustainable development are highly accordant, so that the governing principle of nature protection should be established and popularized. The important work now is to positive avoiding the ill influence, which come from the urbanization in the tourist destination, through the appropriate countermeasure. The tourist industry in the minority region is general behind the developed region. But the proper advanced consciousness of the tourist development are needed. The signification of the "proper advance " could be described in two aspects: 1)the development speed of the tourist industry should match up to the local economic development situation and keep step with it at an appropriate degree; 2) the tourist exploitation should development advanced and it means that the tourism growth is enough to support the scale and earnings of the whole tourist system. The application of the proper advanced principle in tourism is necessary to the minority region and could deal with the backwardness. In the practice, the "government guiding policy " is a well-contented choice to the eco-tourism destination. This policy can be described as : the local government get dominant position to operate the tourist activity and centralized arrange for and harmonize the relationship among of the different industry. The most important work in this system is to develop tourism supported by all social participation and on the faith of the government the tourism can be developed as a precedence industry in the local economic system.

The reason of the application about the "government guiding policy" in the minority eco-tourism destination include the following content: 1) special attributes of the tourism need for overall planning to the different industry. The six main parts of the tourism, traffic, hotel, restaurant, sightseeing, shopping and entertainment are higher correlative. Without the unified management by the government the tourism could not operate well. In long time the tourism has been built up a self-contained system which are composed by the numerous small tourist companies and the main financial source is from the local government in China. Hence the tourism itself could not support the operation of the whole system. At the complex and disorder management situation, the tourism could not get too more benefit. Therefore, the government must realizes the responsibility of the conduction and coordination to the different industry. In the local practice of the application of the above principle, building up a committee of tourism management is necessary and useful. The function of this committee is to carry out and arrange macroscopic behavior relevant to the tourism and finally building up a unitary, open and ordered tourist market system. 2) The tourism marketing also needs the support from the government. The economy of the minority region is in low-level than that of the developed region. The way of the tourist specialization is difficult. The government guiding could concentrate social participation to operate the tourism. According to the situation of the tourist industry in Longshen County, the basic of the tourist specialization is mass tourism since the mass tourism now is an effective way to develop tourism rapidly in the new tourist destination. The advances of the mass tourism are noticeable because it is a kind of the chartered group behaviour created by travel agency and its market aims at the popular. In the new tourist region such as Longshen County, sometimes it does not provide tourist and the tourism development lie on the foreign travellers. The local government through the above principle can enforce the high expenses of the sales promotion and media advertisement. Therefore the contradiction between mass tourism and eco-tourism could be harmonized well and guarantee the sustainable development of the tourism. 3) The quick increase of the holiday tourism needs for guidance by the government. In the past three years, the three long time holidays, Spring Festival, National Days and Labour Days, activate the tourist market and accelerate the development of the holiday economy in China. The gathering and large-scale effect of the tourist industry occurred obviously in more tourist destination cities. But by contrast with the above success the more and more population bring about bad effect to the environment and the restrictive and time sharing enter become the effective ways to control these unflavoured state in some more vacation land.

In general, the government guiding is only one of the positive manners in a special period to development tourism in new travel destination. From the long-term management planning, accompany with the improvement of the tourist law institutionalization and industry specialization the government guiding will gradually transform into the new style something like the "government instruction" or " government coordination".

Protection of the Ecological Environment

The environment protection is equal to the tourist resources conservation in the eco-tourism destination. The core principle of the environmental preservation is to introduce the environment sightseeing program under the guard by the sustainable theory and coordinate the activities between the tourist development and environment protection.

Because of the implication of environmental preservation, the eco-tourism develops soon over the world. More and more scenic area and travel program titled eco-tourism shows the growth tendency and sounds marketing prospect in the future. If just look at the conception of eco-tourism, two fields could be classified: one is in the narrow sense and it means the eco-tourism could be summarized as "return nature tourism", "green tourism", and "environment protection tourism"etc. The broader conception means the eco-tourism, not only contains the nature system implication but also have the meaning of the culture system. Mr.Laixi Guo outlined the essential properties of the eco-tourism including the six aspects: nature, peculiarity, culture, elegant, participation and sustainability, which constitute a sustainable tourist system(ZHANG JIAN-Ping, 2001). More regulation and law are enacted such as (The nature conservation program of China), *(The biodiversity action plan of China), (The regulation of the protection of the national historical relic of China), (The management regulation of the national scenic area of China), (The 21 century agenda of China) and correspondingly building up a serial unit something like the national forest park, national nature conservation, national scenic area, ocean reservation area, national Famous Historical Cultural Cities, national important cultural relic and national resort etc.,* In all these areas could undertake the population pressure from the tourists. The tendency of the spatial movement of the tourist activity gradual approaches the primitive area in the world. From the recent mountainous tourism and forest tourism, the interest of the tourists has been transferred from the east area to the inapprehensive west areas of China. In this situation we can find out that the Longshen County has its resources superiority on the eco-tourism such as the primitive environment and long history of the minorities. It is an apropos time to the tourist development in the west minority area. There are more regions like Longshen County not only show the visible attraction such as landform, river and biodiversity but also have the invisible attraction like the sunshine, clean air and pollution-free nature environment. These special tourist resources have been changed into peculiar tourist attraction and promote the tourism development. Operating of the different theme and type eco-tourism would become a high productibility and potentiality tourist industry especially in the broaden minority area in the west of China.

Refrain from any Rash Urbanization Action in Scenic Zone

The colonial is concomitant phenomenon of the tourist activity. When the tourists come from the developed countries they usually influence the tourist destination with their traditional custom and culture. These foreign tourist behaviours exert an imperceptible influence on the inhabitants of the destination. The people will change the original environment and culture so as to alter the appearance of the eco-tourism in that they pursuit the improvement of the living conditions. This process is the continuousness of the urbanization from the nearby cities and affect the tourist sustainable development. Now the chartered mass tourism is still a mainstream mode in the eco-tourism destination such as Longshen County, because of its convenient and cheap. So many development businesses regard the eco-tourism destination as ordinary resort and get earnings from the mass tourism. The theme of the environment protection is inobservant and therefore the contradictory relations of nature conservation and tourist consumption are exacerbated. The result of the urban culture irruption had changed the

Table—14.2 The Comparison of the Mass Tourism and Eco-tourism (YAN YOU-Bin, 2001)

	Mass tourism	Eco-tourism
Key property	High development speed and economic effect of optimization; it is custom not need strict control for market-development and has relative short tourist time.	Lower development speed and go after the optimal benefit harmonized among of the ecological, environment and society; needed for strict market control and long tourist time.
Tourist behaviour	The generally mode is a group chartered tourist and has steady travel period and has tour guide and comfortable tour; the tourist are just to be sightseeing along the travel rout, have no occasion to communication with foreign language and have to litter more noisy in tour.	Usually the tourist is single or small group and not need tour guide, and they can voluntary action in the destination; sometimes they need communication with foreign language and total tour is quieter than that of the group tourist.
Basic requirement	The activity usually occurs in the peak vacation. The staff often lack of training, the promotion of the tourism has get the way of routine media advertisement and hard selling.	The tourist action takes place in the alternating vacation and need high quality staff. The market-development need to instruct tourist and the marketing way is emphasized in heart selling.
Development strategy	There are not any long time plan and the program about the main mode. The tourist development need to enforce basic construction and the foreign capital are the main-stream of the development company.	The strict plan is needed for the special title of the ecological idea and environment ethical. The tourist development can reuse the old building and the main body of the development is local companies.

heterogeneity of the special eco-tourism community and weakens the tourist attraction. The unsustainable of the tourism would ineluctable take place when the physical ecotop basis dies away. In order to build up a perfect eco-tourism area, we should get correct recognition of the differentiation, superior and inferior between the eco-tourism and mass tourism (looking the Table—14.2) :

Thus the distinction of the eco-tourism and mass tourism can be seen that not only shown in the tourist behaviour but also shown in the manager's idea and marketing-development mode. In China the main target of the eco-tourism is get the local people to make benefit from the tourism. In the mode of mass tourism we can find out that just few people can get earnings from the tourist activity. The step-up tourist would prompt the raise of Social cost in destination and lead to some people bring about opposed emotion and effect the tourist activity. So the community participation is an important principle to the eco-tourism. The marketing development business company is also another factor to bring the success for the tourist development. The foreign company always pursuit short-term action effects and ignore the long-term ecological affect about the environment protection. When leaded by the government guide principle the eco-tourism can keep sustainable development. There is more similar property in the implication of eco-tourism and sustainable development for instance the environment protection, limitation of the development, respect of the local culture and community participation etc. So the sustainable of the tourist development in Longshen County is a goal to the local economic growth and the eco-tourism is a suitable choice.

Conclusion

The economic development level still in a lower level in the minority area of China. The tourist industry developed rapidly after the "operating tourism to relieve the poor" policy has been ascertained. Because there is more Nature Conservation, National Forest Park and scenic area and beauty spot with high quality in minority area. But some key factors which effects the tourist development, such as lack of the capital and professional staff, the management means behind that of the developed area. All of these restrain the sustainability of the tourism and operating the eco-tourism exploitation program in a large scale is not reality. So the approach of the moderately combination marketing-development of the mass tourism and eco-tourism has to be selected as main mode in future in the new tourist destination such as Longshen County.

REFERENCES

Zou Tong-Qian (1999). Tourist Exploitation and Plan. GungDong Tourism Publishing house, Guangzhou, China, 265-275

WAN HUA-Bin, ZHOU Ling (2001). The Development of the Eco-tourism, Science Publishing house, Beijing, China, 50-53

ZHANG JIAN-Ping (2001). The Theory and Practice of the Eco-tourism, Tourism Publishing House of China, Beijing, China, 93-95

YAN YOU-Bin (2001). The Research About the Tourist Development, Hunan Teachers University Publishing House, Changsha, China, 178-186

15

Tourism Marketing in India: An Overview

*Mukesh Ranga**

Abstract

Man is a social animal. Since the dawn of civilization man has been an ardent traveller with the motivations either to expand existing trade or to conquer new places and to pilgrimage. Whatever may be the objectives, man has been sauntering to other areas to know more facts or to acquire more wisdom. India as a Tourist destination provides everything as an attraction to everybody. Present paper discusses tourism development in India along with government efforts for the promotion.

Introduction

Tourism is one of the fastest growing industries in the world today. In some countries with weak national economies, tourism is being regarded as a new primary industry. It creates employment and often brings in foreign currency to economically marginal areas. Sightseers from more affluent

* Lecturer, Institute of Tourism and Hotel Management, Bundelkhand University, Jhansi (India).

nations are ever searching for new places to explore. The trend seems to be growing away from sun, sea, and sand holidays toward adventure, the outdoors, wildlife watching, and cultural interests. Tourism is a major force in global trade. It plays a vital role in the social cultural and economic development of most nations, and has the potential both to preserve heritage and to destroy it. Tourism is a source of income to hundreds of millions of individuals' worldwide. Tourism is a source of income to hundreds of millions of individuals' worldwide. Tourism is not just hundreds of thousands of businesses, but a global industry with major policy implications. One important characteristic of the tourism industry is that it is labour intensive. A given level of revenue or capital investment creates many jobs in tourism than the same level of revenue or investment would in agriculture, automobile manufacturing or petrochemicals. Tourism is not only a major social phenomenon of the modern society with enormous economic consequences but also the world's largest export industry, which accounts for about 8 per cent of the total world's exports, more than 30 per cent of international trade in services, 10.7 per cent of the global work force and about 12 per cent of world GDP. It is also dubbed as the 'Largest Smokeless Industry' and contributors towards preservation of clean environment. Tourism generates employment for guides, restaurateurs, hoteliers, local shopkeepers, mechanics, and so on. Further, tourism helps create a local integrity and sense of oneness among the people of different caste and creed. Human resource development is of vital importance in a service industry like tourism. We may spend crores of rupees on building infrastructure but it is the service people who alone can make them come alive.

India is a centre for two primitive civilizations of the world. One is the Indus-valley civilization and the Aryan civilization. The republic of India is the sixth largest country in the world preceded by China, Canada, Brazil, the United States of America and Australia. It is a country with an area of 32,87,593 square kilometers and the second largest country in the world. It stretches over 3,220 kms. from North to South and 2,980 kms. from East to West. Around 83 per cent of total population is Hindus, 2.5 per cent Muslims, 2 per cent Christians, Sikhs, Buddhists, Jains are 1.5 per cent and others and 11 per cent. Hindi is most important and popular National language spoken by about 50 per cent of the population. There are 17 other regional languages scheduled in the constitution. It is pertinent to mention that no civilization except Indus-valley civilization cover such a vast area. India means not only the prized pearls and valuable stones, but also more than anything that the rest of the world could see only an infinitesimal fraction of knowledge over a period of time and suggested solutions to the complex and multiple problems of man and society now experiences. In spite of many fields throughout the world and even though modern equipment is at the doorstep of Homeo sepins still there are many more things to discern, in mother nature on the one hand and on the other we notice the growing uncertainty, uneasiness and personal problems of the man. The holiest things in life of modern man are very minimal and his scientific knowledge and advancement is not able to solve ever-growing problems. It is the area where Indian culture penetrates and gives an indelible impression in the minds of people with the sage of continuity; solace shows the ways and means for transient problems faced. Ayurveda, Unani and Sidha are the three gifts to India, which are famous to all over the world. Yoga is another great gift endowed by this noble country to the world.

India being a big country has every thing to offer to everybody. Visiting India is an enthralling and memorable experience to one and all. The improvisations about the Oriental wonderland are provided fertile over a period of time and withstand for the time-test and suggesting solutions to the problems faced by the world. The beautiful ancient monuments are fascinating and will be a tourist delight. India is a country where the past and present blend in a systematic manner in the threshold of an exciting future and emerging as International Market. Delhi is the capital of India and is a Gateway city to the vast country. The tourist can find the beautiful sights, the sounds and smells of India through a single window system of tourism. Similarly, sandalwood smell of Karnataka presents a beautiful Panorama to the visitor. The

Karnataka's lush green forests and hills unravel nature and its beautiful products. The ruins at Hampi sing the saga of a glorious past. Bangalore and Mysore are the two great Jewels and the Crown of Bharat Mata (Mother of India). Mysore is a spiritual place and it's holiness Ganpati Sachindanand Swamiji is further making by his preaching. He is an expert in ushering music therapy. Thousands of devotees used to pay homage to this place apart from all parts of India. It is a tourist paradise and has all unique features of modernity and traditional hospitality. Each State has its own cultural glory and historical monuments to visit. Andhra Pradesh is a confluence of many a cultural stream. Assam State is resorting normally and is having beautiful areas to visit. West Bengal's contribution to Indian life is unique and unforgettable. Bihar State is with glamorous past and presents prestigious places to visit. Gujarat is an industrially developed state and offers many products to the visitor. Himachal Pradesh State is a beautiful picnic centre and offers many attractions, Jammu and Kashmir is a diamond studded with many beautiful Gardens and lakes in the crown of Indian and a visit to Jammu and Kashmir gives most enjoyable experiences. Kerala is the most densely populated state in India and offers many attractions to visitors. Tamilnadu is with ancient temples and with modern industrial achievements. Madhya Pradesh is the meeting place of different races and offers many tourist places. Maharashtra is the cradle of Indian freedom and an industrially advanced state having many a splendid picnic sports to visit. Karnataka is the land of Sandal wood and the centre for many historical events. Orissa is a state immortalized by Art. Punjab is both industrially and agriculturally advanced state and searched in our history. Rajasthan is a state with deserts promising to bloom and has many great forts, lakes and desert life is so vivid and also a visit to the State is a unique experience. Uttar Pradesh is the valley of Ganga having unique place in Indian Politics and offers many interesting holy and picnic places to visit. India has been hidden from prying eyes for many thousands of years had has secluded itself for a considerable period of time. India once called as the brightest jewel in the British Crown has developed to such great heights that it has became an example to other countries in many respects.

The present century has witnessed this country rising to higher heights and moving forward with other leading countries of a globe. The main reason is its vast geographical size, big markets and its rich potential resources. The unique feature of Indian society is joint family system where the members of the entire family are having close contacts and certain values are being maintained which is absent in other Western Countries. Many Business firm are run as family concerns. A healthy family is an asset to the society and it is the edifice on which a strong Nation is built. Even though this country is viewed as an orthodox, this system of joint family pays rich dividends and suggests solutions to many sociological problems, which the world is facing. No other country except this country perhaps has so many temples and churches, Gurudwaras and mosques, thus showing devoting towards the guiding and invisible deity in all respects. It is the reason why many people prefer to visit this country to learn intricacies, which they are not aware of, or their society permits.

Tourism Development in India

Tourism Development in this country has been started in the early sixties. By that time, all other countries have achieved a remarkable progress in this area and has exploited to a maximum possible extent. Post Independence era has witnessed Tourism development in this country. Only Great Countries, which have glorious past, can thrive on Tourism Business. Tourism Business is to some extent the product of historical facts of a country. India has been a late starter in tourism. Understandably, after independence in 1947, the attention of the government and people was focused on key areas like agriculture, irrigation, industry, power and the infrastructure. Education literacy, health care, social reform occupied center stage in government and political thinking and so-called 'luxury' activities like tourism were left to their own devises. Tourism thus grew on its own and, from 15,000 tourists in 1950, reached a figure of 2.64 million arrivals in year 2000.

India in world tourism arrivals and world tourism receipts was only 0.38 per cent and 0.39 per cent and 0.68 per cent and

0.71 per cent during 1996 and 1997 respectively, which does not commensurate with the amount and efforts spent on tourist offices abroad and overseas campaign. It creates employment and often brings in foreign currency to economically marginal areas. Sightseers from more affluent nations are ever searching for new places to explore. The trend seems to be growing away from sun, sea, and sand holidays toward adventure, the outdoors, wildlife watching, and cultural interests. The tourist pays for everything in advance in the country.

The international tourist traffic in India during 1951 was just 16,829. Over a period of 47 years since then, the arrivals became 2.4 million in 1998, registering an annual rate of growth of about 17.6 per cent. While the decade from 1951 to 1960 recorded the highest rate of growth of 24.7 per cent per year, the next decade from 1961 to 1970 registered a moderate growth rate of 8.6 per cent. The decade from 1971 to 1980 again registered a higher growth of 11.0 per cent per annum and the total arrivals crossed half-a-million mark in 1976. It, thus, took 25 years since 1951 for tourist arrivals to reach that level. The period from 1981 to 1990 registered wide fluctuations in growth rate which ranged from 5-6 per cent 29.1 per cent. While the growth during the period from 1980 to 1985 was almost negligible, the year 1986 registered a remarkable growth of 29.1 per cent and reached the one million mark. Thus, within a period of 10 years from 1976, the foreign tourist arrivals doubled to cross the one million mark. The tempo in growth was maintained till 1989, with annual increases varying from 6.5 per cent to 7.8 per cent. The year 1990, however, recorded a decline of 0.5 per cent due to various national and international events including the Gulf crisis. The average rate of growth in the decade from 1981 to 1990 was, thus, only 5.2 per cent. Tourism is of a particular significance so far as developing countries are concerned since it contributes to the environment and to the national integration as it helps in the interaction amongst social and cultural lives of the people. Over 160 million domestic tourists visiting different parts of the country every year return with a better understanding of the people living in the other regions of the country and the cultural diversity of India.

The most significant finding of virtually every organisation connected with tourism and aviation is that the focus of travel and tourism is gradually but deliberately shifting from Europe and North America to East South Asia/pacific, Middle East and South Asia recording almost twice the growth in the Americas and Europe.

The WTTC Tourism Satellite Account 2001, confirm this phenomenon and has projected data of far reaching implications for Indian Tourism in coming decade.

The following constitute important element in the tourism profile:

— The main source markets for India are United Kingdom and the United States, followed by Sri Lanka, France, Germany, Canada, Japan, Australia and Singapore.

— Tourists in the age group of 35-44 years constituted 27.5 per cent of total arrivals during 1999 followed by those in age group of 25-35 years (23.4 per cent) and 45-54 years (20.8 per cent). The majority of the visitors to India were, therefore, in the younger age brackets.

— Male tourists far exceeded the female arrivals and accounted for 69.5 per cent of the total tourist arrivals during 1999.

— Delhi and Mumbai were the main international ports of entry and accounted for 72.1 per cent of tourist disembarkation. The Southern Indian airports of Chennai, Hyderabad, Trivandrum, Cochin and Bangalore wee also points of demand, and could take future loads of international traffic.

— A significant percentage of overseas visitors to India are repeat visitors (44.9 per cent) and of these, 32.6 per cent had visited India at least twice in the past.

— About 35.4 per cent of tourists visited India in combination with other countries in the Asian region. The major neighbouring countries, which are combined with a visit to India, are Nepal, Thailand, Hong Kong and Singapore.

India's Arrival figure have kept pace with the global average but have been outstripped by competition from China, Hong Kong (China). Thailand, Dubai and Maldives. India's share in world tourism arrivals (0.38 per cent) has also remained virtually stagnant over a last decade.

	1990	**1995**	**1997**	**1998**	**1999**	**% growth 1999/1990**
World	457,217	565,385	618,2	626,7	650,00	5.03
China	10,484	20,034	23,770	25,073	27,047	17.5
Hong Kong	6,581	10,200	10,406	9,575	11,328	8.0
Dubai	633	1,601	1,792	2,184	2,481	32.4
Maldives	195	315	366	396	430	13.3
Thailand	5,299	6,952	7,294	7,843	8,651	7.02
India	1707	2,124	2,374	2,359	2,482	5.04

***Source*:** **Market Research Division, Department of Tourism, Govt. of India**

In terms of tourism receipts, India has scored above the global average and is clearly the leader in the region. The buoyancy in the tourism earnings are largely on account of shopping and the consolidation of traditional items of handicraft along with the new demand for gems and jewellery, especially diamonds, has put considerable weight in the Indian market.

	1990	**1995**	**1997**	**1998**	**1999**
World	263,647	405,904	439,677	443,000	453,200
China	2,218	8,733	12,074	12,602	14,098
Hong Kong	5,032	9,604	9,424	7,083	7,210
Dubai	169	389	535	562	607
Singapore	4,937	8,390	6,073	5,402	5,974
Thailand	4,326	7,664	7,084	5,984	6,695
India	1,513	2,609	2,913	22,945	3,036

There is, however, a hidden dimension to Indian tourism, one that has figured little in the policy planning or thinking of most government and industrial players. This has been the most almost unobtrusive and yet inexorable rise of domestic tourism in Indian paradigm. In the last ten years alone domestic tourism has increased by more than 100 million travellers, up from 63.8 million visitors in 1990 to 176 million visitors in 1999.

This phenomenal explosion of domestic tourism is an inevitable by-product of economic development in the country. As people acquire more disposable income, the demand for Travel and Tourism grown exponentially. This is because of the well-recognized axiom that travel is the first priority of an income earner after the basic requirement of home, food and essentials.

Domestic tourism in India is also influenced by several factors:

— India is home of leading religions of the world: Hinduism, Buddism, Jainism and Sikhism. It is also home of sizable followers of Islam and Christianity. Important pilgrim sites of different religion are scattered through out the country and Indians from different States travel vast distances to perform pilgrim duties at the shrines. There are great religious places of pilgrimages like Badri Nath, Vaishno Devi, Bodh Gaya, Tirupati, Rameshwaram, The Golden Temple, Jagannath puri, Mount Abu and countless others. The great Kumbh Mela attracted more than 68 million visitors in 2000 to Allahabad, making it the largest international event other than the Haj.

— The average Indian is also an avid sightseer and can travel thousands of miles to different environments. Gujarat and Bengal head this list but Tamil Nadu, Karnataka and Andhra Pradesh are not far behind.

— Each State has its own cultural and historical monuments to visit. Andhra Pradesh is a confluence of many a cultural stream. Rajasthan is a state with Deserts promising to bloom and has many great forts, lakes and desert life is so vivid and also a visit to the State is a unique experience.

Domestic Visits

Year	Domestic
1990	63,817,285
1991	85,864,892
1992	102,465,705
1993	109,237,566
1994	127,116,655
1995	136,648,600
1996	140,119,672
1997	159,871,008
1998	168,196,000
1999	176,082,442

Source: Market Research Division, Department of Tourism, Govt. of India

In recent years tourism has emerged as a major economic activity that is employment oriented and earns foreign exchange. Its share in the worlds GDP in 1994-95 was 10 per cent, which is more than the world military budgets put together. In global terms, the investment in tourism industry and travel trade accounts for 7 per cent of the total capital investment. Today 21.2 crore people around the globe are employed in travel trade and tourism. In future, this industry is likely to see unprecedented growth. According to the World Tourism Council at Bruseels, the revenues from travel and tourism in Asia Pacific region will grow at the rate of 7.8 per cent annually over the next decade.

Amongst the economic sectors, the tourism sector is highly labcur intensive. A survey by the Government of India notes that the rate of employment generation (direct and indirect)

in tourism is 52 persons employed per Rs. 10 lakh investment (based on 1992-93 Consumer Price Index). This is much higher than the rates of employment generation in most other economic sectors. Indian tourism industry has also recorded phenomenal growth. The rate of international arrivals in India in recent years has been to the tune of about 19 lakh arrivals per year. The unprecedented growth in tourism in India has made it the third largest foreign exchange earner after gem and jewellery and ready-made garments. This is not surprising since India possesses a whole range of attractive normally sought by tourists and which includes natural attractions like Landscapes, scenic beauty, mountains, wildlife, beaches, major rivers and man-made attractions such as mountains, forts, places and havelis. However, in global terms, in spite of such attractions, tourist arrivals in India are a mere 0.30 per cent of the world arrivals. Receipts are similarly low, just a 0.50 per cent of the world receipts. We are still quite far from the target of 50 lakh tourist arrivals per year.

International/National Tourist Arrivals

International Tourist Arrivals to India have grown by fits and starts during the last decade to reach a figure of 2.6 million by 2000.

	Tourist arrivals (India)	**Tourist arrivals (World, in Million)**	**Percentage share of India**
1994	1,886,433	550.3	0.34
1995	2,123,683	565.4	0.38
1996	2,287,860	597.4	0.38
1997	2,374,094	618.2	0.38
1998	2,358,629	626.7	0.38
1999	2,481,928	650.0	0.38
2000	2,641,157	698.3	0.38

Source: India Tourist Statistics, 1999, issued by Market Research Division, Department of Tourism, Govt. of India.

Formation of Ministry of Tourism

On March 1, 1958, a separate department was created in Ministry of Transport to deal with all matters concerning tourism. This new department was put under the charge of the Director General who had under him on Deputy Director General and four Directors. Each in charge of Administration, Publicity, Travel Relations and Planning and Development. There was a decline in tourist traffic to India from 1,39,804 in 1961 to 1,34,036 in 1962. This prompted the government to appoint an Ad-hoc committee on Tourism in March 1963, under the Chairmanship of L.K. Jha. In 1965, as a follow-up on the a high level coordination committee was appointed as to suggest ways and means to implement the recommendations, of the Jha Committee with the help of the concerned department of tourist traffic to India. New created corporation was called "India Tourism Development Corporation Limited". On March 13,1067 a Separate Ministry of Tourism and Civil Aviation, India tourism was created. This was a significant step as it brought Tourism and Civil Aviation together under one administration. Since the formation of the Ministry of Tourism and Civil aviation. Indian tourism has been developing in spite of limited resources and relatively low priority given to this economic activity.

The Department of Tourism is under the charge of Director General of the rank of an Additional Secretary and reports directly to the minister. Under him there are divisions of Planning, administration, Publicity, Hotels, Marketing Research, Wildlife, supplementary accommodation etc.

The activities of the Department of Tourism include:

- Compilation collection, and dissemination of tourist information in India and abroad and attending to enquiries from international tourists, tour operators and travel industry sectors such as airlines, steamship, companies and hotels, production of tourist literature posters, brochures, information directories, tourist guide maps-for wide distribution;

- Cooperation with international travel and tourist organisations at government and non-government levels;
- Facilities work such as simplification of frontier formalities in respect of international tourists;
- Development of tourist facilities of interest to international tourists;
- Publicity at home and abroad with the object of creating an overall awareness of the importance of tourism;
- Regulation of the activities of various segments of the travel trade, such as hotels, youth hostels travel agents, wild life outfitters, tourists car operators and, shopkeepers catering to tourists needs; and
- Compilation of statistics and market research on international tourist traffic to India and their utilisation for more effective tourist promotion.

Organisation Chart of the Department of Tourism

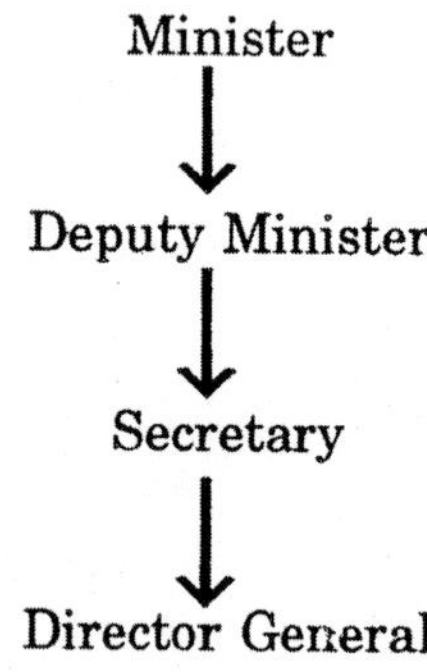

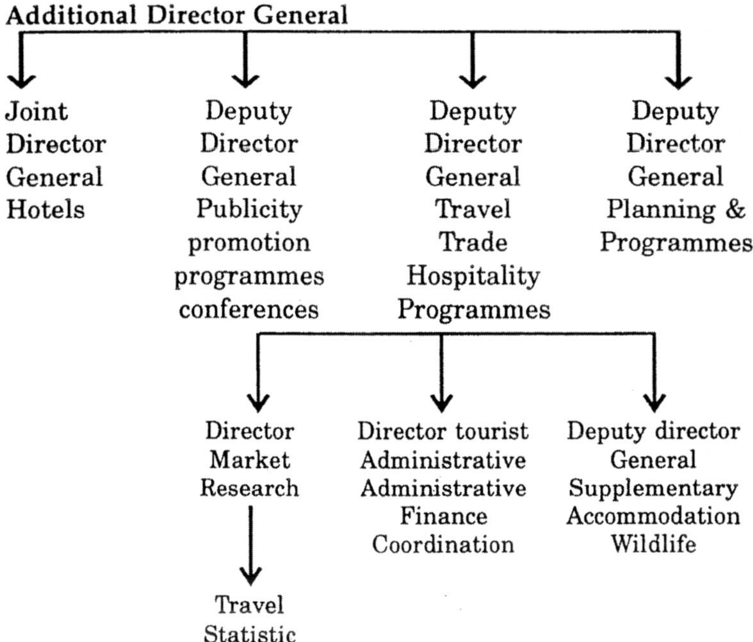

Tourism Marketing of India

Having understood the current profile of Indian tourism, it is possible to analyse the marketing efforts put in by the Department of Tourism, Government of India. While starting tourism promotion in a modest way in the early fifties, the Government of India had no clear-cut objectives and goals about how to go about it. Tourism promotion was considered an information service like information on any other aspect of a country *i.e.* trade, economy, etc. Nothing more.

To most government officials involved in tourism promotion in the early fifties, international tourism meant that some affluent people form rice countries with a lot of money and some curiosity (especially from the US) were willing to travel to foreign lands. It was recognized that the first preference of such people in North America would be Europe, which they considered the cradle of Western civilization. However, the retired and more affluent among them could be persuaded to take round-the-world trips either by ship or by air, which sometimes included India. That was the India's target group in the fifties and sixties.

In North America, or for that matter in the entire Western world, India, if known at all, at the time had the image primary of an exotic country-hot and humid, poor and backward, a land of snake charmers and ropewalkers—an image, which the British authors like, Kipling had built up over the decades. The British rulers projected this image, as they had to stand the heat of long summers in India to administer the country. Their families retired to the hills with cooks, bearers, nannies and gardners and there was little attempt at meeting the people of India and understanding their rich culture.

In the early fifties, the government decided that India should have overseas offices to project a new image of the country as a tourist destination. The markets chosen were the USA, the UK followed by West Germany, France and Australia. These officers were essentially information offices whose job was to distribute and disseminate tourist information through brochures printed in India. In an effort to do everything in India, they forgot that their publicity material exported out of India was not attractive enough and of the best quality.

Although these offices were useful in projecting the new image on an independent India, some of the offices were perhaps opened a little too soon. For instances, an India tourist office was opened in Germany in 1957 at a time when the Germans had just undertaken travelling outside their country. They were not ready for India. It took them a decade before they began taking long distance holiday trips to countries like India and that too only when holidays to India became relatively inexpensive due to the introduction of characters and the cheaper inclusive group fares on scheduled carriers. Similarly, India opened a tourist office in Japan in 1964, when Japan first liberalized its foreign exchange restrictions and allowed the Japanese to take only three hundred dollars for travel overseas. But traffic from Japan to India remained static for five years as the Japanese did not think beyond the USA and Europe as their preferred holiday or business destinations. In Australia also, the story was more or less repeated as

Australians started taking India holidays or stopovers on the way to Europe only in the early seventies. However, these tourist offices were useful in paving the way for tourism from these markets in later decades.

The tourist offices overseas within their limited resources launched modest advertising campaigns. It was generally a well thought out activity undertaken on the advice of the professional advertising agencies hired by each tourist office locally to improve the image of India as a land of Ajanta-Ellora, the Taj Mahal, the Himalayas and Mahabalipuram. Cultural tourism relating to monuments and an ancient civilization was the initial thrust of promotion as people in the Western world could more readily identify India with such an image. The frequency and the size of advertisements were inadequate. Advertisements were released mostly in black and white, as colour advertising was considered too expensive. At the same time, tourist offices, however, established contacts with the tour-operators and travel agents to persuade them to send their clients to India.

Conclusion

A particular irritant affecting any visitor to the country is the lack of reliable telecommunication facilities. With the entire world emerging as a single market place, where production centres and distribution networks are spread over continents, immediate contact with business associates, relatives and friends, and travel agents becomes an imperative need for any foreign traveller. The group working on the I.T. sector, it is hoped, will look into this aspect.

The publication of educational materials and maps for tourists so that they can be easily informed about the places to be visit. In that material there should be information regarding availability of transport, its fares of transport accommodation facility along with charges etc. should also be mentioned.

The government should immediately get out of the tourist infrastructure and leave this to the private sector. Else park directors will continue to spend more of their time booking accommodation for all and sundry VIPs from state capitals and Delhi. It should be clear is to be done to Forest Rest Houses, which are regularly being used, by politicians and conservation celebrities. The infrastructure should definitely be improved, though the clientele might have to be restricted.

Availability of information helps parks more approachable. In this regard, the construction of forest roads should be done in such a manner that it does not harm the wildlife. Tourism can also be developed in the buffers to increase vigilance there and to take pressure away from the central attractions. Tourism at each park should be restricted to its carrying capacity already identified and publicized in advance, so there should not be long queues at park entrances.

The Government should also explore the possibility of utilising the services of professional agencies abroad to boost the image of India as tourist destination instead of having separate tourist offices overseas. The Committee recommends that immediate necessary action may be taken upon all the recommendations of the World Tourism Organisations and the action taken upon them may be brought to the notice of the Committee.

Before launching new projects and expanding the tourism potential of the destination it is necessary to study the impact such activities. In this regard educational institutes should be involved for a proper study to promote a destination.

REFERENCES

Babu, A. Satish (1999) *Tourism Development in India*, A.P.H. Publishing Corporation, New Delhi, pp. 20-48, 23-25.

Business Inc. (1997) 'Dream Holidays which remains a dream'. *Indian Express*, 30th March.

Chopra, S. 1991 *Tourism and Development in India*. Ashish Publishing House, New Delhi.

Fennell, D. (1999) Ecotourism—An Introduction. Routledge, London, *HRAI Magazine and Newsletter* 2000, Vol. 2; 1 March: 12.

Kaur, J. (1985) *Himalayan Pilgrimages and the New Tourism*, Himalayan Books, New Delhi.

Misra, S.K. (1998) 'Public-Private Partnerships: New Ways of Managing Tourism in India', *Journal of Tourism*, Vol. 3: 5-12.

Ranga, Mukesh (2003), *Tourism Potential in India*, Abhijeet Publications, New Delhi. pp. 45-48.

Ravendran, G. (1988) 'Development of Ecotourism in India,' *Journal of Travel and Tourism* 2(1): 137-140.

Sengupta, N.K. (1997) 'Tourism and Balance of Payments Crisis'. In *Journal of Travel and Tourism* 1 (1): 14-21.

Singh, S and Singh T.V. (1996) 'Preface', in Shalini Singh (ed) *Profiles of Indian Tourism Industry*, Ashish Publishing Corporation, New Delhi.

Stephen L.J. Smith (1995), *An Overview of Tourism Research, Tourism Analysis—A Handbook*, pp. 6-12.

Tourism in India: The Traditional Approach, India: The Tourism Imperative, *WTTC India Initiative; A Status Paper* August 2001, p. 6.

Zulfikar Mohammed (1999), *Tourism and Hotel Industry*, Vikas Publishing House Pvt. Ltd., New Delhi, pp. 41-43.

16

An Introduction to Urban Tourism Destination Management

*Walter Jamieson**

Introduction

Tourism is the world's largest industry and encompasses one of every ten jobs worldwide. Southeast Asia alone received more than 31 million international tourists in 1999. Forecasts are for ever larger numbers of domestic and international tourists. How tourism destinations will cope with these visitor numbers in a sustainable manner is a crucial urban management issue.

For many Asian cities and countries, tourism development provides much-needed employment and foreign exchange earnings and, in some cases, this increased wealth is directed toward the improvement of social and physical conditions. There can be negative impacts from tourism and the costs to a local society and environment can be significant: the influx of tourists and workers from outside a destination can change

* Ph.D Professor of Planning, University of Calgary, Visiting Professor, Institute For Tourism Studies, Macao, Heritage Resource Management and Tourism Consultant, UNESCO

the local community's social fabric; development can cause pollution, habitat destruction and associated health risks. With poor management of tourism destinations, the future of many destinations is threatened.

Experience has clearly demonstrated strategic planning and sound management are crucial in achieving sustainable development goals. Those responsible for managing destinations need to begin thinking in an integrated manner about everyday municipal concerns of tourism and cultural and heritage dimensions of a community. Stakeholders at all levels have a common objective to preserve resources that make a destination unique and appealing to tourists. Sustainable tourism destination management views destinations as more than the sum of their parts and seeks to create destinations that are healthy and viable in the long term for tourists and residents.

The sustainable, integrated view of destination management serves to:

- Address the needs of tourists and the economic interests of the tourism industry
- Approach tourism development in a way which reduces negative impacts
- Protect local people's business interests, heritage and environment
- Protect the local environment in part because it is the livelihood of the destination

This chapter provides an overview of the complex web of issues to be addressed to manage a destination sustainably. It does not seek to provide solutions but to identify areas of focus and tools for management that may relate to a destination.

Sustainable Tourism

A sustainable approach to tourism destination management is based on globally applicable principles of sustainability. Any action toward managing a destination should be considered in terms of the values of sustainable development.

Over the past two decades, the inter-relatedness of all earth and human systems has become abundantly clear. We now understand no human action occurs in total isolation from other natural systems. We appreciate the reality that humans are dependent on limited resources of the earth.

The global community has been primed for some fundamental changes, including a search for "sustainable development" based on new modes of resource allocation and accounting, new attitudes toward preservation of environmental integrity and new ways of making decisions in all sectors.

Among the imperatives that promote and enhance the vision of sustainable futures, including that of a sustainable future for tourism, are:

- Prudent use of the earth's resources within the limits of the planet's carrying capacity
- Devolution of top-down decision-making responsibilities and capabilities to a broader range of a destination's stakeholders
- Abatement of poverty and gender inequalities and respect for fundamental human rights
- Enhancement of the quality of life for residents through improved health care, shelter, nutrition and access to education and income-generating skills
- Preservation of biodiversity and life support systems for all natural habitats
- Preservation of indigenous knowledge and ways of living and respect for the spiritual and cultural traditions of different peoples

In fulfilling these imperatives, governments and other societal agents must struggle to find an appropriate balance between different, sometimes apparently conflicting, needs and value systems. Whatever the situation, sustainable development must meet three fundamental and equal objectives:

- *Economic*: production of goods and services (the overriding criterion in fulfilling this objective is efficiency)
- *Environmental*: conservation and prudent management of natural resources (the overriding criterion is preservation of biodiversity and maintenance of ecological integrity)
- *Social*: the maintenance and enhancement of quality of life (equity is the main consideration in meeting this objective) and inter-generational, as well as intra-generational, equity in the distribution of wealth

Achieving sustainable tourism development requires that the private sector and community co-operate as partners in working toward a sustainable society. Making decisions about sustainable tourism development also requires that communities work within a broad framework developing decisions that are:

- Long-term, allowing communities to better anticipate and prevent problems and make risk-reducing decisions
- Multi-sectoral, including the full range of interest and activities in a tourism environment
- Ecosystem-based, recognizing the cumulative and synergistic effects of all actions on the ecological integrity of a community and region
- Integrated, identifying impact of actions on other sectors, regions and communities
- Cognizant, recognizing the cause and consequence of problems communities seek to solve that may involve others and other institutions
- Full-cycle, thereby understanding the full context of resource use from extraction to end use

Individual tourist resource management decisions have to be made with increased understanding of all these dimensions if the goal of sustainable futures is to be attained. To achieve profitability and environmental sustainability in the tourism industry, the industry as a whole must take a different approach to planning and development.

Evidence shows an integrated approach to tourism planning and management is now required to achieve sustainable tourism. Only recently has there been a growing recognition of the importance of combining the needs of traditional urban management (transportation, land-use planning, marketing, economic development, fire and safety, etc.) with the need to plan for tourism.

Principles of Sustainable Tourism

Some of the most important principles of sustainable tourism development:

- Tourism should be initiated with the help of broad-based community inputs and the community should maintain control of tourism development.
- Tourism should provide quality employment to community residents, and linkage between local businesses and tourism should be established.
- A code of practice should be established for tourism at all levels - national, regional and local - based on internationally acceptable standards; guidelines for tourism operations, impact assessment, monitoring of cumulative impacts and limits to acceptable change should be established.
- Education and training programs to improve and manage heritage and natural resources should be established.

The following sections demonstrate the range of factors to be considered when managing destinations - practical steps to be undertaken before a destination can enable a vision of sustainable tourism to become a reality. This should not be considered a prescription for success as there are alternative ways to manage destinations. The process featured in this chapter, however, presents a valuable model when it is paired with initiative and strategic thinking.

The Need for a Tourism Destination Management Approach

In order to ensure sustainable development in a destination this chapter advocates a destination management and planning approach that is organized around a conceptual framework with four major dimensions as illustrated in Fig. 16.1.

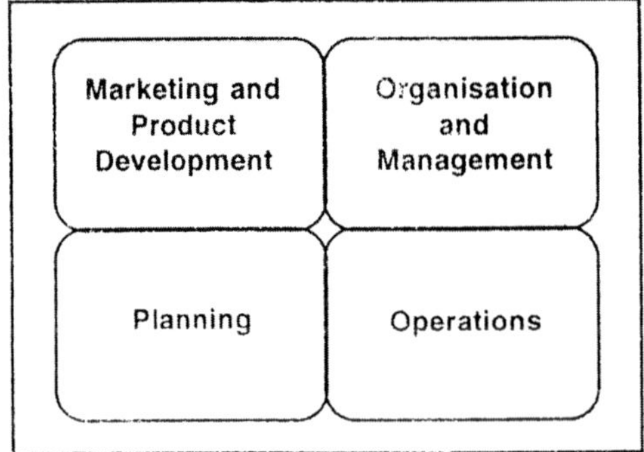

Fig. 16.1 Tourism Destination Management Approach

Destination Product Development and Marketing

The product development and marketing process has a number of dimensions as illustrated in Fig. 16.2 and which will be discussed in this section.

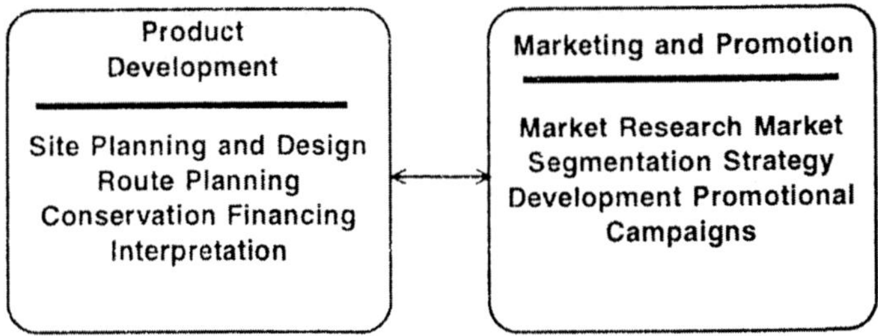

Fig. 16.2 Destination Product Development and Marketing

Product Development

The destination management process requires that a destination should develop products, cultural, natural or intangible in nature, to meet market demands. It is not acceptable to develop an approach based on the assumption that "if we build facilities and products, the market will come." Rather, there must be a clear relationship between the nature of the product and the market. The process is more complex than with other forms of product since tourism planners and managers are often dealing with irreplaceable and fragile resources. The challenge is to achieve a match between product and market. This chapter presents some issues to be addressed in the product/market matching process.

Product Design

"Product" is a general term which covers all attractions and services which can be "sold" to visitors. A destination's "product" consists of built and natural attractions, tours and packages, services for travelers (e.g. shopping, restaurants, accommodation) and activities. Destinations may choose to concentrate on services such as tour packages, guiding and interpretation. Natural resources are generally not thought of as "product," but an ecotour in a natural park is a product. The heritage architecture of a community is not a product but its interpretation, through a guided tour, can be seen as a product.

Approaching a destination as product, however, does not mean only attractions which appeal to tourists, regardless of their appropriateness, should be developed. Rather, it means the product should be seen as a community's livelihood and marketed and protected accordingly. Control must be exercised to prevent developments which do not fit the community or cause undesirable impacts. Each destination has its own unique product mix, based on its resources, values, needs and preferences. The result should be an authentic community tourism product attractive to travelers seeking hospitable and unique experiences.

The following elements should be considered when developing a destination's product:

- Choose authentic themes which reflect the local culture(s) and environment-human relationships
- Keep development in scale with the community and environment
- Ensure developments also meet community needs (e.g. through joint use)
- Develop attractions that are attractive and competitive in the long run, not faddish
- Require strong community support (not imposing new ideas on an unreceptive population)
- Avoid "parachuting" successful ideas from other places since success comes from strong local commitment and enthusiasm
- Choose themes to position the destination within sustainable development principles
- Consider sports since many competitions and fun events can be held using existing facilities
- Inform all visitors of tourism plans, goals and management approach
- Ask local clubs, associations and businesses to generate meetings and conventions to the extent permitted by infrastructure
- Provide high-quality experiences

Site Planning

To develop attractions and facilities, every destination needs a design plan including issues of visitor management and flow, parking and access to the attractions. Site designs should be compatible with local heritage and lifestyles to maintain a sense of place and should enhance local architecture and culture.

Site planning refers to the specific location (or siting) of buildings and related development forms on the land and considers functions of buildings, their physical interrelationships and characteristics of the natural environmental setting. Site planning also includes the location of roads, parking areas, landscaped and open space areas, footpaths and recreational facilities, all of which are integrated with building locations. At more general levels of planning, an ecological approach to site planning is essential to ensure developments are well integrated into the natural environment and environmental problems are not generated. Detailed surveys and analysis of the environmental characteristics of a site are some of the first steps in the site planning process, along with determination of specific types, functions and size of buildings and other development forms being planned. This section reviews some basic considerations that must be made in site planning of tourist facilities.

Building Relationships

The grouping of buildings, e.g. accommodations and their relationships to amenity and recreational facilities, is an important concern of site planning. The type of grouping depends on the density and character of the development desired as related to the natural environment.

Types of Development Standards

There are several types of specific standards applicable to the controlled development of tourist facilities. These standards typically include:

- Density of development
- Heights of buildings
- Setbacks of buildings from amenity features, shorelines, roads, lot lines and other buildings
- Ratio of the building floor area to the site area
- Coverage of the site by buildings and other structures

- Parking requirements
- Other requirements, e.g. landscaping and open space, public access to amenity features, signs and utility lines

Design Standards

Design standards should respect the following key elements:

- Local styles and motifs
- Roof lines
- Use of local building materials
- Environmental relationships
- Landscaping design

Designing Tourism Products

Tourism products such as accommodation, hospitality, attractions, events and other tourist services should be considered in a site plan. These tourist facilities include hotels, restaurants, hospitals and public restrooms. When developing a site plan, the following factors should be considered:

- The scale and type of development - sustainable development would favor small scale developments to minimize impacts and encourage incremental (staged) development.
- The kind of tourism activities (ecotourism, heritage tours), facilities, attractions and amenities to be included in a site plan - tourism products to be developed will ideally be based on competitive analysis, market research, ecological assessment.
- Approaches that minimize negative impacts through design, land-use planning, zoning and management.
- Development of project financing strategies that focus on local control and minimize economic leakage from the community.

- Tourism vision statements and goals communicated to commercial and other stakeholders of the sites should be included in the planning.
- Policies that allow room for future growth and alteration in the plan and sites themselves.

Since tourists want to visit the main attractions in a destination, tourist flows should be established to ensure they are able to see and experience everything they want within a reasonable period of time. Walking tours and promotional material can alert the visitor to possibilities provided by a site and avoid those not appropriate for tourist use.

Regional route planning can be developed in conjunction with other district or municipal planners so attractions throughout the region can be developed, creating a broader and more varied tourism experience.

Financing

Financing is a major issue facing those responsible for managing destinations. Public budgets are often not adequate to cover rising costs of such basics as increasing waste disposal due to increased tourism, ensuring low priority funding for management of historic sites and enforcement of building restrictions. Financial sustainability most often involves multiple funding sources with a focus on earned income and measures that contain operating and restoration costs. Resources for financing include:

- Public sector grants and tax breaks
- Community initiatives and investment
- Self-help and self-build approaches
- Joint public/private ventures and partnerships where often the public sector contributes land or other resources
- Financing from various organizations such as non-profits, trusts, foundations, revolving funds and community development corporations

- Build-operate-transfer arrangements
- The private sector

Since governments are playing a smaller role in providing financing to tourism projects because of limited financial resources, the private sector must supply the majority of financing. These private sources include individuals, banks, trust companies, credit unions and insurance companies.

Achieving the right funding "mix" by increasing efficiency without compromising the destination's attractiveness is a "sustainable issue" for many destinations. One possible option is to combine market economy and public interventions. In this type of financing situation, public authorities are able to retain ownership of resources such as facilities or historic buildings - but the development or renovation responsibility is transferred to private managers. Build-operate-transfer (BOT) procedures are a good example. However, these transfers present other problems. Commercial management is concerned primarily with the facility's ability to attract tourism, which may compromise other considerations such as its larger role within the destination or conservation concerns. Any attempt at BOT approaches requires the public sector interest group responsible for the facility to be sophisticated in developing management policies and contracts that respect the local community and its environment, while providing a reasonable rate of return.

In some situations, it may be inappropriate to contract out the development or management of a particular site. However, supplementary commercial enterprises can be allowed such as photography, shops or restaurants - the revenue from these activities can be put toward the ongoing development and protection of the site.

Park and site admission fees, hotel and entertainment taxes and fundraising events can be used to raise money directly for tourism management. A community tourism development corporation can be established to attract investors, identify potential funding sources and manage funds.

Private corporate sponsorships of events, sites or even clean-up projects and other public awareness campaigns may be possible. Sponsorships may also be available in the form of expertise or organizational assistance. However, this type of non-profit sponsorship is often driven primarily by the desire to improve a company's image. As long as the destination's stakeholders retain control over the terms of sponsorship, this type of support has the potential to be beneficial for all concerned.

Donations of aid for specific restoration or preservation projects may also be available from international organizations or foreign governments. However, these are often one-time funds and cannot be depended on as long term. Often capital funds are available but operational financing is difficult, if not impossible, to obtain.

Marketing

Attractions can change over time. The level of importance of any attraction can change due to two main influences. First, physical characteristics can change since cities may improve or deteriorate in quality and developed destinations may wear out. Secondly, market conditions can change. Popularity is as much a function of market forces as a physical factor. Influences such as terrorism activity, international monetary exchange rates, fashion, personal interests, public policy and competition can change market segment interest in attractions.

There are many factors within the control of the destination or site manager. Others, as suggested above, result from international or national decisions or changing consumer behavior. It is vital that destinations understand the motivation and expectation of visitors in order to maintain the viability of the destination. This requires destination mangers to have a good understanding of market research and promotion and maintain a timely database of tourism trends and the ability of their site to meet visitor expectations.

Marketing for Sustainability

While traditional marketing places heavy emphasis on the potential customer's needs and desires, sustainable tourism marketing begins with consideration of a community's values, goals and needs. Preserving the integrity of the natural and cultural resource base is the foundation of such an approach. Attention must also be given to ensuring the destination's tourism industry is competitive and economically sustainable, and the community will continue to support tourism and the changes it often brings.

Tourists are not always interested in the host culture or its environment. Not all forms of tourism or types of visitor are compatible with local goals and conditions. Careful attention to high-quality, high-yield visitors will benefit the community much more than indiscriminate mass marketing.

For the most part, mass tourism is incompatible with a sustainable tourism marketing strategy. We can define "mass tourism" as being large-scaled and oriented toward the widest possible range of customers. Many destinations are quite successfully pursuing mass tourism. However, the cost is high and negative impacts can easily outweigh the benefits, at least from the residents' perspective. Furthermore, once set in motion, it is difficult, or impossible, to reverse the process of mass tourism development. It can result in external control and often local businesses and residents are pushed aside.

The alternative strategy is niche marketing or the pursuit of market segments that will meet the community's sustainable tourism goals. Most people can be attracted to a popular beach resort because of the universal appeal of sun, sea and sand, but not everyone is particularly interested in bird watching, local festivals or home stays. The more focused the marketing efforts, the more control can be retained over the process.

At times, it is argued the tourism industry needs constant growth and maximum amounts of promotion to sustain profits and jobs. This is simply not the case. Mass marketing sows the seeds of its own problems, namely the "boom and bust" cycle that typically results when high levels of demand lead to oversupply, resulting in low levels of use and inefficient operations. From the point of view of the destinations, and especially the residents, it is far better to concentrate on a single or a few prime segments and avoid the pitfalls of mass marketing. Furthermore, much less development and servicing is required if year-round occupancy/use can be assured, as opposed to constantly building new infrastructure to cater to growing peak-season demand.

A sustainable approach to tourism marketing still requires good market research, detailed segmentation to find the best target markets, attention to customer needs and preferences and delivery of high-quality products and services. The difference between a sustainable and standard approach is that sustainable marketing favors the community and its environment; industry and community must be in partnership to agree on the goals and process.

Marketing for sustainable tourism involves the same process and elements used by all businesses and destinations but the orientation is quite different. Sustainable tourism marketing stresses the following:

- Meeting the needs and goals of the community
- Matching locally supported "products" to appropriate segments
- Attracting high yield and high-quality visitors, not large numbers
- Cultivating the right image to convey environmentally and culturally sensitive messages by employing unique selling propositions
- Communicating effectively with and educating all visitors
- Employing environmental and cultural interpretation
- Managing the visitor and encouraging the adoption of codes of conduct
- Achieving efficiency by avoiding high peaks of demand and overuse
- Offering high-quality attractions and services

- Researching appropriate segments, communication effectiveness and resultant impacts
- Building repeat trade

Market Research

Market research has a number of important aims:

- Understanding what existing and potential visitors want in terms of benefits and experiences, products and services
- Identifying the appropriate target market segments
- Matching products to potential market segments
- Knowing what the competition is doing
- Understanding the relative importance of all elements in the marketing mix (e.g. how important is price?)

In marketing, the key is always to focus on what potential customers want, need and will demand. For example, if a destination wishes to develop ecotourism, two questions must be addressed: Who will purchase ecotours? and Will demand be sufficient to justify the investment? Niche marketing requires that very careful attention be given to measuring potential demand from target segments and ways of effectively reaching them.

Market potential can be evaluated in several ways. Basic research into tourism trends is the starting point; usually government agencies, industry associations and educational institutions can provide this data. It will be more difficult, however, to obtain demand-related information specific to certain areas, communities or businesses. In these cases, original market research is likely necessary.

It is not sufficient to know if demand for a product or experience exists. It must be shown through research and a feasibility study that the proposed development can capture an adequate share of the market. Many good ideas fail because of a mistaken assumption that demand follows supply. Always remember a great deal of competition exists for the consumer's attention, time and money.

Segmentation and selection of target markets are crucial parts of this process because demand will come from specific segments of the global marketplace. Because sustainable tourism marketing is the opposite of mass marketing, extra care must be taken to identify and attract appropriate market segments.

Development of a Marketing Strategy

A summary of the research and analysis should be included in the actual marketing plan. Goals and objectives should be clearly stated, strategies articulated and an action plan and budget outlined. The marketing plan is usually revised annually in light of ongoing research and evaluation of its effectiveness. It should incorporate a multi-year strategy for each element of the marketing mix as few strategies can be fully implemented in one year.

The following is an outline of a typical marketing plan for a destination marketing organization:

- Vision and goals for the destination
- General marketing goals
- Situation analysis and market research
- Resource and supply appraisal
- Market potential
- Strategies, goals and objectives
- Action plan and budget
- Evaluation of key performance criteria

Monitoring, Evaluation and Revisions

Every marketing planning process requires ongoing monitoring of results and constant attention to improvements.

Monitoring usually requires specific research efforts and establishment of indicators using the following types of research instruments:

- Tracking studies which determine the effectiveness and efficiency of marketing, awareness levels, attitudes, travel patterns and satisfaction levels of visitors
- Impact assessment which measures concrete and qualitative results from marketing efforts in particular and tourism in general, including economic, social, cultural and environmental effects
- Measuring costs and benefits often using statistical analysis

Development of a Promotion Strategy

Image-making is an essential part of sustainable tourism marketing. The sustainable tourism destination wants to portray itself using attractive symbols and messages. On the other hand, the words "green", "eco-tourism" and "environmentally friendly" have often been abused, so clichés must be avoided. Most often the best approach stresses authenticity, uniqueness and sound visitor management practices. The focus should be on image-making for precise targets.

From a sustainability point of view, a number of factors must be considered:

- Promotion must be targeted and fully informative, otherwise false expectations are generated.
- Quality products are marketed differently from mass tourism products (e.g. value is more important than price).
- Information and interpretation are important elements in the travel experience.

Destination Planning

The intricacy of the tourism system is demonstrated by the many individuals and groups which can affect a destination's future. This complexity makes destination planning vital but also difficult. Clearly some form of co-operative and proactive direction is required to guide planning and development. This section will identify actions required for developing and implementing effective sustainable tourism strategies. The character of the process can be described as dynamic, participative and adaptable to the needs and concerns of the destination's many stakeholders. The destination planning process has a number of dimensions as illustrated in Fig. 16.3 and which will be discussed in this section.

Fig. 16.3 Destination Planning

There is no formula for the amount of planning a particular situation needs. Clearly each societal context will determine what is appropriate. Similarly, although sustainable tourism calls for a high level of local involvement in planning and developing tourism, the amount and quality of resident participation will vary depending on cultural and political factors in the destination. It is not useful to develop a sophisticated planning system if there is no political or community support for it. In these cases, one might first have to generate an appropriate setting or structure for a planning process.

A strategic planning approach is essential for sustainable tourism, whereby the disparate planning and development activities related to tourism are linked to an overall, broad strategic tourism plan to provide an integrated framework for directing tourism. Strategic planning seeks an optimal fit between the system and its environment and should possess the following characteristics:

- A long-term perspective
- A vision
- Stated goals and specific actions and resources necessary to achieve those goals
- Dynamic, flexible and adaptable
- Formulation and implementation of the strategic plan linked closely through constant monitoring, environmental scanning, evaluation and adjustment
- Close co-ordination between local and regional legislative and political structures
- Community participation and support
- Support by an informed, educated and aware community
- Innovative and inclusive organizational structure for joint planning
- Application of principles of sustainable tourism development to ensure the long-term sustainability of the ecology, local economy and the socio-cultural values of the community, and distribution of benefits equitably among stakeholders

There are many approaches to planning, from none at all to a centralized, top-down method. Despite this variety, good planning generally contains the following elements and action steps:

- Defining a vision and mission statement
- Implementing a situational analysis
- Developing strategic goals

- Evaluating strategic alternatives to achieve these goals
- Developing strategies
- Implementing strategies including measurable objectives and detailed action plans
- Monitoring and evaluating strategies and action plans
- Adjusting strategic and operational plans based on information and feedback from evaluation and constant scanning of the external environment

Destination Analysis

Once a destination has decided it is ready for tourism, it is important to conduct a destination analysis to assess the community's infrastructure and tourism resources. Carrying out this task in a comprehensive manner can benefit everyone. The objectives of the process are to:

- Determine what the destination possesses in terms of tourism attractions
- Determine the location of tourism resources, infrastructure and attractions
- Assess the tourism qualities of resources and attractions
- Determine what stage of readiness for tourism the attractions and resources are in
- Develop some initial priorities
- Outline an action plan

Policy Development

To plan for sustainable guidelines, a destination needs a policy that reflects all the stakeholders' concerns and objectives. Developing this policy can be a long, complex process due to different and often competing interests of diverse groups which make up the stakeholders in any destination. Even if it is not a binding document, a destination-based policy can be used by constituents to demonstrate and confirm the desires and goals of all stakeholders.

Consideration of a destination policy as a relevant implementation tool requires support of local government, stakeholders and businesses. It also needs to fit well with regional, national and global tourism policies. There is potential for conflict in some destinations. Destinations must determine what can be done locally and what requires regional and national government assistance. Depending on political and economic considerations, there may be a need for new political and legislative structures to establish sustainable tourism development frameworks.

Public Participation

Managing tourism in a sustainable way requires that everyone affected by tourism is informed and involved in tourism, both in the planning process and implementation of policies and action plans.

Local people can be involved in tourism to varying degrees, ranging from information gathering to direct decision-making, ownership, and employment in planning, project development and service delivery. In the context of sustainable tourism development, a clear distinction must be made between consultation and participation. While community consultation is highly recommended, it is not synonymous with participation. Sustainable tourism development requires participation that allows people the right to order and influence their world. To accomplish this, opportunities need to be created to enable community members to participate as fully as possible in directing the development of their community.

Local citizenry can get involved directly in the tourism planning process (via committees, workshops) and indirectly through public meetings, surveys, etc. Direct participation in tourism-related projects is also highly recommended since this creates a sense of ownership in the outcome of the process. Participation may also allow the benefits of tourism to be distributed more widely among community members, both directly and indirectly. More direct local involvement in decision-making, for example, may enable residents to request a specific portion of tax benefits from tourism to be allocated toward community development and the protection of the tourism resource base.

Determination of Carrying Capacity

In its simplest form, carrying capacity measures the sustainable level of destination use. In fact, carrying capacity is a complex concept, particularly when a range of products and services must come from the same environment (as in the case of tourism). Yet the question remains similar: how many tourists/visitors can be accommodated in a destination and within specific portions of the destination without threatening the long-term sustainability of a specific site and destination?

Carrying capacity has value particularly because it draws attention to limits and thresholds beyond which a site does not wish to tread. But in dealing with the reality, we need to consider the following:

- Tourism depends on many attributes of an environment: aesthetic qualities, maintenance of wildlife and access to shoreline or ability to support active uses. Each has its own response to different levels of use.
- The impact of human activity on a system may be gradual and affect different parts of the system at different rates. While some environmental resources may be highly sensitive to human impact (e.g. habitats for fragile or endangered species), others degrade gradually in response to different use levels.
- Every environment serves multiple purposes and its sensitivity to different use levels depends on the values of all users.

- Different types of use have different impacts.
- Tourism managers need some form of measure to reduce the risk of unknowingly stepping over biological or cultural thresholds with results that degrade the product, cause other adverse effects or discourage customers.

The success of the tourism planning effort greatly depends on the ability of a destination to monitor the implementation of action plans, the achievement of its objectives, and the setting and monitoring of critical indicators and carrying capacity thresholds related to the resources being used. Carrying capacity in this context refers to the level or threshold of use or impact a resource can handle without seriously affecting the health or survival of that resource. Indicators and thresholds need to be established which provide decision-makers with information enabling them to evaluate and make timely decisions on changes caused by tourism.

Destination Organisational Structure and Management

Establishing the right organizational and management structure is often a key to success. While each situation

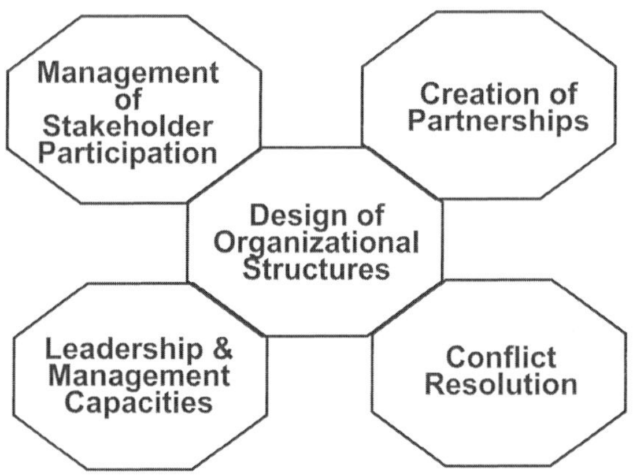

Fig. 16.4 Destination Organization and Management

requires a distinct organizational structure, the importance of stakeholder involvement cannot be overemphasized. Generally speaking, every destination needs a structure for the management of tourism and its many related issues. The organizational and management process has a number of dimensions as illustrated in Fig. 16.4 and which will be discussed in this section.

Design of Organisational Structures

Establishing ongoing leadership will facilitate future planning-related actions such as constant scanning of the environment, identifying opportunities and managing problems as they emerge, thereby increasing the probability for sustainable tourism development.

Regardless of the structure of the existing or newly-created destination management organization, some major areas of responsibility can be:

- Participating in community tourism strategy planning
- Guiding and evaluating physical development, programs and activities
- Ongoing monitoring of tourism development and impacts
- Guiding impact mitigation and adjusting tourism strategies
- Ensuring sustainable tourism practices are implemented including economic incentives for local ownership and control of tourism, education and training of locals to participate in the tourism industry, and equitable access for residents to tourism facilities and activities
- Establishing sub-committees for managing various aspects of the overall tourism strategy
- Assisting with ongoing community education and awareness of tourism activities

Creation of Partnerships

One of the most important lessons established in all areas of development is the considerable influence of partnerships on the success of any initiative. Public/private partnerships among government, public organizations, community organizations, industry and commerce are seen as the key to success in many destination initiatives. Partnerships can bring together many different sets of ideas, points of view and contributions of various kinds, whether financial, social or political in nature, helping to achieve a successful heritage area strategy.

Conflict Management

Managing objectives and opinions of stakeholders is critical for tourism organizations involved in development. Controversy can be harmful to tourism proposals; lengthy delays may ensue. Adverse media attention could harm the image or reputation of the developer and community resistance to proposals (due to perceived threats of negative impacts) can make it difficult for developers to establish a mutually beneficial working relationship in the destination. While a detailed treatment of this vital issue of conflict management is not possible in this manual, the following points provide some useful direction:

- Anticipate and prevent conflicts where possible
- Establish mechanisms to enable effective communication, consultation and participation of stakeholders in development decision-making
- Investigate community values and attitudes and involve the community (through consultation and more direct participation) prior to making commitments on issues that can have a significant impact on the community and environment
- Identify and involve key stakeholders in the conflict management and conflict resolution processes

- Be as inclusive as possible when dealing with the local community. This will require managing a diversity of opinions, interests, attitudes and values of stakeholders with varying knowledge and communication skills. The participation mechanisms developed must deal with these challenges

In addition, stakeholders who are involved in conflict management/resolution must have the necessary information to provide an informed decision or opinion in a timely manner. It is also important to ensure the information is comprehensible to everyone.

Training of Public and Private Sector Staff

Training is important to ensure all stakeholders can be involved in the actual implementation and management of tourism in the destination. Their involvement reduces leakage of revenue, enables import substitution and generates employment.

Sustainable tourism development requires the establishment of education and training programs to improve public understanding and enhance business, vocational and professional skills. Training should include courses in tourism, hotel management and other relevant topics. Training can be developed through linkages with area and regional educational institutions such as community colleges or universities.

Training staff in tourists' needs and views is important in any situation where there is interaction between visitor and staff. This requires an investment of time and resources which may be difficult to justify in a restricted budget situation. However, training dimensions cannot be neglected if the site is to be protected and the message transmitted to the visitor.

It is important to note that training and education can take many forms ranging from formal, in-class instruction and distance education to self-paced, computer-based learning, and publications and manuals.

Achieving the right kind of organizational structure and management is essential in allowing a destination to achieve a sustainable future. There are many approaches to creating a management structure, but the principles previously identified should be seen as important dimensions of any organizational structure. The most important consideration is that all stakeholders from the community, public and private sectors be seen as essential actors in the overall management of the tourism destination.

Destination and Site Management/Opportunities

Once destinations have developed policies, plans and management structures, they need to develop management operation policies and procedures to ensure the ongoing attractiveness of the destination and protection of local cultures and environments. This control should involve cooperation of all stakeholders in the community and should not be seen solely as the responsibility of local authorities. The organizational and management process has a number of dimensions as illustrated in Fig. 16.5 and which will be discussed in this section.

Fig. 16.5 Destination and Site Management/Operations

Environmental Management

A major task for any destination is to ensure the urban environment is improved and does not negatively impact the surrounding environment. This is a topic for significant discussion but certainly any ongoing management of tourism destinations must take into account the following physical factors:

- Roads
- Drainage
- Water supply
- Electric power
- Sewage disposal
- Solid waste disposal
- Telecommunications
- Sanitation and public health standards

Urban Environmental Management for Facilities

Part of developing a destination's product is ensuring sustainable values are held throughout the tourism industry. Environmental Management Systems (EMS) are designed to assist facilities such as hotels and restaurants to improve their overall environmental performance. The main benefit of using a system such as EMS is that it takes a holistic approach to the facility by monitoring its environmental behavior from the beginning of the process (e.g. inflow of resources and products into the facility) through to the end. The EMS monitors all environmentally-sensitive areas such as solid waste generation, consumption of water, disposal of wastewater and consumption of energy (electricity and other fuels).

Heritage Resource Conservation

As discussed earlier, a destination's historic, cultural and natural heritages environments are often its main attractions. These resources must be protected and managed in order to ensure their conservation. A conservation plan to address the detailed needs of a destination should be drafted during the planning phase of tourism development.

Site/Attraction Management

One major site management task is to deal with visitor numbers, behavior and impacts. As discussed earlier, there are limits on the use of any kind of site. When those limits are exceeded, damage begins to occur and the visitor experience is compromised. Visitor impact, therefore, can be seen to be the result of the number of people using a site, type of activity and the ability of particular environments to withstand use.

Managing use would be fairly straightforward if there were not the need to balance visitor volumes and the positive economic impact generated from those volumes. The ideal level of use might be unrealistic when attempting to meet the economic objectives of a site. It is the role of the site management team to ensure the least possible damage while guaranteeing the financial viability of the site.

Managing Visitors

If the site is to maintain its financial viability and protect its integrity, there has to be an ongoing process of understanding the visitor and his/her expectations. This can be done through a series of techniques.

There are a number of possible management strategies for dealing with visitor numbers. The task can be simply one of reducing the number of visitors to the site, reducing the number of people at any one time or limiting the number of people in a particular place. There are softer techniques such as helping to change visitor behavior through education. There are also physical strategies to make the site more resistant to change. Typically in any situation, all of these strategies must coalesce in a management plan. Some management strategies appropriate to any of these approaches are:

- Restricting or limiting entry to the area

- Reducing numbers of large groups
- Implementing a quota system
- Using pricing techniques to reduce demand
- Directing visitors to other areas
- Having different pricing policies for different times of the week and year
- Developing a reservations system
- Using a system of lotteries to determine who can use a site
- Extending hours at particularly busy times of the year
- Limiting accommodation near the site

Each of these management strategies brings with it certain costs and benefits and has important political realities that must be reconciled as part of a management process.

Managing the Site and Surrounding Environment

No one site exists in isolation and many depend on the surrounding community for financial and social support. In addition, the surrounding community most often provides a wide range of visitor services and attractions essential to meet the full visitor experience. The site management plan must take into account how the relationship between the site itself and the surrounding community is to be handled. It is useful to think of the destination in its many dimensions as one of the many stakeholders involved in overall site management. Various forms of participation are possible but it is essential the relationship with the surrounding community is well considered and incorporated into any planning and management exercise.

Visitors Amenities and Services

Once visitors arrive at the site or destination, they must be treated in the best possible manner to ensure their satisfaction, willingness to return and recommendation of the site to others. Site services and amenities can range from simple things like drinking fountains and benches to a well-cared for environment.

Visitor amenities and services exist both on and offsite. On-site amenities and services include:

- Drinking water
- Toilets
- Public telephones
- Postal services
- Emergency medical services
- Garbage removal and disposal

The range of on-site amenities is obviously a function of the scale of the site. Larger sites can offer a full range of eating and accommodation services. If these services are contracted out, there is a need for leasing and contract administration. Off-site amenities can include:

- Accommodation of various kinds
- Restaurants
- Retail activities
- Services such as car repair, e-mail
- Recreational facilities
- Entertainment possibilities
- Healthcare

While site managers do not control these amenities, they can influence community and regional private sector interests to provide some of these amenities through their public relations programs.

Security

No matter what the destination, most tourists want to feel safe and secure not only from theft and crime, but in the ability of the destination to deal with any problems that may arise. It is often more of a sense of security, than anything tangible, that tourists are seeking.

Concerns of a destination's fire, police and hospital facilities are paramount. This includes, for example, concerns that doctors or police speak the tourist's language and are trustworthy and sympathetic. If any problems do arise for tourists, lack of preparation on the part of the destination will not support the image of a tourist-friendly destination.

When visiting a foreign or even a domestic destination, tourists want to feel confident the water they are drinking is safe and the food free of disease. Strategies to promote these feelings of security revolve around training and awareness campaigns for locals. For example, hotel and restaurant workers may need training about what tourists find acceptable and unacceptable in terms of hygiene and food preparation. The most important strategy, however, is to communicate with tourists. The unknown is frightening; honest, straightforward information will reassure them about what is and is not safe in a destination. For example, if tap water is not safe to drink - but is safe for brushing teeth - explain to visitors why and where they can purchase bottled water. Many tourists to Asia worry about malaria. If malaria prophylactics are necessary, it is important tourists are aware of this before they arrive and they are confident the destination would be able to cope with any potential problems.

Disaster Planning

The Asia-Pacific region is prone to major disasters such as fires, typhoons and particularly floods. Destinations should be concerned about the impact of disasters not only for safety of local people but because the destination's ability to deal with the situation effectively and professionally is important in terms of tourists' perceptions of safety. Disaster planning is crucial so the destination is prepared to deal with most possible eventualities.

There are limitations to traditional top-down relief-based disaster management. During times of disaster, local governments are in the best position to provide leadership, supervise distribution of relief goods and medicine and manage evacuations. Since local governments have the most at stake and are the most closely involved in local development, they can be effective in planning long-term risk reduction.

Public relations "damage control" is of the utmost importance in mitigating a disaster's negative effects on the tourism industry. For example, if a typhoon hits one corner of an island and images of the damage reach the international press, the destination must mobilize to publicize that only one portion of the island has been affected and the rest is open for business as usual.

A destination must also be physically prepared to respond to emergencies. Planning should look at how to preserve the resources themselves along with the well-being of the host community and guests. Disasters can destroy both natural and cultural heritage. A good disaster plan can reduce the impact on heritage and natural resources and minimize damage. For example, in the case of fire, are local fire brigades trained on how to salvage ancient paintings from a burning museum?

Considerations of water, transport and communication in times of crisis are internal dimensions that must be planned ahead of time and cannot be managed by a damage control public relations team.

Conclusion

Along with sound planning, policymaking and the development of realizable marketing strategies, it is essential to treat the ongoing operation of the entire destination and specific sites as a crucial element in the overall destination management process. This chapter has attempted to provide an indication of some elements that must be considered.

REFERENCES

Getz, D. *Event Management and Event Tourism*. New York: Cognisant Communication Corp. 1997.

Jamieson, Walter and Pallavi Mandke. "An Exploration of the National Policy Issues Related to the Use of Tourism Development in Poverty Reduction in Southeast Asia", *Conference Proceedings, Tourism In Asia: Development, Marketing and Sustainability*, The Fifth Annual Biennial Conference, Kaye Chon et al. (eds.), 2002.

Jamieson, Walter and Pawinee Sunalai. *The Management of Urban Tourism Destinations: The Cases of Klong Khwang and Phimai, Thailand*, UMP-Asia Occasional Paper No. 56. 2002.

Jamieson, Walter (ed.). *Community Tourism Destination Management: Principles and Practices*, Canadian Universities Consortium Urban Environmental Management Project. 2001.

Jamieson, Walter. "Interpretation and Tourism", *Community Tourism Destination Management: Principles and Practices*, Walter Jamieson (ed.), Canadian Universities Consortium Urban Environmental Management Project. 2001.

Jamieson, Walter. "Defining Urban Tourism Destination Management", Walter Jamieson (ed.), *Community Tourism Destination Management: Principles and Practices*, Canadian Universities Consortium Urban Environmental Management Project. 2001.

Jamieson, Walter. "Managing Urban Heritage Resources Within a Cultural Tourism Context, Walter Jamieson (ed.), *Community Tourism Destination Management: Principles and Practices*, Canadian Universities Consortium Urban Environmental Management Project. 2001.

Jamieson, Walter. *Promotion of Investment in Tourism Infrastructure*, New York: United Nations Economic and Social Commission for Asia and the Pacific. 2001.

Jamieson, Walter and Alix Noble. *A Manual for Sustainable Tourism Destination Management*, Training and Technology Transfer Program, Canadian Universities Consortium Urban Environmental Management Project at AIT. 2000.

Jamieson, Walter and Alix Noble. *A Manual for Interpreting Community Heritage for Tourism*, Training and Technology Transfer Program, Canadian Universities Consortium Urban Environmental Management Project at AIT. 2000.

Jamieson, Walter and Don Getz, Tazim Jamal, and Alix Noble. *Local Level Planning for Sustainable Tourism Development*, Canadian Universities Consortium Urban Environmental Management Project at AIT. 2000.

Jamieson, Walter and Pallavi Mandke. "Urban tourism and environmental sustainability - taking an integrated approach", *Developments in Urban and Regional Tourism*, M. Robinson, R. Sharpley, N. Evans, P. Long and J. Swarbrooke, Sunderland: The Centre for Travel and Tourism and Distance Education Publishers Ltd. 2000.

Jamieson, Walter and Pallavi Mandke. " The Role of Urban Environmental Management in Resolving Urban Tourism Destination Management Problems", in Conference Proceedings, *Tourism—A Strategic Industry in Asia and Pacific: Defining Problems and Creating Solutions*, Asia Pacific Tourism Association. 2000.

Jamieson, Walter. *Guidelines on Integrated Planning for Sustainable Tourism Development*, New York: United Nations Economic and Social Commission for Asia and the Pacific. 1999.

Jamieson, Walter and Adela Galloway-Cosijn. "Towards Sustainable Cultural Tourism Planning and Development Training Programs for Aboriginal Communities", *Teoros*. Summer 1998.

Jamieson, Walter and Tazim Jamal. "Contributions of Tourism to Economic Development" in *International Tourism: A Global Perspective*, Chuck Gee and Eduardo Fayos-Sola (eds.), Madrid: World Tourism Organization. 1997.

Jamieson, Walter and Tazim Jamal. "Tourism Planning and Destination Management" in *International Tourism: A Global Perspective*, Chuck Gee and Eduardo Fayos-Sola (eds.), Madrid: World Tourism Organization. 1997.

Jamieson, Walter (ed.). "The Challenge of Cultural Tourism", *Monuments and Sites—Canada*, published by the Sri Lanka National Committee of ICOMOS and the Central Cultural Fund of the Government of Sri Lanka and UNESCO for the International Council on Monuments and Sites (ICOMOS), Sri Lanka. 1996.

Jamieson, Walter. "The Use of Indicators in Monitoring: The Economic Impact of Cultural Tourism Initiatives", *ICOMOS Momentum 1995.*

Levy, Richard M. and Elizabeth E. Dickson. "GIS, Remote Sensing and Tourism Destination Management", Jamieson, Walter (ed.). *Community Tourism Destination Management: Principles and Practices*, Canadian Universities Consortium Urban Environmental Management Project. 2001.

Lindberg, Kreg, Arild Molstad, Donald Hawkins, Walter Jamieson. "International Development Assistance in Tourism", *Annals of Tourism Research.* 2001.

Mandke, Pallavi. "Carrying Capacity as a Tool for Tourism Destination Management", Jamieson, Walter (ed.). *Community Tourism Destination Management: Principles and Practices*, Canadian Universities Consortium Urban Environmental Management Project. 2001.

Ross, William, Jason Husack, Glenda Koh, Hans Luu, and Kelly Skeith Cumulative Impact Assessment of Hotel Development in Siem Reap,Cambodia, Jamieson, Walter (ed.). *Community Tourism Destination Management:*

Principles and Practices, Canadian Universities Consortium Urban Environmental Management Project. 2001.

Wall, Geoffrey. The Nature of Urban and Community Tourism, Jamieson, Walter (ed.). *Community Tourism Destination Management: Principles and Practices*, Canadian Universities Consortium Urban Environmental Management Project. 2001.

Zimmerman, Willi and Beatriz Mayer. "Good Governance in Destination Management", Jamieson, Walter (ed.). *Community Tourism Destination Management: Principles and Practices*, Canadian Universities Consortium Urban Environmental Management Project. 2001.

17

New Tourism Enterprises and the Complexities of Sustainable Development Policy: The Case of the Cairngorm Funicular Railway

*David M. Silbergh**

Abstract

One of the longest-running and most contested in recent years about whether or not a British tourism development can be regarded as sustainable has been focused on the case of the Cairngorm Funicular Railway in Scotland. This tourism development has caused disagreement between a number of public authorities and interest groups. It is now in situ, operational and, according to its supporters at least, contributing to the sustainable development of the Cairngorm area. The author will not wish to comment at length in this chapter on whether or not he is supportive of the funicular's development. Rather, he will reflect upon the policy framework within which the project was conceived, summarise the debate that has surrounded the initiative and draw conclusions in

* Dr. David Silbergh is a Lecturer in the Division of Management at Glasgow Caledonian University, United Kingdom.

relation to the lessons that can be usefully learned for future policy implementation in relation to sustainable tourism development.

Across the globe, most public, commercial and voluntary organisations now at least state a commitment, through a variety of policy statements, strategy documents and charters, to the pursuit of sustainable development. Of course, as both this author and others have charted elsewhere, the meaning of sustainable development remains multifarious (Kidd, 1992; Silbergh, 1999, 2002a, 2002b). Whilst different actors are often able to agree on the meaning of this complex concept at the most general of levels e.g. the Brundtland definition (see World Commission on Environment and Development, 1987), there tends to be far less agreement on how the concept should be operationalised when planning, implementing or evaluating projects in the empirical world. Thus, a new enterprise may be adjudged a sustainable development by one person and regarded as the antithesis of a sustainable development by another. There is probably no quick or easy solution to this issue and when new tourism developments are proposed, battles can occur between groups adopting opposing stances. Even when there is agreement at the most general of levels as to sustainable development's meaning, underlying differences in conceptualisation and/or operationalisation are unlikely to disappear in the near future. Indeed, for Hegelians and others who take a dialectical view of the development of human knowledge, such a state of affairs would be seen as nothing more than the onward march of history.

In this chapter, a Scottish case study that demonstrates the complexity of the issues that can surround new tourism developments is considered, i.e. the Cairngorm Funicular Railway (hereafter abbreviated to 'the funicular'). The funicular has been designed to transport tourists up Cairngorm (one of the largest mountains in Scotland) to marvel at the landscape and wildlife in the summer and to take them to the ski slopes that are to be found in operation there during the winter. The development of this new tourism enterprise has undoubtedly been one of the most controversial witnessed in recent years in the United Kingdom. As a result, its story merits further attention. For any reader interested in investigating this case further, there is certainly no shortage of material available. Typing 'Cairngorm funicular' into any internet search engine will throw up an amazing array of commentary and simply to read it all is a considerable task.

This chapter will therefore progress by way of brief consideration of the complex conceptual nature of sustainable development and provide a summarised overview of the over-arching international and UK/Scottish policy frameworks within which the Cairngorm Funicular Railway project was conceived and built. The case itself will then be outlined and examined with reference to the policy frameworks that guide the development of new tourism enterprises in Scotland and conclusions will be presented regarding the lessons that can be learned from the story of the funicular. These conclusions will draw upon literature that has been published in relation to the sustainable development of enterprises that rely on the exploitation of an inherited resource, which can be equally usefully be applied in relation to enterprises dependent on either a natural or a built resource.

Sustainable Development

As noted above, how one should define 'sustainable development', whether conceptually or operationally, has exercised many a mind in recent decades. The complex concept of sustainable development appears to have developed (according to Kidd, 1992) from initial references that first appeared in print in *A Blueprint for Survival* (Goldsmith *et al*, 1972). The central tenet of this seminal piece of work (now available re-printed in book format) was that, "The principal defect of the industrial way of life is that it is not sustainable." (*ibid.*). Some fifteen years after the publication of *Blueprint* the concept was to gain currency with the world's public policy community, following the report of the UN-sponsored World Commission on Environment and Development that had been chaired by Gro Harlem Brundtland, later to become Prime

Minister of Norway (WCED, 1987). The name of Brundtland has subsequently been used as a shorthand prefix to describe for the Commission, its report, and the definition of sustainable development that is contained within it.

This so-called Brundtland definition of sustainable development is, "development which meets the needs of the present without compromising the ability of future generations to meet their own needs" (*ibid.*). As suggested in the introduction to this chapter, although the general thrust of the Brundtland Commission's definition has a few detractors, most commentators are willing to agree that the pursuit of such a long-term approach to development is both sensible and desirable. As was also noted in the introduction though, far less agreement is evident when it comes to questions of how this notion of sustainable development should be unpacked into its most basic conceptual components and of how it should be operationalised thereafter. Such disagreement has led to an extensive literature on the issue of defining sustainable development. This literature sets out a very wide range of sometimes competing and sometimes complementary perspectives, addressing issues both of conceptualisation and operationalisation. This chapter is not the appropriate place in which to discuss these alternative perspectives at length.

To give some measure of the complexity of 'sustainable development' as an idea however, it is worth mentioning that the present author has identified elsewhere no fewer than thirty different sub-dimensions of the notion (Silbergh, 1999). Yet, even when thirty such sub-dimensions are enumerated, this is still far from being equal to a full listing. One way in which sustainable development can be viewed then is as follows, "In the final analysis, the end result of seeking to define sustainable development is to find that the concept is too large an unwieldy to capture in a generic sense . . ." (*ibid.*). This is not to say that one cannot usefully employ notions of sustainable development in more limited contexts though e.g. sustainable tourism development, sustainable agricultural development etc. Indeed, this is the approach that has been taken by most organisations and individuals. That is, they have tended to define its meaning in relation to their own sphere of interest, whilst maintaining regard for the general Brundtland definition. A good example of this approach can be seen by referring to the outputs of the United Nations Conference on Environment and Development held in Rio de Janeiro in 1992 (UN, 1992). The general statement of international principles of sustainable development agreed at the conference (known as the Rio Declaration) is a very slender document and has been described as "ambiguous" (Grubb *et al*, 1993). When it came to applying these general principles to more specific issues however, the Rio output was more voluminous and had considerably more effect. Amongst other things it resulted in two international treaties (the Climate Change Convention and Convention on Biological Diversity).

Thus, to conclude this section of the chapter, sustainable development is best regarded as a guiding principle that can be used to shape one's thinking in relation to most spheres of human activity. Defining it *in toto* is difficult, but that does not necessarily render it as useless. Thus, it is to the relevant international and domestic policy frameworks within which the Cairngorm Funicular Railway was conceived and built that this chapter will now turn.

International Sustainable Development Policy

From the time of *Blueprint for Survival* in 1972 the concept of sustainable development made little impact in terms of public policy until the publication of the *World Conservation Strategy: Living Resource Conservation for Sustainable Development* (1980). This report had a truly international pedigree, having been authored by IUCN (The World Conservation Union), UNEP (United Nations Environment Programme) and WWF (the World Wide Fund for Nature). As is evident from the publication's title, the advancement of conservation was its main purpose, not the promotion of sustainable development. Nevertheless, the *World Conservation Strategy* was a significant publication, aiming as it did to encourage international co-operation and the pursuit of environmental action on a supra-national level. The *Strategy* contains a few passages where sustainable development is pointedly addressed. Clear reference is made to the idea that, "Human beings, in their quest for economic development and enjoyment of the riches of nature, must come to terms with the reality of resource limitation and the carrying capacity of ecosystems, and must take account of the needs of future generations." (IUCN *et al*, 1980). It can be seen by looking at the 1987 report of the World Commission on Environment and Development that the standard Brundtland definition of sustainable development and the international policy agenda that it shaped thereafter have thus been at least in part shaped by the *World Conservation Strategy*.

It is the work of the Brundtland Commission and the subsequent United Nations Conference on Environment and Development or 'Earth Summit' held in Rio in 1992 that can most accurately be said to form the basis for current policy on sustainable development. With three basic tenets of sustainable development in mind (inter-generational equity, man considered as fully part of the planetary ecosystem and the need for appropriate action to be taken in each and every nation), the Brundland Commission's 1987 report established a list of fundamental principles for sustainable development. This set of fundamental principles formed the foundation for the UN Conference on Environment and Development in 1992 and are (WCED, 1987) :

1. Revive growth;
2. Change the quality of growth;
3. Conserve and enhance the resource base;
4. Ensure a sustainable level of population;
5. Re-orientate technological advancement and manage risks better;
6. Integrate environment and economics in decision-making;

7. Reform international economic relations;

8. Strengthen international co-operation.

Welcoming the Brundtland report, the UN began to organise the Conference on Environment and Development (or UNCED). UNCED involved a massive global effort to compile the social, economic and environmental concerns which form the agenda for sustainable development. It was not however convened with a view to solving all the problems of the world. There was a realisation, even beforehand that, "Not everything will be solved in Rio - sustainable development is a long-term process with the need for flexible or incremental approaches which can be reviewed and developed as monitoring and evaluation provides information on progress and effects." (Thomson, 1991). Such a flexible and incremental approach has subsequently transpired.

As previously noted, UNCED led to a number of outputs including the Rio Declaration, the Climate Change Convention and the Convention on Biological Diversity. It also led to the generation of a set of Principles of Forestry Management. The best known outcome from Rio however, and the one that is most important in relation to tourism development, was Agenda 21. In 1992 the then Secretary-General of the United Nations, Dr. Boutros-Ghali, described Agenda 21 as (UN, 1992),

> A comprehensive and far-reaching programme for sustainable development . . . which constitutes the centrepiece of international cooperation and coordination activities within the United Nations system for many years to come . . . Building on the spirit of Rio, the implementation of Agenda 21 must be seen as an investment in our future.

A terser description is given by Maurice Strong who had been Secretary General to UNCED, "Agenda 21 - a comprehensive blueprint for the global actions to affect the transition to sustainable development," (UN, 1992). Agenda 21 was devised as *the* international Agenda for the Twenty-First Century, an Agenda that is to help define the future shape of social, environmental and economic spheres in the world community. It is an international call to action for sustainable development, and requires governments to formulate and implement their own national policies in order to achieve this.

In comparison with more transient policy initiatives, the longevity of what was agreed at Rio is to be welcomed. The 2002 Johannesburg World Summit on Sustainable Development was a repeat UNCED, reviewing progress against Agenda 21. Indeed, the *World Summit on Sustainable Development: Plan of Implementation* (UNEP, 2002) notes that the international community's policy on sustainable development did not change radically in Johannesburg,

> The United Nations Conference on Environment and Development (UNCED), held in Rio de Janeiro in 1992, provided the fundamental principles and the programme of action for achieving sustainable development. We strongly reaffirm our commitment to the Rio principles, the full implementation of Agenda 21 and the Programme for the Further Implementation of Agenda 21 . . . The present plan of implementation will further build on the achievements made since UNCED and expedite the realization of the remaining goals.

Although mainly concerned with extending the achievements of Rio, the outputs from the Johannesburg summit did also include a range of decisions made in relation to nine specific areas of activity (UNEP, 2002) :

1. Poverty eradication;
2. Changing unsustainable patterns of consumption and production;
3. Protecting and managing the resource base of economic and social development;
4. Sustainable development in a globalizing world;
5. Health and sustainable development;
6. Sustainable development of small island developing States;
7. Sustainable development for Africa;

8. Means of implementation;
9. Institutional frameworks for sustainable development.

Although it was the first of these areas (poverty eradication) that was to receive the most coverage in the press, it is the third which is especially important in relation to tourism developments such as the Cairngorm Funicular Railway. In relation to tourism and protecting/managing the resource base of economic/social development the conclusion that came out of the Johannesburg World Summit was that the international community should (UNEP, 2002),

> Promote sustainable tourism development, including non-consumptive and eco-tourism . . . . . . in order to increase the benefits from tourism resources for the population in host communities while maintaining the cultural and environmental integrity of the host communities and enhancing the protection of ecologically sensitive areas and natural heritages. Promote sustainable tourism development and capacity-building in order to contribute to the strengthening of rural and local communities.

Thus, this statement underpins international policy on sustainable tourism today.

Sustainable Development Policy And Scottish Tourism

Within the international policy framework for sustainable development the Government of the United Kingdom has developed its own agenda, designed to meet the challenges agreed upon at Rio and Johannesburg. This is not of course in any way peculiar to the United Kingdom and nearly all countries on the planet have acted in a similar manner to their meet Agenda 21 commitments and treaty obligations. At time of writing, the UK's policy on sustainable development was articulated in a White Paper entitled *A Better Quality of Life: A Strategy for Sustainable Development in the UK* (Deputy Prime Minister, 1999). It is however likely that this document will to be subject to revisions as a result of the recent World Summit in Johannesburg.

The over-arching aim of the UK Government as regards sustainable tourism development is set out in *A Better Quality of Life* and states, "The Government wishes to see the UK tourism industry grow significantly, in ways which are economically, socially and environmentally beneficial." (Deputy Prime Minister, 1999). The objectives identified that will serve to achieve this aim are (*ibid.*) :

- *establishing an effective policy framework*: a new strategic body will lead in developing sustainable tourism . . .
- *maximising tourism's potential to benefit communities*, by encouraging local goods, services and employment, and tourism's role in improving local environments;
- *managing visitor flows*, through more effective visitor management plans;
- *addressing transport and planning issues*: integrating tourism with public transport, and ensuring that tourism development respects the local built and natural environment;
- *building partnerships* between public, private and voluntary sectors . . .

These UK objectives will later be used as a basis for evaluating the case of the Cairngorm Funicular Railway. Finally, although it complicates matters further, at time of writing the UK has a non-Federal and inconsistent system of devolved government, quite unlike anything that exists elsewhere, and this must be briefly explained in order that the case of the Cairngorm Funicular can be set in context.

Since the Labour Party returned to government in 1997, the traditional centralised system of British government has been modified. In some parts of the UK devolved assemblies have taken over some of the powers previously held at Westminster. The development of devolved assemblies has not however been consistent and the lives of the majority of British citizens are still subject to government from Westminster. Ignoring Northern Ireland (where the system of devolved government has in its short life been suspended on more than one occasion) the areas of the country which currently have assemblies are Scotland, Wales and London. To confuse matters more, these assemblies all have powers that differ considerably, with the London Assembly having fewer powers than the Welsh Assembly. The Edinburgh-based Scottish Parliament is the most powerful of the three devolved assemblies and has law-making and tax-raising powers in relation to all areas of activity that have not been specifically retained at Westminster. Similarly, a Scottish Executive, led by Members of the Scottish Parliament, now carries out all central public administration functions that have not been specifically retained by the UK Government Tourism and sustainable development are functions that have been almost entirely devolved from London to Edinburgh.

Consequently, the over-arching aim of the UK Government as regards sustainable tourism development is complemented by a further set of detailed and specifically Scottish aims. These are set out in *A New Strategy for Scottish Tourism* (Scottish Executive, 2000). This document contains the Executive's vision for tourism development, i.e. to achieve the following for Scotland (*ibid.*),

- A modern tourist industry in touch with its customers
- A skilled and enterprising industry which has embraced the culture of lifelong learning
- An industry dedicated to providing the high quality of service our visitors demand.

If we realise this vision, tourism can take its rightful place at the heart of Scotland's economy. It will be a sustainable industry.

Thus, both the UK Government and the Scottish Executive have wedded themselves to the pursuit of sustainable tourism development. This is important to note for two reasons:

(a) in relation to those functions for which it has responsibility, the Scottish Executive is no way bound to follow the policy direction of the UK Government (and regularly chooses not to do so); and,

(b) the Cairngorm Funicular Railway project was initially planned and granted planning permission under the old centralised Westminster system of government, its construction was begun during a transitional phase and it was completed and opened under a fully operative devolved system of government.

These points simply serve to add further to the complexity of the case, which will now be considered.

The Complexities of the Case of the Cairngorm Funicular

Over and above the Parliaments in Westminster and Edinburgh, the UK Government and the Scottish Executive, a myriad of actors have been involved in the case of the Cairngorm Funicular Railway, including the judiciary. Other organisations that have played a central role in the story of this tourism development (and this is by no means an exhaustive list) are shown below in Table—17.1. All of the non-departmental public bodies shown now report to the Scottish Executive rather than the UK Government.

Please note that this table is intended as a brief summary only. As a result of the complexity of the funicular's development the list of the roles of actors shown have been simplified. For a full account of the funicular's development see both CairnGorm Mountain (2002) and Cairngorms Campaign (2002). Taken together these documents explain the case in further detail than can be achieved in this chapter, without overloading the reader with minutiae.

When the first passengers ascended Cairngorm using the funicular at Christmas 2001 (Grant, 2001), it marked the end of a battle of wills between groups in favour of and groups against its development as a replacement for an older chairlift system. Despite this battle of wills having lasted

Table 17.1 Some Key Actors in the Development of the Cairngorm Funicular

Organisation	Responsibilities	Role
CairnGorm Mountain Ltd.	The Funicular's operating company	Applicant for planning permission. Leases and operates the funicular
European Union	In regard to this case, European sustainable development (both economic and environment).	Both designer of protective designations in place on Cairngorm and co-funder.
Highland Council	The local government body with land-use planning among its many responsibilities.	Responsible for granting planning permission. Co-funder of the funicular project.
Highlands and Islands Enterprise	Non-departmental public body with the responsibility of encouraging economic and social development in Highland Scotland (including tourism).	Owner of the Cairngorm ski area land, the funicular itself and associated buildings. The main financial backer of the funicular project.
Royal Society for the Protection of Birds (RSPB)	Voluntary sector body with interest in promoting sustainable development.	Co-litigant with WWF-UK in legal bid to stop the funicular's development.
Scottish Natural Heritage	Non-departmental public body with a wide range of advisory and executive functions in relation to the sustainable management of the natural heritage of Scotland.	Responsible for providing expert advice on sustainable development in relation to both protective designations and the consideration of the planning application for the funicular.
World Wide Fund for Nature (WWF-UK)	Voluntary sector body with interest in promoting sustainable development.	Co-litigant with REPB in legal bid to stop the funicular's development.

approximately a full decade prior to the funicular's opening (CairnGorm Mountain, 2002), the debate is not *passé* now that it is in full operation. It remains a controversial development, and is one from which lessons about sustainable tourism development can be learned. To get an idea of just how controversial, see the Appendix to this chapter, which shows the type of questions that were still being asked of the Scottish Executive in relation to the funicular's development just as construction work was due to start. The Appendix lists ten questions (Rumbles, 1999) all asked in a one-week period, by one Member of the Scottish Parliament alone. When one considers that this is only a week's output from one MSP (Mike Rumbles) and that he was by no means the only Member (there are 129) who was hostile to the funicular, it gives an indication of the scale of the controversy surrounding this development.

As highlighted earlier in this chapter (and as can so often be the case when interpreting the meaning of a complex concept such as sustainable development in a 'real-life' situation) the battle of wills between the competing groups came about as a result of their having drawn separate conclusions about both the concept's meaning and how it should be operationalised. Thus, for one group the funicular was a sustainable development, for the other it was the antithesis of such.

The funicular's champions (including CairnGorm Mountain Limited, the Highland Council and Highlands and Islands Enterprise) promoted their vision of the funicular as an example of a sustainable development, a tourism resource that would not unduly impinge upon the natural environment or upon 'quiet' forms of outdoor recreation such as walking. For example, Tim Whittome of the Cairngorm Chairlift Company (now CairnGorm Ltd.) noted in 1995 that,

> The Cairngorm Ski Area has provided both a recreational facility and the key to the economic prosperity of Badenoch and Strathspey for nearly 35 years . . . Much has been made in the past of the conflict between the needs of tourism and of quiet informal recreation. I suspect that much of this conflict is in the mind.

Other supporters of the project such as the Highland Council (2001) have described the funicular as an, "environmentally sustainable tourist attraction," and the Chief Executive of Highlands and Islands Enterprise was quoted as stating, "the funicular project presented significant economic and environmental gains of national significance." (HIE, 1999).

Supporters of the funicular would point out its credentials as a sustainable development as it: would be have less visual impact on the landscape than the chairlifts which it replaced; and, would be socially inclusive as it could convey small children, frail and disabled people up the mountain to enjoy the natural environment in a way which the chairlifts could not. Moreover, it was argued that as the chairlifts had reached the end of their useful life and needed to be replaced anyway, a funicular would be an ideal replacement as it would be: a major tourist attraction in its own right in the summer, re-vitalising the tourism industry; and, a major driver in re-vitalising the ski-ing and winter tourism industries in the Badenoch and Strathspey area as the funicular would be able to convey skiers up the mountain in most conditions, which the chairlifts could not, thus extending the number of days that the ski area could be open for business. Both summer and winter tourism would help to secure local jobs.

On the other hand, those opposed to the funicular's development also claimed to be acting in accordance with the interests of sustainable development. In the paper *Montane Concerns* the RSPB (which together with WWF-UK launched legal challenges aimed at halting the funicular's development) noted that they, ". . . together with all other conservation and recreation NGOs in Scotland, have opposed this development." Their concerns can be summarised as: worries in relation to undertaking such a large scale civil engineering project in an environmentally sensitive area (including railway cuttings); the dangers to habitat and wildlife that would be caused by larger numbers of people than ever before being given easy access to the mountain's plateau; and, worries that the financial viability of the scheme was not quite as suggested by its promoters. Indeed, one of the strongest arguments advanced by the funicular's detractors related to the inter-play between the latter two concerns. The RSPB and WWF-UK felt that the funicular project was anything but an example of a sustainable development, arguing that the funicular would either cause, "consequent environmental damage – or the project will be unable to deliver the promised economic benefits to the community, or both." (RSPB, undated). Put simply, the argument was that for the funicular to be a sustainable development it would need to be justifiable on both economic and environmental grounds and that the two were incompatible. The number of visitors required to secure financial viability would be too great to avoid serious and irreversible damage to the environment. Conversely, at environmentally 'safe' levels, too few visitors would be using the funicular to generate sufficient income for the project to be viable.

The government's statutory advisers, Scottish Natural Heritage sought to find a middle way between the two competing camps, recommending that tourists using the funicular in the summer months would not be allowed to take the funicular all the way up to the fragile plateau of Cairngorm, nor would they be able to access it on foot from the funicular station at which they would alight. In other words, Scottish Natural Heritage took a third view of what constituted sustainable development, in partial agreement with both pro- and anti-funicular camps but in total agreement with neither. Although criticisms of this approach to sustainable development through visitor management was to result in legal actions by the funicular's detractors (a long and complex story in itself), it was this approach which was finally to win the day.

Conclusion

In retrospect, it is perhaps the case that all sides (i.e. pro, anti and SNH) were 'right' in the sense that they could provide evidence to the effect that their view of the funicular was a view of sustainable tourism development. Given that the meaning of sustainable development remains multifarious and given the consequently significant problems encountered in trying to operationalise the concept, this is perhaps inevitable.

However, in the author's opinion, a number of lessons can be learned from the case of the funicular. The positive lesson is that consideration and debate, even if it takes a decade, can result in what most commentators can at least agree is a *more* sustainable tourism development than that which had initially been planned (i.e. the SNH middle way). On the other hand, by considering some well-established principles of sustainable development, whilst it is undoubtedly the case that whilst the funicular is not as appalling a development as has been painted by some of its more vehement critics, its claim to being a sustainable tourism development could have been further strengthened.

Most importantly of all, the Brundtland definition of sustainable development places an emphasis on not undertaking activities that will compromise future generations. In the case of Cairngorm the construction of the funicular has not needed a generational timescale to compromise the decision-making and management options open to others. At time of writing Cairngorm and its environs are in the process of being included in a new National Park (see APRS, 2002). The very fact of the funicular's existence means that the authorities that will run this National Park have had their options for deciding upon / managing the shape and nature of activities that will go on there compromised.

As many authors have noted, the pursuit of sustainable development relies on "*The precautionary principle.* Damage caused . . . by inappropriate development is irreversible on anything other than geological timescales" (Silbergh, 1999). The civil engineering works including railway cuttings that have been undertaken on Cairngorm would certainly fall into this category. Whilst the chairlifts which the funicular replaced were undoubtedly unsightly, they could always be removed more easily, leaving less trace of their having been there. This area of concern has recently been giving concern to researchers concerned with the sustainable development of the built heritage resource, and some of their conclusions have resonance in regard to the case of the funicular. Baxter and Chippindale (2002a, 2002b) have traced the continuing re-development of transportation and tourism facilities at and around the Stonehenge site and drawn the conclusion that perceptions of the visual impacts of development are fickle, and that it is therefore more sensible to build temporary and not permanent structures in sensitive areas and to do so in a way that involves building on top of the existing ground level rather than cutting into it. That way they argue, when the tide of opinion in relation to what is visually intrusive changes, the physical infrastructure of a tourism development can also be changed, with minimal long-term damage caused. This of course would be truer for a chairlift than a funicular.

To conclude this chapter, the case of the Cairngorm funicular is immensely complex and its development has been by no means perfect as an example of sustainable tourism. It could however have been far more damaging to the natural environment had SNH's middle way not prevailed and, since it has come into use, there have been further tourism developments planned for the area (Ross, 2002), although it is difficult to judge to what extent the funicular's existence has helped to make these a reality. Finally, in terms of the UK Government's objectives sustainable tourism development as set out in Cm4345 *A Better Quality of Life* (Deputy Prime Minister, 1999) and reproduced earlier in this chapter, it may be fair to say that the funicular has managed (to some extent at least) to maximise tourism's potential to benefit the community and to manage visitor flows through a visitor management plans. In terms of its role in improving local built and natural environment environments and addressing transport and planning issues it could be said to have been less successful. In terms of the Government's sustainable tourism objective of building partnerships between public, private and voluntary sectors the funicular has been something of a disaster, resulting in a decade of squabbling between (and within) sectors, ending up in the Courts. On balance, a mixed report. Given the problems of defining and operationalising the complex concept of sustainable development however, could it ever be otherwise?

Appendix – Reproduced from *Scottish Parliament Business Bulletin* 37/1999

S1W-700 : To ask the Scottish Executive what is the average cost of each tourism-related job supported or created by grants from Highlands and Islands Enterprise.

S1W-701 : To ask the Scottish Executive what is the average estimated cost of each job supported or created by Highlands and Islands Enterprise, Highland Council or European Union grants to the proposed funicular railway on Cairn Gorm.

S1W-702 : To ask the Scottish Executive what financial provisions have been agreed with Highlands and Islands Enterprise to provide future support to the proposed Cairn Gorm funicular railway in the event that it attracts insufficient visitors to be profitable.

S1W-703 : To ask the Scottish Executive whether it will publish the assessment made by Highlands and Islands Enterprise of the number of likely visitors to the proposed funicular railway on Cairn Gorm.

S1W-704 : To ask the Scottish Executive how many representations it has received over the last six years opposing the proposed funicular railway on Cairn Gorm or calling for a review and how many it has received in support of the development.

S1W-705 : To ask the Scottish Executive what financial or other provisions have been made by Highlands and Islands Enterprise to find an alternative operator, to become the operator itself or to dismantle the development should the proposed funicular railway on Cairn Gorm attract insufficient visitors to be viable and the Cairngorm Chairlift Company cease trading.

S1W-706 : To ask the Scottish Executive how much public money has been spent by Highlands and Islands Enterprise on studies, research and other preparatory work regarding the proposed funicular railway in Cairn Gorm.

S1W-707 : To ask the Scottish Executive whether it will publish details of any current or former Highlands and Islands Enterprise Board members who are shareholders of the Cairngorm Chairlift Company.

S1W-708 : To ask the Scottish Executive whether Highland and Islands Enterprise's estimate of the likely numbers of visitors to the proposed funicular railway on Cairn Gorm is based on the estimated or actual number of visitors to other existing Highland tourist attractions.

S1W-709 : To ask the Scottish Executive how Highland and Islands Enterprise's estimate of the likely number of visitors to the proposed funicular railway on Cairn Gorm compares with the independent assessment carried out by the former Chief Executive of the Scottish Tourist Board and the reason for any difference between these two figures.

REFERENCES

Association for the Protection of Rural Scotland (2002), *Annual Report and Accounts 2001*, Edinburgh, APRS.

Baxter, I. and Chippindale, C. (2002a), *A Sustainable and Green Approach to Stonehenge Visitation: The 'Brownfield' Option: A Discussion Paper*, Glasgow, Glasgow Caledonian University, 6 pp.

Baxter, I. and Chippindale, C. (2002b), *From 'National Disgrace' to Flagship Monument: Recent Attempts to Manage the Future of Stonehenge*, in *Conservation and Management of Archaeological Sites*, Vol. 5, No. 3, pp. 151-184.

CairnGorm Mountain (2002), *The Funicular: Chronology*, 7 pp. Online. Available at: <http://www.cairngormmountain.com/chronology.htm> (accessed 2 December 2002).

Cairngorms Campaign (2002), *The Cairngorm Funicular Controversy* 2 pp. Online. Available at: <http://www.cairngorms.demon.co.uk/cairngorm_funicular.htm> (accessed 2 December 2002).

Deputy Prime Minister (1999), *A Better Quality of Life: A Strategy for Sustainable Development in the UK* Cm 4345, London, The Stationery Office.

Goldsmith, E. *et al* (1972), *A Blueprint for Survival*, in *The Ecologist*, Vol. 2, No. 1.

Grant, C. (2001), *Cairngorm Funicular Railway Opens at Last*, in *The Scotsman*, 24 December, p. 9.

Grubb, M. *et al* (1993), *The 'Earth Summit' Agreements: A Guide and Assessment: An Analysis of the Rio '92 UN Conference on Environment and Development*, London, Earthscan.

Highland Council (2001), *Investment Achieves Full Public Ownership of Funicular Railway*. Online. Available at: *http://www.highland.gov.uk/cx/pressreleases/archive2001/august2001/funicular.htm* (accessed 16 May 2002).

Highlands and Islands Enterprise (1999), *Cairngorm Funicular Funding Finalised*. Online. Available at: *http://www.hie.co.uk/welcome.asp.LocID-new185.htm* (accessed 16 May 2002).

IUCN/UNEP/WWF (1980), *World Conservation Strategy: Living Resource Conservation for Sustainable Development*, Gland, Switzerland, IUCN.

Kidd, C.V. (1992), *The Evolution of Sustainability*, in *Journal of Agricultural and Environmental Ethics*, Vol. 5, pp. 1-26.

Ross, J. (2002), *£26.5m Plan to Revitalise the Aviemore Centre*, in *The Scotsman*, 19 December, p. 4.

Rumbles, M. (1999), *Written Questions Lodged Between 23 and 29 July 1999*, in *The Scottish Parliament Business Bulletin* 37/1999, Edinburgh, The Stationery Office.

Scottish Executive (2000), *A New Strategy for Scottish Tourism*, Edinburgh, The Stationery Office.

Silbergh, D. (1999), *Sustainability and Sustainable Development*, in McDowell, E. and McCormick, J. (eds.) Environment Scotland: Prospects for Sustainability, Aldershot, Ashgate, pp. 16-41.

Silbergh, D. (2002a), *The Cairngorm Funicular and the Meaning of Sustainable Development*, in Leisure Studies Association Newsletter, No. 62, pp. 20-22.

Silbergh, D. (2002b), *Sustainable Development: Environmental Thinking in the North*, in Fladmark, J.M. (ed.) *Heritage & Identity: Shaping the Nations of the North*, Shaftesbury, Dorset, pp. 305-326.

Thomson, K. (ed.) (1991), *Agenda 21 'Building Blocks': Preliminary Submissions from UK Non Governmental Organisations for the Third Preparatory Committee of UNCED: An Interim Report from the UNEP-UK National Committee Draft II*, London, UNEP-UK.

United Nations (1992), *Earth Summit '92: The UN Conference on Environment and Development: Rio de Janeiro 1992*, London, Regency Press Corporation.

United Nations Environment Programme (2002), *World Summit on Sustainable Development: Plan of Implementation*, Nairobi, United Nations Environment Programme, 54 pp. Online. Available HTTP: <http://

www.johannesburgsummit.org/html/documents/summit_docs/plan_final1009.doc> (accessed 2 December 2002).

Whittome, T. (1995), *The Cairngorm Mountain Railway Project*, in Association for the Protection of Rural Scotland, *Tourism and Recreation, A Sustainable Approach for Rural Areas: Papers Presented at APRS Conference, Station Hotel, Perth, 21 March 1995*, Edinburgh, APRS.

World Commission on Environment and Development (1987), *Our Common Future*, Oxford, Oxford University Press.

18

The Web As a Strategic Marketing Tool for Independent Tourism and Hospitality Businesses: Branding and the Battle on the Search Engines

*Mohammed Nassar**
*Dr. Eleri Jones**and*
*Dr. Nigel Morgan****

Introduction

The Web is revolutionising the rourism and hospitality industries through all phases of product marketing, sales and distribution, affecting the way that business reach customers and cutting out supply chain intermediaries. Many businesses have involved themselves in web marketing (Gilbert *et. al.*, 1999). Hotel companies, for example, aggressively utilise the Web to market room inventories and other products, disseminate information, correspond interactively and instantaneously with their customers, and extend their booking channels. Tourism business, whther small independents or

Research*, Head of School**and Principal Lecturer,*** Welsh School of Hospitality, Tourism and Leisure Management, University of Wales Institute, Cardiff, Cardiff, CF23, 9XR.

larger multinational corporations, can have equal presence on the Web at comparatively low cost. A site on the Web has the potential not only to save administration costs, but also to reduce marketing expenses. Accordingly, the Web has become a major distribution channel and strategic marketing took for the tourism industry.

Multinational companies

Multinational companies around the world spend billions promoting and supporting their brands to deliver consistent messages to their customers and the Web has become an integral part of the marketing mix. Successful marketing programmes have led to loyal customer bases. However, independent tourism businesses do not benefit from economies of scale afforded to chains. Moreover, their names are not 'known' and reinforced through a presence around the world. Thus, whilst, independent businesses can register on the major search engines and appear high on the list of products resulting from customer searches, brand awareness and brand loyalty kick in and non-brands are likely to be bypassed as customers click onto familiar brands. Multinational businesses have developed products to respond to specific market segments and these products are delivered consistently around the globe. Thus, the customer knows what to expect and can be confident that she understands the nature of the product being presented—branding enhances consumer confidence and promotes sales.

So, whilst the Web offers independent tourism businesses a cost-effective channel to market their products in a global marketplace, it is not as simple as getting onto the search engines. The power of brand names, particularly in the global marketplace, favours the selection of branded products. Independent tourism business are disadvantaged in attracting customers to click onto their website to even consider their product, let alone taking the next step and making a purchase unless they have invested time and effort in putting their businesses into the consumer's evoked set (Hoyer and MacInnis, 1997). The challenge, therefore, for independent businesses is to build their brands in the minds of potential customers, which mandates an enhanced understanding of the new business paradigms afforded by the Web. Little attention has been paid to how websites can be used to build brands, an issue that is critically important to the survival of independent tourism businesses and the focus of this chapter. How can independent tourism businesses with their limited resources benefit from the cost-effectiveness and global reach of the Web and compete against the superbrands? The answer has to come from understanding more about the unique communications potential of the Web and how it can be used for brand-building. It is evident from surfing the Web that many tourism businesses do not harness the full power of the Web, as will be explained in the next section.

The Unique Communications Potential of the Web

The Web, unlike traditional media, is characterized by its interaction, global reach and 24 hours a day, 7 days a week (24/7) accessibility (Pitt et al., 1996; Peterson et al., 1997; Hanson, 2000) and has distinct advantages over other media (Berthon et al., 1996) - it is relatively easy and inexpensive to get onto the Web and access the global market which integrates information representation, collaboration, communication, interactivity and transactions (Gretzel et al., 2000). It has been proposed that the marketing paradigm itself will evolve towards interactive web marketing due to its efficient and cost-effective integration of advertising, marketing and distribution (Rayport and Sviokla, 1994, 1995; Hoffman and Novak, 1996b; Deighton, 1997; Wigand, 1997; Br_nnback, 1997; Peterson et al, 1997). The Web blurs traditional distinctions between interpersonal and mass communication and frees consumers from passive roles, allowing them to become active participants in the marketing process (Hoffman and Novak, 1996a). Hoffman et al. (1995) contrast two communication models to emphasise the communications potential of the Web - a traditional, passive model of marketing in which businesses broadcast information through a medium to a mass market of consumers and a new interactive multimedia many-to-many marketing model which can achieve narrow-casting in the extreme.

Traditional communications models would show tourism businesses producing content, which they disseminate through a communication medium, in this case the Web, to consumers. There are numerous examples of tourism businesses that treat the Web as if it were an on-line brochure, providing static pages adapted from existing collateral. Some are enhanced with 'bells and whistles' to provide a semblance of dynamism, possibly allowing potential customers to view rooms and other facilities. However, many websites do not provide price information, are not e-commerce enabled, do not support e-mail interaction or, if they do, do not respond within customer-meaningful timescales and do nothing to develop relationships with customers.

Hoffman et al. (1995) present a new model in which both consumers and firms can interact with the medium, providing content, communicating in one-to-one or one-to-many modes with more direct control over the way they communicate. Not only do old communication models become obsolete, but also the business structures and communication channels based on them (Evans and Thomas, 1999). Interactive marketing communication differs from traditional marketing by being based on dialogue and targeting individual consumers not mass markets (Parsons et al., 1998). Web marketing success requires: attracting and engaging user interest and participation, retaining users and ensuring they return, learning about user preferences and providing customized interactions (Gretzel et al., 2000). The Web mandates a paradigm shift (King et al., 1997) to reconstruct traditional marketing activities for the new medium (Hoffman and Novak, 1996a; Br_nnback, 1997; Janal, 1997). The next section describes the development of a model for a brand-building website and is described in more detail in Nassar (2002).

A Unified Model for Brand-Building Websites

The literature provides a number of perspectives on website design. Pollock (1996, 1999) and Hamill and Gregory (1997) suggest the key elements for success are the ability to form strategic partnerships, the support of user information gathering and integration with other marketing channels. Morrison et al. (1999) identify 25 critical success factors in four perspectives: technical; marketing; internal; customer, to achieve a dynamic interactive relationship. Reid and Bojanic (2001) advise that a website needs to be creative and grab attention, avoiding overly complex layouts and balancing use of graphics and speed of movement. The most valuable Web applications allow companies to transcend communication barriers and establish direct dialogue with customers (Gilbert et al., 1999). Sigala (2001, 2002) emphasises three capabilities: interactivity, connectivity and convergence. Morgan and Pritchard (2000) emphasise the integration of web marketing in an overall marketing strategy. Useful though these comments are they scarcely provide a pragmatic steer for effective design for a brand-building website to win the battle on the search engines.

One way to develop a model for a brand-building website would be to return to marketing basics and the 4 Ps - product, place (distribution), promotion, and price. Dutta et al.'s (1998) model comprises two dimensions: a technological dimension comprising interactivity and connectivity and a strategic business dimension reflecting the 4Ps and 'C' (customer relationships) and was taken as the starting point for the development of a unified model for a brand-building website. However, their separation of interactivity and connectivity, i.e. the Internet (the hardware) from the Web (the functionality that sits on top of the hardware), is arguably artificial as the interoperability of different platforms makes hardware transparent to the user.

Dutta et al. (1998) and Dutta and Segev (1999) identify features for each of the model's elements that can be extended through a review of the literature. McLachlan (1996) focuses on information currency and information quality. Nielsen (1999c) emphasizes logical site layout and minimal clicks for easy navigation and access. Lemay (1996) stresses conciseness and clarity, consistent layout and design, the use of reduced-size graphics and breaking up large amounts of text. Venditto

(1997) and Bell and Tang (1998) focus on coherent layout, ease of navigation, useful content, and updated information. Pitt et al. (1996) and Nielsen (1999 a, b) comment on the use of multimedia features to create an interactive and user-friendly environment turning prospective buyers into interactive customers. Nielsen and Molich (1990) and Nielsen (1994 a, b) provide a total of ten general heuristics challenging websites throughout design. Gilbert et al. (1999) list a number of relationship marketing considerations. Thus 48 web-site features were identified (see Table—18.1) and tested for completeness without redundancy through an evaluation of four different hotel websites randomly selected from lists generated by typing the key words "*Hotels+Egypt*", "*Hotels+UK*", "*Hotels+USA*", into the search engine "Yahoo".

Any system must be 'user-driven' rather than 'technology-driven' or 'content-driven', thus a consumer focus was developed through a series of semi-structured interviews and an on-line survey. As a result the 48 website features identified in phase 1 were reduced to 28 user-relevant features (see Table—18.2).

The 28 user-relevant features were organized under six headings: accessibility; information; credibility; e-commerce; immediacy; customer relationship, and further into a pyramid emphasising how a website can support brand development (see Fig. 18.1). The lower in the pyramid the consideration is, the more fundamental it is. Thus, accessibility is a more fundamental concern than customer relationship - there is little point focusing on customer relationships if the website is not accessible. The issues of accessibility and information, credibility, and immediacy, e-commerce and customer relationship are not mutually exclusive and cannot be considered individually, but rather should be considered complementary and synergistic, reinforcing each other to enhance the customer relationship and build the brand.

Table—18.1 **48 Website Features**

Interactivity	**Product**	**Price**
Accessibility	Basic product information	Price information available on-line
Downloading time	Additional (expended) product information	Customer participation in pricing
Navigation	On-line-brochure	Currency converters
Flow and design	On-line help for choosing products	
Languages	Customer participation in new product design	
URL address	Group bookings	
Rank on search engines	Destination contents	
Updates		
Graphics		
Multimedia		
Reliable hyper links		
Security.		
Search		
Place (Distribution)	**Promotion**	**Customer**
Product availability	On-line advertising	Relationship
E-mail reservation	Downloadable coupons	Feedback form
On-line reservation	Special packages and offers	On-line customer service
Real time processing of orders	Frequent guest programs	Customer identification (profiling)
Confirmation	Membership clubs	Customer communities
On-line payment	Discounts	FAQ
Third party booking (GDSs)		Mailing lists
Credit cards used		News letters
Privacy and security		Direct E-mail
		Suggestions and/or complaints
		What's new

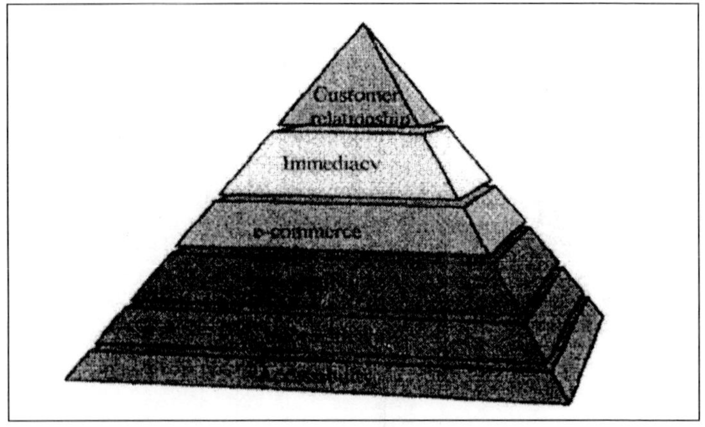

Fig. 18.1 A pyramid of consideration for the development of a brand-building website

Accessibility

Unless a website is easy to locate and responds to customer searches on major search engines (e.g. Yahoo) it will be unable to communicate information to its audience. However accessibility on its own is not enough, the website must download reasonably quickly and 'grab' the attention of the user before s/he 'surfs on' to another site. Navigation is an important accessibility feature - a website should provide clear and consistent navigation mechanisms (e.g. orientation information, navigation bars, site maps) to ensure users find what they are looking for instantly and conveniently.

Information

Content is a critical element of a website's usefulness. Useful information ranges from basic destination contents, e.g. maps, restaurant facilities, local attractions and community events, to detailed information about products and services and their availability and up-to-date price information.

Credibility (reliability)

Proper website design is largely a matter of balancing the structure and relationship of a menu or "home pages" and individual content pages or other linked graphics and documents. The goal is to build a hierarchy of menus and pages that feels natural and well structured to the user, and does not interfere with website use. Links should be carefully labelled and consistently working. Updated and revised content is also important; the site should never contain outdated information that may turn users away to a different site.

E-commerce

An e-commerce enabled website offers the speed and convenience of a one-stop availability check, instant purchase and confirmation. It should enable guests to confirm their rooms' bookings in 'real-time'. It should also allow them to close a sale immediately through an on-line booking engine which is branded to have the look and feel of the website, and is customized to communicate the property's specific terms of the reservation, room views, property directions and other important features.

Immediacy

Good use of the Web recognises its potential immediacy. The Web fuels an increasing demand for immediacy. It is vital that operators quickly confirm receipt of on-line reservations and immediately confirm or identify problems quickly.

Customer Relationship

A website should effectively function as a powerful tool to sustain a good relationship with customer and support brand-building. There are many features to perform this, for example, websites can provide electronic forms for customer completion and operators can respond via e-mail. This kind of rapport improves customer relations and promotes customer loyalty. Strategies to enhance customer relationships will be discussed later in the chapter.

Finally, each of the 28 individual website design dimensions were rated on a performance scale of 0-5 to give three degrees of performance: sub-optimal (0+1), satisfactory (2+3), and good (4+5) (see Table—18.2). The performance ratings were determined from the literature, from the on-line survey and from semi-structured interviews with web consumers (see Notes column in Table— 18.2). Using spreadsheet software the performance of a website was visualized using a radar chart as a representational tool. Radar charts, sometimes known as a 'radar plots' or 'spider webs', are well-established management tools and are particularly useful for visualizing performance on multiple dimensions simultaneously and for comparing multiple cases. A point close to the centre indicates a low value and 'sub-optimal performance' on that dimension, whereas a point near the edge indicates a high value and 'good' performance. Figure 2 shows a screen shot of the radar plot developed from an evaluation of two hotel websites using the performance criteria from Table—18.2 and facilitates the identification of performance gaps and enables prioritisation of response. Hotel 1 is a typical example of a fully-transactional and user-friendly hotel chain website projecting the 'look and feel' of the brand and is designed from a user perspective with no major weaknesses. In contrast, Hotel 2 has a number of major weaknesses and is effectively an on-line brochure adapted from existing collateral.

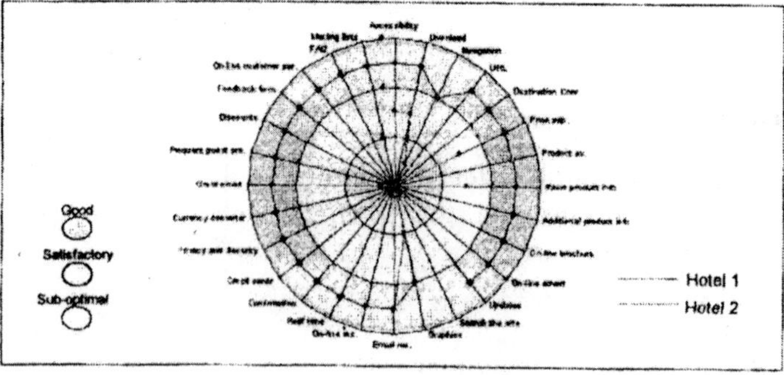

Fig. 18.2 Analysis of two Exemplar Websites

The Web as a Strategic Marketing Tool for Independent Tourism Businesses

This section suggests some pragmatic strategies for brand-building which can be customised by independent tourism businesses according to their specific context and is presented under four sub-headings: think strategic; think international; think destination; think consumer. For all the reasons outlined earlier in this chapter, independent tourism businesses that have not invested in brand-building are likely to be disadvantaged on the search engines. However, once a business has got a customer it should work hard to keep that customer and ensure that the customer not only remains loyal but also becomes an advocate for the business. The Hoffman et al. (1995) model needs to be extended to represent such customer-customer interactions and advocacy. The list is supposed to offer some creative solutions to website development that enhance customer relationships rather than being exhaustive.

Think Strategic

As already pointed out, web marketing should be an integrated part of the overall marketing, and wider business, strategy (Morgan and Pritchard, 2000). Having made a decision to invest in web marketing, organisational culture shifts and changes in operational practices may be required to maximise the benefits achieved from the Web, e.g. ensuring that there is a strategy for responding effectively and efficiently with e-mails from customers, which may require investment in training. The need for updating a website regularly so that it is a dynamic part of an overall business communications strategy has implications for in-house web development skills and again may require investment in training. Simple, 'no frills' websites download quickly and are less likely to be surfed past by potential customers, but perhaps more importantly are easier to maintain.

Think International

Global tourism is rising in Asian markets, whereas across Europe and North America demand is clearly limited by the already high level of tourism activity and by demography (Arlt, 2002). The Web is the cheapest, most convenient and efficient way to address potential international customers and can be an effective communication tool for independent tourism businesses (Arlt, 2002). However, as pointed out by Arlt (2002), approximately 50% of web users have no working command of English and less than 10% are able to understand the languages of other major European countries (e.g. German, French, Spanish). This has major implications for the promotion of tourism products in an international context and the languages that are supported on tourism websites. Cross-cultural marketing needs to be handled extremely sensitively (Arlt, 2002) - humour, for example, is not something that travels well and may be best avoided (Ansholt, 1999).

Think Destination

Tourism and hospitality products have a number of unique characteristics that differentiate them from manufactured products: intangibility (Shostack, 1977; Lovelock et al., 1981); perishability (Zeithaml et al., 1985; Onkvisit and Shaw, 1991; Hartman and Lindgren, 1993); inseparability of production and consumption (Grönroos, 1978; Zeithaml, 1981; Bowen, 1990; Onkvisit and Shaw, 1991); heterogeneity (Zeithaml et al., 1985; Onkvisit and Shaw, 1991); and perhaps most importantly in the context of brand-building - interdependence (O'Connor, 1999). Interdependence is particularly important because tourism products are rarely bought individually, but are generally bought in combination with other products. People on holiday often want to buy somewhere to stay and things to do as well as food, transport and other products. Thus, a tourism business can benefit by considering the products that are likely to be bought in combination and to provide links to and from related websites, e.g. a business located in a destination suitable for cycling holidays may find it useful to link to the Sustrans (a sustainable transport charity that works on practical projects to encourage people to walk, cycle and use public transport in order to reduce motor traffic and its adverse effects) site (http://www.sustrans.org.uk/webcode/home.asp) and negotiate a reciprocal link back to the business. Links from event sites to tourism businesses can provide spin-off business opportunities. Many destination management organisations have now developed web-based destination management systems at regional and national levels and tourism businesses can benefit from participating in these developments.

Think Consumer

The real opportunity on the Web is not to do things faster and cheaper; it is the chance to rethink the business models that organizations employ, both in terms of delivering value to the customer and in building relationships with customers, suppliers, and other business partners - through a new interactive business model called 'collaboration marketing' to build a virtual community for tourists with considerable economic potential (Hagel, 1999). Virtual communities of consumers are 24/7 focus groups offering an enormous learning opportunity for organizations that can then implement appropriate actions (Hagel, 1999). As such consumers can provide useful feedback on business websites and can contribute to the development of these websites. As pointed out by Arlt (2002), international customers may locate articles on the destination written in other languages which can be incorporated into a tourism business website. This may minimise the need for extensive translation. Indeed, customers may be prepared, even keen, to get involved in writing for websites in their own languages. As Arlt (2002) suggests— 'they thought of me!' is a powerful motivator.

Conclusion

The chapter has attempted to demonstrate the inherent dilemma for non-branded tourism products, i.e. that although they can get onto the major search engines and compete alongside the branded products of multinational companies, their non-branded status may mean that they are 'surfed past'. The battle on the search engines is won by enhancing brand awareness. The chapter describes a unified model for website design that enhances understanding of the critical role of

Table—18.2 Summary of Performance for Each of the 28 website Design Considerations

Design Features	Sub-optimal	Satisfactory	Good	Notes
ACCESSIBILITY				
Accessibility	Website is always offline, not accessible from most search engines, ranks low on search engines.	Website is generally accessible, accessible from at least major search engines, ranks high (top 20 sites) on major search engines.	Website consistently accessible from all search engines, ranks high (top 10 sites) on search engines, accessible from other parent (chain) sites.	Foster (1999); Guenther (1999); User interviews.
Downloading	Downloads in more than 30 seconds, downloads with many missing elements (e.g. graphics), not compatible with user's web browser.	Site downloads in 10 to 30 seconds, site downloads with incomplete elements, downloads directly on user's web browser	Downloads in 10 seconds or less, downloads complete with no missing elements, downloads directly on user's web browser.	GVU (1998); Dellaert and Kahn (1999); Nielsen (1999b); Nielsen (2000a); Bailey and Schaffer (2001).
Navigation	Difficult to navigate, does not include any navigation tools, very difficult to move between pages, includes dead or inactive hyperlinks.	Easy to navigate, Includes navigation tools, easy to move between pages, includes active hyperlinks.	Very easy to navigate, includes interesting and interactive navigation tools, all hyperlinks are active and live.	Lemay (1995); Murphy *et al.* (1996a); Hamill and Gregory (1997); Standing and Vasudavan (1999); User interviews.
URL	Does not operate under its own URL, URL address is long and difficult to remember, does not reflect the brand.	N/A	Operates under its own URL, short and easy to remember, reflects the brand.	Murphy *et al.* (1996a); Lederer and Maupin (1997); Foster (1999); Farris (1999); Weeks and Crouch (1999).
INFORMATION				
Destination contents	No destination contents available	N/A	Detailed destination contents available	On-line survey.
Price information available on-line	Price information is not available or vague.	Price information available, but no details.	Price information available with more details.	On-line survey
Basic product information	Lacks basic information about the product.	Basic information about the product is available.	Many items of basic information about the product are available.	Murphy *et al.* (1996a); Gilbert *et al.* (1999); User interviews.
Additional product information	Lacks additional product information.	N/A	Detailed product information is available.	Foster (1999); Lodging news (2001); Bakos (2001); User interviews.
Product availability	Not possible to check.	Only possible to check by email.	Can be checked instantly on-line.	Gilbert *et al.* (1999); On-line survey.
On-line advertising	No on-line advertising items.	Some advertising items available.	Advertising items are well used.	Dutta *et al.* (1998); On-line survey.
On-line brochure	No on-line brochure.	N/A	On-line brochure available to download instantly on-line.	Silverstien (1999)
CREDIBILITY				
Search the site	Not possible.	N/A	It is possible to search the site.	Nielsen (1997); Loban (1998a,b).
Updates	Not updated, Never show when last updated.	Not frequently updated, shows when it is last updated.	Frequently updated, shows when it is last updated.	Murphy *et al.* (1996a,b); Nielsen (1999b); Ghosh (1997); McCune (1998); User interviews.
Graphics	General misuse of Graphics, no consistency in using fonts and colours, contains complex backgrounds, large image blocks; many moving useless item.	Good use of graphics but overly dependent on them.	Graphics are used to provide a dynamic, attractive feel to the site	Tittel and James (1995); DeAngelis (1996); Burns (1997); User interviews.

Table 2: Summary of performance for each of the 28 website design considerations (continues overleaf)

E-COMMERCE/ IMMEDIACY				
The e-commerce and immediacy sections are combined here to avoid duplication.				
Real time confirmation	Not available	Confirmation available by email but usually takes few days to respond to confirmation.	Instant real time confirmation available.	Gilbert *et al.* (1999); Weeks and Crouch (1999); On-line survey.
Real time processing of orders	Not provided.	N/A	Instant real time processing of orders provided.	Ellsworth and Ellsworth (1997); Gilbert *et al.* (1999).
Currency converter	Not included.	Show prices in two or more currencies.	Currency converter available.	On-line survey.
Email reservation	Not available.	Available but slow and takes long time to confirm.	Available and usually confirms the same/next day.	Gilbert *et al.* (1999); Price and Starkov (2002).
On-line reservation	Not available.	Available but not active.	Available instantly on-line and interactive.	Murphy *et al.* (1996a); Gilbert *et al.* (1999); Starkov (2001).
Privacy and security	Security and encryption systems are not employed, no sign of security standards on site.	N/A	Security encryption systems are not employed.	Ellsworth and Ellsworth (1997); Silverstien (1999); Klemow (1999).
Credit cards used	Not applicable.	N/A.	Provided	On-line survey.
CUSTOMER RELATIONSHIP				
FAQ (Frequently Asked Questions)	Not available.	N/A	Available	Heinen (1996); Gilbert *et al.* (1999); Gee (2000).
Direct email	Not possible.	Possible but reply always late.	Possible with immediate response.	On-line survey.
Discounts	Not available	N/A	Available.	Murphy *et al* (1996a); Forrester Research (2001).
Feedback form	Not available.	N/A	Available	Pitt *et al.* (1996); Spalter (1996); Gilbert *et al.* (1999); Standing and Vasudavan (1999); Morgan and Pritchard (2000).
Mailing lists	Not available.	N/A	Available and active.	Gilbert *et al.* (1999); On-line survey.
Frequently guest programs	Not available	N/A	Available	Gilbert *et al.* (1999); Weeks and Crouch (1999); Nielsen (2000b).
On-line customer service	Not available.	N/A	Available in different forms such as: help function, frequently asked questions page, feedback mechanism, and customer service information.	Gilbert *et al.* (1999); User interviews.

developing customer relationships in brand-building - the Nassar et al. pyramid, which places customer relationships at the top of a pyramid of six considerations: accessibility, information, credibility, e-commerce, immediacy and customer relationship and identifies 28 customer-relevant features which can be codified in terms of 'good', 'satisfactory' and 'sub-optimal' performance onto a radar plot for visual presentation of the results. The radar plot helps identify areas of weakness in website design. Returning to Hoffman et al.'s new model of communication a number of strategies for developing the Web as a strategic marketing tool for independent business are suggested under four headings; think strategic; think international; think destination; think customer. The chapter concludes that there are considerable opportunities for creatively enhancing independent tourism business websites to develop relationships with customers and thus build the product brand. Such brand development should enhance the chances of independent tourism businesses winning the battle on the search engines.

REFERENCES

Ansholt, S. (1999) Travel and Tourism Companies: *Global Brands, Journal of Vacation Marketing*, 5 (3), 290-295.

Arlt, W. (2002) *Internet as a Cross Culture Incoming Tourism Communication Tool for SMEs*, Tourism Research 2002, Proceedings of an International Interdisciplinary Conference in Wales, University of Wales Institute, Cardiff, Cardiff 4th-7th September 2002.

Bailey, B. and Schaffer, E. (2001) *Acceptable Computer Response Times, UI Design Update Newsletter*, URL: http://www.humanfactors.com/downloads/apr01.asp, Accessed 02/09/2002.

Bakos, Y. (2001) The Emerging Landscape for Retail e-commerce, *Journal of Economic Perspectives*, 5 (1), 69-80.

Bell, H. and Tang, N. (1998) The Effectiveness of Commercial Internet Web sites: A User's Perspective, *Internet Research: Electronic Networking Applications and Policy*, 8 (3), 219-228.

Berthon, P., Pitt, L., and Watson, R. (1996) The World Wide Web as an Advertising Medium: Towards an understanding of Conversion Efficiency, *Journal of Advertising Research*, 60 (1), 43-54.

Bowen, J. (1990) Development of a Taxonomy of Services to Gain Strategic Marketing Insights, *Journal of the Academy of Marketing Science*, 18 (1), 43-49.

Brännback, M. (1997) Is the Internet Changing the Dominant Logic of Marketing? *European Management Journal*, 15 (6), 698-707.

Burns, H. (1997) *The Top Fifteen Mistakes of First Time Web Design*, URL: http://www.doghause.com/top15.html, Accessed 18/01/1999.

DeAngelis, M. (1996) *Marketing on the Internet*, URL: www.netresource.com/itp/repch1.html, Accessed 14/09/1999.

Deighton, J. (1997) Commentary on "Exploring the Implications of the Internet for Consumer Marketing", *Journal of the Academy of Marketing Science*, 25 (4), 347-351.

Dellaert, B. and Kahn, B. (1999) How Tolerate is Delay? Consumers' Evaluations of Internet web sites after Waiting, *Journal of Interactive Marketing*, 13 (1), 41-54.

Dutta, S. and Segev, A. (1999) Business Transformation on the Internet, *European Management Journal*, 17 (5), 466-476.

Dutta, S., Kwan, S., and Segev, A. (1998) Business Transformation in Electronic Commerce: A Study of Sectoral and Regional Trends, *European Management Journal*, 16 (5), 540-551.

Ellsworth, J. and Ellsworth, M. (1995) *Marketing on the Internet: Multimedia Strategies for the World Wide Web*, New York: John Wiley and Sons Inc.

Evans, P. and Thomas, S. (1999) Getting real about Virtual Commerce, Harvard *Business Review*, November-December, 84-94.

Farris, R. (1999) Web site Marketing Basics, *Mortgage Banking*, 59, 53-58.

Forrester Research (2001) *Web Travel will hold up in an Industry Downturn*, URL: http://www.forrester.com/ER/Research/Brief/Excerpt/0,1317,13516,00.html, Accessed 14/01/2002.

Foster, E. (1999) Building web site, *Business and Economic Review*, 46,33-35.

Gee, V. (2000) *Using FAQs to Build a Superior Support Center*, ebiz, URL: http://www.digitrends.net/ebiz/13646_12863.html, Accessed 21/03/2002.

Ghosh, S. (1997) Selling on the Internet: Achieving Competitive Advantage and Market Lead, *Planning Review*, 25,3,53-55.

Gilbert, D., Powell-Perry, J., and Widijoso, S. (1999) Approaches by Hotels to the Use of the Internet as a Relationship Marketing Tool, *Journal of Marketing Practice—Applied Marketing Science*, 5, 1, 21-38.

Gretzel, U., Yuan, Y., and Fesenmaier, D. (2000) Preparing for the New Economy: Advertising and Change in Destination Marketing Organisations, *Journal of Travel Research*, 39 (2), 146-156.

Grönroos, C. (1978) A Service Oriented Approach to Marketing of Services, *European Journal of Marketing*, 12 (8), 588 - 601.

Guenther, K. (1999) Publicity through Better web site Design, *Computers in Libraries*, 19, 62-67.

GVU (1998) *WWW User Surveys*, URL: http://www.gvu.gatech.edu, Accessed 13/07/2000.

Hagel, J. (1999) Net gain: Expanding Markets through Virtual Communities, *Journal of Interactive Marketing*, 13 (1), 55-65.

Hamill, J. and Gregory, K. (1997) Internet Marketing in the Internationalisation of UK SMEs, *Journal of Marketing Management*, 13, 9-28.

Hanson, W. (2000) *Principles of Internet Marketing*, Ohio: South -Western College Publishing, Thomson Learning.

Hartman, D. and Lindgren, J. (1993) Consumer Evaluations of Goods and Services -Implications for Services Marketing, *Journal of Services Marketing*, 7 (2), 4 -15.

Heinen, J. (1996) Internet Marketing Practices, *Information Management and Computer Security*, 4 (5), 7-14.

Hoffman, D. and Novak, T. (1996a) *A New Marketing Paradigm for Electronic Commerce*, Paper Submitted for the Special issue on Electronic Commerce for The Information Society, URL: http://www2000.ogsm.vanderbilt.edu, Accessed 22/09/1999.

Hoffman, D. and Novak, T. (1996b) Marketing in Hypermedia Computer-Mediated Environments: Conceptual Foundations, *Journal of Marketing*, 60 (3), 50-68.

Hoffman, D., Novak, T., and Chatterjee, P. (1995) Commercial Scenarios for the Web: Opportunities and Challenges, *Journal of Computer Mediated Communication, Special Issue on Electronic Commerce*, 1,3, URL: http://jcmc.huji.ac.il/vol1/issue3/hoffman.html, Accessed 02/02/1999.

Hoyer, W. and Maclnnis, D. (1997) *Consumer behavior*, Boston: Houghton Mifflin Co.

Janal, D. (1997) *Online Marketing Handbook: How to Promote, Advertise, and Sell your Products and Services on the Internet*, New York: Van Nostrand Reinhold.

King, J., Knight, P., and Mason, J. (1997) *Web Marketing: Cookbook*, New York: Chichester: Wiley.

Klemow, J. (1999) Credit Card Via the Internet, *TMA Journal,* 19, 10-14.

Lederer, A. and Maupin, D. (1997) A World Wide Web Primer for Small Business, *Journal of Small Business Strategy,* 8, 1-11.

Lemay, L. (1996) *Teach Yourself Web Publishing with HTML 3.2 in a Week* (3rd ed.), Indianapolis, Indiana: Sams Publishing.

Loban, S. (1998a) *Designing Effective Documents for Destination Information Systems.* In Buhalis, D., Tjoa, A., and Jafari, J. (eds.), *Information and Communication Technologies in Tourism* 1998, Wien: Springer-Verlag.

Loban, S. (1998b) Effective Documents for Tourist Information Systems, *Information Technology and Tourism*, 1 (1), 59-71.

Lodging News (2001) *From Surfing to Booking: The Qualities that Appeal to your Web guests*, URL: http://www.lodgingnews.com/lodgingmag/2001_10/2001_10_27.asp?zone=12.

Lovelock, C., Langeard, E., Bateson, J., and Eiglier, P. (1981) *Some Organisational Problems Facing Marketing in the Service Sector.* In Donnelly, J. and George, W. (eds.), Marketing of Services, Chicago: American Marketing Association.

McCune, J. (1998) Making Web sites pay, *Management Review*, 87 (6),36-38.

McLachlan, K. (1996) *WWW CyberGuide Ratings for Content Evaluation*, URL: http:// http://www.cyberbee.com/guide.html, Accessed, 18/03/2000.

Morgan, N. and Pritchard, A. (2000) *Advertising in Tourism and Leisure*, Oxford: Butterworth Heinemann.

Morrison, A.M., Morrison, A. J., Morrison, A. D., Taylor, S. (1999) Marketing Small Hotels on the World Wide Web, *Information Technology and Tourism*, 2 (2), 97-113.

Murphy, J., Forrest, E., Wotring, C., and Brymer, R. (1996a) Hotel Management and Marketing on the Internet, *Cornell Hotel and Restaurant Administration Quarterly*, 37 (3), 70-82.

Nassar, M. (2002), *The Web as a Strategic Marketing Tool for the Egyptian Hotel Sector*, PhD Thesis, University of Wales.

Nielsen, J. (1994a) *How to Conduct a Heuristic Evaluation*, URL: http://www.useit.com/papers/heuristic/heuristic_evaluation.html, Accessed 14/05/1999.

Nielsen, J. (1994b) *Heuristic Evaluation*. In Nielsen, J. and Mack, R. (eds.), Usability Inspection Methods, New York: John Wiley and Sons, Inc.

Nielsen, J. (1997) *Search and You May Find*, URL: http://www.useit.com/alertbox/9707b.html, Accessed 22/09/2000.

Nielsen, J. (1999a) *Ten Good Deeds in Web Design*, URL: http://www.useit.com/alertbox/991003.html, Accessed 19/03/2002.

Nielsen, J. (1999b) *Top Ten Mistakes Revisited Three Years later*, URL: http://www.useit.com/alertbox/990502.html, Accessed 19/03/2002.

Nielsen, J. (1999c) *Why People Shop on the Web*, http://www.useit.com/alertbox/990207.html, Accessed 14/09/2001.

Nielsen, J. (2000a) *Designing Web Usability: The Practice of Simplicity*, Indianapolis: New Riders Publishing.

Nielsen, J. (2000b) *Profit Maximization vs. User loyalty*, URL: http://www.useit.com/alertbox/20000305.html, Accessed 13/09/2001.

Nielsen, J. and Molich R. (1990) *Heuristic Evaluation of User Interfaces*, in Proceedings of CHI'90 (Seattle WA, April 1990), ACM Press.

O'Connor, P. (1999) *Electronic Information Distribution in Tourism and Hospitality*, Wallingford: CABI Publishing.

Onkvisit, S. and Shaw, J. (1991) Is Services Marketing Really Different?, *Journal of Professional Services Marketing*, 7 (2), 3-17.

Parsons, A., Zeisser, M., and Waitman, R. (1998) Organising Today for the Digital Marketing of Tomorrow, *Journal of Interactive Marketing*, 12 (1), 31-46.

Peterson, R., Balasubramanian, S., and Bronnenberg, B. (1997) Exploring the Implications of the Internet for Consumer marketing, *Journal of the Academy of Marketing Science*, 25 (4), 329-346.

Pitt, L., Berthon, P., and Watson, R. (1996) From Surfer to Buyer on the WWW: What Marketing Managers Might want to know, *Journal of General Management*, 22 (1), 1-13.

Pollock, A. (1996) The Role of Electronic Brochures in Selling Travel: Implications for Businesses and Destinations, *Australian Journal of Hospitality Management*, 3 (1), 25-30.

Price, J. and Starkov, M. (2002) *Developing a Total email Marketing Strategy*, URL: http://www.eurhotec.com/news/4012285.2000346.htm, Accessed 10/08/2000.

Rayport, J. and Sviokla, J. (1994) Managing in the Marketspace, *Harvard Business Review*, November-December, 141-150.

Rayport, J., and Sviokla, J. (1995) Exploiting the Virtual Value Chain. *Harvard Business Review* November-December, 75-85.

Reid, R. and Bojanic, D. (2001) *Hospitality Marketing Management* (3rd ed), New York: John Wiley and Sons, Inc.

Shostack, G. (1977) Breaking Free from Product Marketing, *Journal of Marketing*, 41, 73-80.

Sigala, M. (2001) Modelling e-marketing Strategies: Internet Presence and Exploitation of Greek Hotels, *Journal of Travel and Tourism Marketing*, 11 (2/3),83-104.

Sigala, M. (2002) *Internet and the Virtual Marketspace: Implications for Building Competitive e-commerce Strategies in the Hospitality Industry,* Proceedings of CHME Spring Conference, CHME Hospitality Research Conference, Leeds, UK.

Silverstien, B. (1999) *Business-to-Business Internet Marketing,* Florida: Maximum Press.

Spalter, M. (1996) *Maintaining a Customer Focus in An Interactive Age,* Advertising age, May 5, 24-31.

Standing, C. and Vasudavan, V. (1999) Internet Marketing Strategies used by Travel Agencies in Australia, *Journal of Vacation Marketing,* 6 (1), 21-32.

Tittel, E. and James, S. (1995) *HTML for Dummies,* Foster City, California: IDG Books.

Venditto, G. (1997) Critic's choice: Six Sites that Rate the Web. *Internet World,* January 82-96.

Weeks, P. and Crouch, I. (1999) Sites for Sore eyes: An Analysis of Australian Tourism and Hospitality Web Sites, *Information Technology and Tourism,* 2, 153-172.

Wigand, R. (1997) Electronic Commerce: Definition, Theory, and Context, *The Information Society,* 13 (1), 1-16.

Zeithaml, V. (1981) *How Consumer Evaluation Processes Differ between Goods and Services.* In Donnelly J. and George, W. (eds.), Marketing of services, Chicago: American Marketing Association.

Zeithaml, V., Parasuraman, A. and Berry, L. (1985) Problems and Strategies in Services Marketing, *Journal of Marketing,* 491, 33-46.